ST. THOMAS AQUINAS

Treatise on the Virtues

ST. THOMAS AQUINAS

Treatise on the Virtues

Translated by

JOHN A. OESTERLE

University of Notre Dame Press
Notre Dame, Indiana 46556

Library of Congress Cataloging in Publication Data

Thomas, Aquinas, Saint, 1225?–1274.
   Treatise on the virtues.

   Reprint. Originally published: Englewood Cliffs,
N.J.: Prentice Hall, 1966
   Includes bibliographical references.
   1. Virtues. 2. Virtue. 3. Habit. I. Oesterle,
John A. II. Title.
BV4630.T473   1984   241'.4   84–10691
ISBN 0-268-01855-3 (pbk.)

Manufactured in the United States of America

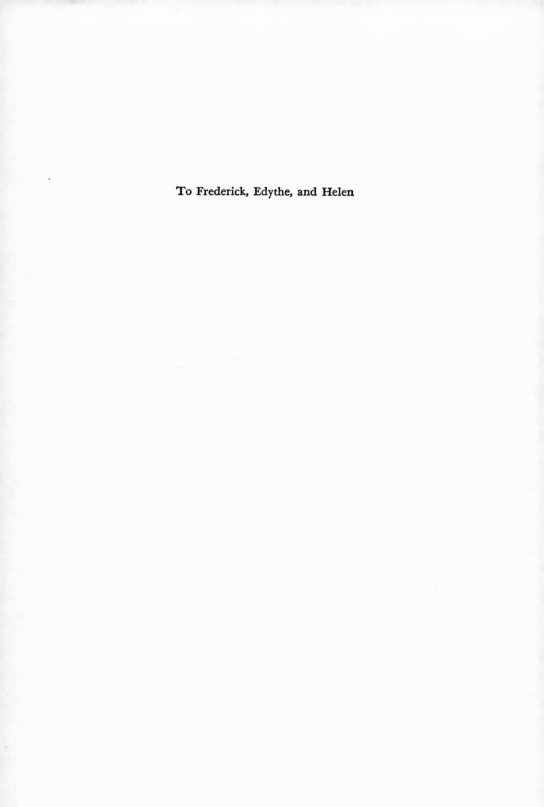

To Frederick, Edythe, and Helen

Table of Contents

vii

QUESTION LXII   118

The Theological Virtues

QUESTION LXIII   124

The Cause of Virtue

QUESTION LXIV   131

The Mean of Virtue

INTRODUCTION

The meaning of virtue in modern time has lost some of the original force it once had. Thanks in part to an extremely rigid moral tradition, stretching perhaps back at least to Puritan times, virtuous living has been linked with joyless living, and the very notion of virtue has been narrowed to signify principally some form of temperate conduct. And just as temperance, in turn, has been primarily restricted to restraining the appetite for alcoholic drink (in which respect, temperance has sometimes been confused with abstinence) so virtue, though actually much broader in meaning than temperance, has been largely confined, in the minds of many, to another area of temperance, restraint or even abstinence in regard to matters pertaining to sex; it is in this sense, for example, that some speak of a woman's "virtue," as the dictionary acknowledges.

However, the dictionary also indicates, and first of all, the more basic meaning of virtue, supported by etymology as well: manliness or worth, and hence *general* moral excellence based on right action and right thinking, which produce goodness of character. The English word *virtue* derives from the Latin *virtus,* and *virtus* signifies at once strength and power (*vir*). It is this broad, positive, strong meaning of virtue that St. Thomas Aquinas has in mind when he discusses and analyzes virtue at great length in the *Summa Theologiae.* Thus when St. Thomas begins to consider what virtue *essentially* is and how it is to be defined (question 55), his first point is that virtue implies perfection of a power. This phrase already lays the groundwork for the complete definition of virtue, by locating precisely where virtue is found, namely, in distinctively human powers, and by emphasizing the wholly positive character of virtue, that it is a *perfection,* the activity of human powers at their best.

In the course of his extensive analysis of virtue, St. Thomas constantly points out that reason is the first principle of all human acts, not reason in some purely abstract state, but reason precisely as determining the direction and formation of the activity of other human powers. Some of these other powers follow the direction of reason at once and without any opposition; thus our power of locomotion, if not physically impeded, responds instantaneously to the command of reason. Hence there is no need for the formation of virtue in these powers. Other powers, however, follow reason's direction while retaining their capacity to act on their own, even in opposition to reason, and accordingly the need of virtue arises. Such are the appetitive powers in man, both the will and sense appetite; and given that, appetite in man has, so to speak, a life of its own. St. Thomas, borrowing a happy phrase from Aristotle, says that reason commands the appetitive part in man by political rule, in the manner in which a man rules over subjects that are free and have a certain right of opposition.

We have here the whole clue to a sound doctrine on man's moral life and the beneficent role virtue plays in it. To be morally good, it is not enough merely to refrain from evil and injurious acts, and so perhaps only reluctantly follow out what we know we should do. The morally *virtuous* person is one whose appetite has the order of reason realized in it; his very appetite, in other words, operates with perfection, and the infallible sign that a person has reached this state of human excellence is that he *enjoys* acting virtuously. The virtuous person, accordingly, is not grim; on the contrary, he experiences genuine pleasure in choosing morally good actions. True enough, there is considerable difficulty in acting in accord with virtue, even for the person approaching moral excellence. But the difficulty often associated with moral excellence is at the level of *acquiring* virtue (and here the difficulty cannot be underestimated); *having acquired* the level of virtue, such difficulty is dissipated, and man is then free to lead the good human life with a proportionate degree of enjoyable accomplishment.

Now "in order that man's actions be good, not only must his reason be well disposed by a habit of intellectual virtue but also his appetitive power by a habit of moral virtue. Accordingly, just as appetite is distinguished from reason so moral virtue is distinguished from intellectual virtue. And hence just as the appetite is the principle of human acts insofar as it participates in reason in some way, so moral habit is considered a human virtue inasmuch as it is in conformity with reason," (question 58, article 2).

Virtue, as this passage indicates, is both intellectual and moral, this division following from the fact that man has two principles of human action, reason and appetite. The primary meaning of virtue is moral, primary not only as to what virtue first means to us (for when we say someone is virtuous we usually refer to moral excellence), but primary also in that moral virtue is virtue in its complete sense, that is, it not only gives an aptitude to act well but also induces good use of that aptitude. Intellectual virtue, on the other hand, only confers an aptitude to operate well, that is, an aptitude for acquiring true knowledge, and hence is virtue in a secondary sense. Nonetheless, St. Thomas treats the intellectual virtues (question 57) before the moral virtues (questions 59-61), for although moral virtue realizes the nature of virtue more perfectly, yet intellectual virtue, which perfects reason, man's power, is in this respect superior to virtue which perfects the appetite (question 66, article 3). The intellectual virtues perfect reason in regard to acquiring theoretical knowledge (and thus we have the three virtues of wisdom, science and understanding) or in regard to making or doing (and thus we have the two virtues of art and prudence). The moral virtues, in the present treatise, are discussed primarily in terms of the four cardinal virtues: justice, fortitude, temperance and prudence, the latter being included again because of its intrinsic relation to appetite, wherein it has a moral dimension.

A full understanding of St. Thomas' treatise on the virtues must take into account both what precedes the analysis of the virtues as well as the role of the theological virtues, discussed after the intellectual and moral virtues. This treatise therefore begins with an analysis of habit (questions 49-54), since habit is the proximate genus under which virtue falls. Here again, as with virtue, St. Thomas in an extensive treatment shows the positive and strong meaning the word conveys. Habit, far from being a restriction placed upon human activity, is shown to be a perfection enabling man to act better, more firmly, and with a greater facility than would otherwise be possible. From a consideration of habit in its broadest scope, St. Thomas moves to a treatment of distinctively human habits, their need and desirability in the intellect, will and appetite. Interlaced with the analytic account of the nature of habit is a perceptive psychological account of the function of habits in our lives, how they are acquired and developed as well as lost, and how habits become good or bad. This extended treatment of habits serves as well today for an understanding of their role in human activity as when it was written.

The *Summa Theologiae*, as its name indicates, is a theological work. Even though the present treatise is highly philosophical in exposition and understanding, the theological ordering of the work is evident on every page. Hence it is that the theological virtues need to be treated (question 62). The whole purpose of virtue is to achieve happiness, but happiness is twofold. The happiness which is proportioned to man's nature, and obtainable by means of man's natural capacities, is the happiness to which the moral and intellectual virtues are immediately ordered. But man is directed ultimately and primarily to a happiness surpassing the capacity of human nature, and obtainable from God alone. Accordingly, man needs additional principles to act well and attain such an end. These additional principles, directing him to supernatural happiness, are the theological virtues of faith, hope and charity. Contrary to the moral and intellectual virtues, which are acquired by our own efforts though not without divine assistance, the theological virtues are wholly infused in us by God. Having thus distinguished the theological virtues from other virtues, St. Thomas can then discuss the cause of virtue (question 63), the mean of virtue (question 64), the connection of the virtues (question 65), and the equality of virtue (question 66), for in regard to these matters theological virtues differ from moral and intellectual virtues. The final question in this treatise discusses some interesting points relative to the duration of the various virtues in the state after this life.

This treatise on the virtues should be seen in the context of the *Summa Theologiae* as a whole. The *Summa* is divided into three main parts. Part I treats God and the procession of creatures from God. Part III treats Christ Who, as divine and human, is our way to God. The large middle part, treating the movement of rational creatures back to God, is divided into I-II, the consideration of human acts and virtues generally, and II-II, in detail. The treatise on the virtues covers questions 49-67 of I-II. The first twenty-one questions of I-II discuss happiness and the human acts needed as means to attain such happiness (this treatise, translated by the present author, was published by Prentice-Hall in 1964 under the title, *Treatise on Happiness*). Questions 22-48 form a treatise on the human emotions, and consequent to this, the present treatise occurs.

Those who have engaged in the fascinating but demanding task of translating appreciate the varied difficulties which arise. It is particularly appropriate, in connection with this treatise on the virtues, to speak of aiming at the mean; in translating St. Thomas, the mean would seem to be to express the original into readable English without sacrificing accuracy of meaning. Much of current philosophical vocabulary has derived from Latin, and where precision of expression is required, such English words, often familiar in ordinary discourse, have been retained. At other times, somewhat more informal synonyms and expressions have been employed. No translation can measure up to the expectations of the translator or the discerning reader, but my hope is that the present rendition will make the concise thought of St. Thomas both intelligible and interesting. Of one thing I am sure. What merit this translation may have comes chiefly from my wife's ability to edit as well as translate, which she has conscientiously and patiently exercised throughout the treatise; the net result invariably has been an advance in clarification and intelligibility.

The text from which this translation has been made is the critical Leonine edition as it appears in the manual edition of the *Biblioteca de Autores Christianos*, Madrid, Spain, 1955, although other editions have also been consulted. I should like to acknowledge also the English Dominican translation of the *Summa Theologiae*, a monumental effort made over a half century ago, which rendered great assistance for one engaged in the same pursuit. I have added some notes, in addition to references, designed chiefly to offer further explanation of certain points which may be helpful for readers, whether they are using the book in philosophy or theology courses or are reading the book on their own.

J. A. O.

Habits in General, with Respect to What They Are

(In Four Articles)

Now that we have treated human acts and passions, the next point to consider is the principles of human acts.[1] First we shall consider intrinsic principles, then extrinsic principles.[2] The intrinsic principles are power and habit, but as we have already taken up powers,[3] only habits remain to be considered. We shall treat them first in general, and then take up in particular the virtues and vices, and other like habits, which are the principles of human acts.[4]

There are four things to be considered about habits in general. First, the nature of habits; second, their subject;[5] third, the cause of their formation, their increase, and their degeneration;[6] fourth, the distinction of one from another.[7] We consider first what habits are.

First Article

IS HABIT A QUALITY?

It seems that a habit is not a quality.

1. Augustine says that "the word *habit* is taken from the verb *to have*." [8] But *to have* belongs to other categories than quality, for we are said to have quantity, money, and other things of this kind. Therefore habit is not a quality.

2. Habit is itself regarded as a category, as is clear in the book on the *Categories*.[9] But one category is not contained under another. Therefore habit is not a quality.

---

[1] The introduction to question 6 of this part of the *Summa Theologiae* gives the order of treatment in general for I-II and II-II of this work. The topics treated prior to the present one beginning with question 49 on Habits were: I, Happiness (Qq. 1-5); II, Human Acts (Qq. 6-21); III, Human Passions or Emotions (Qq. 22-48).

[2] Question 90. This question begins the treatise on law. Law and grace are extrinsic principles of human acts; habit and virtue, which we now consider, are intrinsic principles.

[3] I, question 77.   [4] Question 55.   [5] Question 50.   [6] Question 51.   [7] Question 54.

[8] *Book of Eighty-Three Questions,* q. 73.

[9] Aristotle, *Categories,* 8 (8b 27). This is "habit" in the sense of being clothed. See note 18.

3. "Every habit is a disposition," as is said in the *Categories.*[10] But disposition is "the order of a thing having parts." [11] However, this belongs in the category *Position.* Therefore habit is not a quality.[12]

On the contrary: The Philosopher speaks of a habit as "a quality of long duration and difficult to change." [13]

Response: The name "habit" is taken from *having,*[14] from which it is derived in two ways: in one way, inasmuch as a man, or anything else, is said *to have* something; in another way, inasmuch as a thing is conditioned in a certain way, either in itself or in regard to something else.

Apropos of the first way, we must note that *to have,* as said regarding whatever a thing has, is common to various categories. Hence the Philosopher puts *to have* among the postpredicaments along with opposition, priority, posteriority, and other things of this kind, which follow upon the various predicaments.[15] But there seems to be a distinction to be noted among things had. There are some things in which there is nothing in between the one having and that which is had; for example, nothing intervenes between a subject and its quality or its quantity.[16] There are other things in which there is something intermediate, but only a relation, as, for instance, a man is said to have a companion or a friend. Finally, there are some things in which something is intermediate, not indeed an action or passion, but something in the manner of an action or passion; for example, something adorns or covers and something else is adorned or covered. Hence the Philosopher says that " 'having' is a kind of actuality of the haver and of what he has," [17] as in the case of those things which we have on our person. Therefore, in regard to these, there is a special genus which is called the category *Habit,* of which the Philosopher says, "between the one who has a garment and the garment which he has there is a having." [18]

But if *to have* refers to a thing's being conditioned in a certain way in

---

[10] *Ibid.,* (9a 10).   [11] Aristotle, *Metaphysics* V, 19 (1022b 1).

[12] These opening arguments should be seen as attempts to place habit in some ultimate genus, as a first step toward understanding the nature of habit. Once such an ultimate genus is established, and this is what a category is, then habit can be distinguished from anything else in the same genus, and eventually a definition of habit can be formulated. St. Thomas presupposes familiarity with Aristotle's work on *Categories,* a logical treatise designed to establish the ultimate genera under which can be found all the finite, natural objects we know. This first question is therefore asking what category should habit be placed in, and this is the initial step to take in trying to understand what a habit is.

[13] *Categories,* 8 (9a 3; a 9).

[14] "Hoc nomen *habitus* ab habendo est sumptum." The derivation is clearer in Latin.

[15] Cf. *Categories,* 11 (14a 26-15b 31). The word "predicaments" derives from the Latin *predicamenta,* which means the same as "categories," deriving from the Greek.

[16] For example, a body and its weight or a surface and its color.

[17] *Metaphysics* V, 20 (1022b 4).

[18] *Ibid.,* (1022b 7). Hence we speak of *having* on clothes. Note also the sense of a riding *habit* or a religious sister's *habit.*

itself or in regard to something else, then habit is a quality, since this way of having is one type of quality. Of this, the Philosopher says, " 'having' or 'habit' means a disposition by which that which is disposed is either well or ill disposed, either in itself or with reference to something else; for example, health is a habit." [19] It is in this sense that we now speak of habit. Hence it must be said that habit is a quality.

Reply to 1: This argument is based on *to have* taken in general; in this sense, it is common to many categories, as we have just said.

Reply to 2: The reasoning of this argument takes habit as meaning something between the one having and that which is had, and in this sense it is a special category.

Reply to 3: A disposition does always imply an ordering of a thing having parts, but there are three such possibilities. Thus the Philosopher, where he speaks of this, goes on to say "either as to place or power or kind." [20] "In saying this," Simplicius says in his Commentary,[21] "he includes all dispositions. He includes the disposition of a body in saying 'as to place,' " and this belongs to the category *Position*, which is the ordering of parts in a place. "When he says 'as to power,' he includes those dispositions which are in process but not yet completely formed," such as incipient science and virtue. "When he says 'as to kind,' he includes perfect dispositions, which are called habits," such as perfect science and virtue.

Second Article

IS HABIT A DISTINCT SPECIES OF QUALITY?[22]

It seems that habit is not a distinct species of quality.

1. As we have noted,[23] habit, as a quality, is "a disposition by which that which is disposed is either well or ill disposed." But this applies to any quality, for a thing is well or ill disposed with respect to shape, or warm and cold, and so of all other qualities. Therefore a habit is not a distinct kind or species of quality.

2. The Philosopher says that heat and cold, as well as sickness and health, are dispositions, or habits.[24] But warm and cold are in the third species of quality. Therefore habit, or disposition, is not distinct from other species of quality.

3. Difficult to change[25] is not a difference which belongs to the genus

---

[19] *Ibid.,* (1022b 10).   [20] *Ibid.,* (1022b 1).

[21] *On the Categories,* 8. Simplicius was a sixth-century Greek commentator on Aristotle.

[22] Cf. Aristotle, *Categories,* 8. Quality, as "that in virtue of which people are said to be such and such," is divided into four kinds or species. The question, therefore, is whether habit is one of these species of quality.

[23] Article 1.   [24] *Categories,* 8 (8b 36).

[25] *Ibid.,* (9a 3; a 9). Cf. *On the contrary* of the preceding article.

of quality but, rather, to movement or to being moved. But no genus is contracted to a species by a difference belonging to another genus; rather, the differences must be proper to the genus in question, as the Philosopher says.[26] Therefore, since habit is said to be a "quality difficult to change," [27] it does not seem to be a distinct species of quality.

On the contrary: The Philosopher says that "habit and disposition are one species of quality." [28]

Response: In the *Categories,* the Philosopher posits disposition and habit as the first of four species of quality.[29] Simplicius explains the differences of these species in the following way. "Some qualities are natural —those that are in their subject by nature and always; others come from without—those that are caused extrinsically and can be lost. Now the latter are habits and dispositions, and they differ insofar as they can be lost easily or with difficulty. Regarding the natural qualities, some belong to a thing insofar as it is in potentiality to something, and thus we have the second species of quality. Others belong to a thing insofar as it is in act, and these are either deep-rooted or only on the surface. If deep-rooted, we have the third species of quality. If on the surface, we have the fourth species of quality, such as figure, and form, which is the shape of the living being." [30]

This distinction of the species of quality, however, does not seem to be appropriate, for there are many shapes and passive qualities which are not natural but from without, and many dispositions are not from without, but natural, for example, health, beauty, and the like. Furthermore, this distinction does not correspond to the order of the species, for what is natural is always prior.

Hence the distinction of dispositions and habits from other qualities must be explained in another way. Now quality, properly speaking, implies some mode of a substance. But a mode, as Augustine says, "is that which a measure fixes," [31] and hence it implies a determination according to some measure. Accordingly, just as that by which the potentiality of matter is determined in regard to substantial being is called a quality, which is a difference of substance, so that by which the potentiality of the subject is determined in regard to accidental being is called an accidental quality, which is also a kind of difference, as the Philosopher explains.[32]

Now the mode or determination of the subject by way of accidental being can be taken in relation to the very nature of the subject, or according to the action and passion which follow upon its natural principles, which are matter and form, or according to quantity. If we take the mode or determination of the subject in regard to quantity, we have

---

[26] *Metaphysics* VII, 12 (1038a 9).   [27] Aristotle, *Categories,* 8 (9a 3; 9).
[28] *Ibid.,* (8b 26).   [29] *Ibid.*   [30] *Commentary on the Categories,* 8.
[31] *A Literal Commentary on "Genesis"* IV, 3.   [32] *Metaphysics* V, 14 (1020a 33).

the fourth species of quality. Now because quantity, considered in itself, is without movement, and has not an aspect of good or evil, it is not relevant to the fourth species of quality that a thing is well or ill disposed, or changing quickly or slowly.

But in the second and third species of quantity we are concerned with the mode or determination of the subject in regard to action and passion. Hence in both species we take into account whether something is done easily or with difficulty, whether it is transitory or lasting. But we do not consider in them anything pertaining to the notion of good or evil, because movements and passions are not regarded as ends whereas good and evil are said in reference to an end.

The mode or determination of the subject in view of the nature of the thing, however, belongs to the first species of quality, which is habit and disposition. Thus the Philosopher, speaking of the habits of the soul and body, says that they are "certain dispositions of what is perfect to what is best for it [i.e., to the end, or operation] in accord with nature." [33] And because "the form itself and the nature of the thing is the end, or that for the sake of which it comes to be," [34] hence in the first species we consider both good and evil, and also easily changeable and changeable with difficulty, inasmuch as a nature is the end of generation and movement. Accordingly, the Philosopher defines habit as "a disposition by which one is well or ill disposed." [35] He also says that "by habits we stand well or badly with reference to the passions." [36] For when a mode or determination is appropriate to the thing's nature, then it has the aspect of good, and when inappropriate, the aspect of evil. And since nature is what is first considered in a thing, habit is regarded as the first species of quality.[37]

Reply to 1: Disposition implies a certain kind of order, as we have said.[38] Hence one is not said to be disposed by some quality except in relation to something. And if "well or ill" is added, which belongs to the notion of habit, we must take into account the ordering to the thing's na-

---

[33] *Physics* VII, 3 (246a 13).   [34] *Op. cit.*, II, 7 (198b 3).
[35] *Metaphysics* V, 20 (1022b 10).   [36] *Nicomachean Ethics* II, 5 (1105b 25).
[37] The response of St. Thomas can be summarized as follows. We know from the first article that habit is a quality. In this second article we want to find out what *kind* of quality, which species of quality, habit is. Habit is not the shape or form of some thing, the fourth species of quality, which qualifies the quantity of a thing. Likewise, habit is not the second species of quality (a capacity or potency for operation) nor the third species of quality (a quality directly sensed, like a color or a flavor). Hence habit is the first kind or species of quality. Such a quality modifies the very nature of something so that it is well or ill disposed, and so we speak of good or bad habits. If such a quality is changeable with difficulty, it is a habit; if it is somewhat readily changeable, it is only a disposition. A moral virtue like temperance would be a good habit; being continent, however, would be only a good disposition, since a continent person is still subject to being led readily astray by inordinate desire.
[38] Article 1, reply to 3.

ture, which is the end. Thus, one is not said to be disposed well or ill with regard to shape, or heat, or cold, except insofar as it is appropriate or inappropriate in relation to the nature of the thing. Hence even shapes and passive qualities, considered as appropriate or inappropriate to the nature of the thing, belong to habits or dispositions. For shape, in proportion to its suitability to the thing's nature, and color also, pertain to beauty; heat and cold, in proportion to their suitability to the nature of the thing, pertain to health. It is on this basis that heat and cold are put by the Philosopher in the first species of quality.[39]

Reply to 2: The solution to this argument is now clear, although some solve it otherwise, as Simplicius says in his *Commentary.*[40]

Reply to 3: The difference *difficult to change* does not set off habit from other species of quality, but from disposition. Now disposition can be taken in two ways: in one way, as the genus of habit, for it is stated in the definition of habit;[41] in another way, as opposed to habit. Again, disposition in its proper sense can be distinguished from habit in two ways. First, as perfect and imperfect within the same species. We then retain the common name, calling it a disposition when it is present imperfectly such that it is easily lost, and calling it a habit when it is present perfectly such that it is not easily lost. Taken in this way, a disposition becomes a habit just as a body becomes a man. Second, they can be distinguished as different species of one subalternate genus.[42] In this division, those qualities of the first species, which by reason of their very nature are easily lost because they have variable causes, are called dispositions—for example, sickness and health; those qualities which by reason of their nature are not easily changeable because their causes are not variable, are called habits—for example, sciences and virtues. In this case, a disposition does not become a habit.

This way of putting the matter seems more in agreement with the intention of Aristotle.[43] For, in order to show that this way of distinguishing habit and disposition is sound, he refers to the ordinary usage of the words. Qualities by nature easily changeable, which through some accident[44] become difficult to change, we call habits, while in regard to qualities which by their nature are changeable with difficulty, the reverse is the case. For if a man has a science imperfectly and as a consequence could easily lose it, he is said to be disposed toward that science rather than to have it. It is evident from this that the name "habit" implies something lasting, but not the name "disposition."

---

[39] *Categories,* 8 (8b 36).   [40] Chapter 8.   [41] Cf. Aristotle, *Metaphysics* V, 20 (1022b 4).

[42] This is a genus ranked below another more universal genus. Thus disposition and habit are distinct species of the first species of quality, which is a genus under the higher genus of quality itself.

[43] Cf. *Categories,* 8 (8b 27).

[44] Not accident in the sense of happening by chance, but in the sense of some accidental, as opposed to essential, characteristic.

Moreover, there is no difficulty about *easy and difficult to change* being the specific differences in this division even though they belong to passion and movement, and not to the genus *quality*. For these differences, even though they seem to be accidental, nevertheless designate proper and per se differences of quality. In a similar way, in the genus *substance* we often use accidental differences in place of substantial differences, to the extent that essential principles are designated by them.

Third Article

DOES HABIT IMPLY ORDERING TOWARD ACT?

It seems that habit does not imply ordering toward act.

1. A thing acts insofar as it is in act. But the Philosopher says that "when one has science as a habit, he is still in a state of potentiality, but not in the same sense as before he learns." [45] Therefore habit does not imply the relation of a principle to its act.

2. What is stated in the definition of a thing belongs to it essentially. But to be a principle of action is put in the definition of a power or a potency.[46] Therefore to be the principle of action belongs essentially to a power. But in any genus that which is essential is primary. If, therefore, habit also is a principle of act, it follows that it is posterior to power. Hence habit or disposition will not be the first species of quality.

3. Health is sometimes a habit, and likewise leanness and beauty. But we do not say that these refer to an act. Therefore, to be the principle of an act is not of the essence of habit.

On the contrary: Augustine says that "habit is that by which something is done when there is work to do." [47] And the Commentator says that "habit is that whereby we act as we will." [48]

Response: To have an ordering toward act can belong to habit both from the viewpoint of the notion of habit and of the subject in which the habit is. From the point of view of the notion of habit, it belongs to every habit in some way to have an ordering toward act. For the notion of habit implies a characteristic condition relevant to a thing's nature as appropriate or inappropriate to it. But the nature of the thing, which is the end of generation, is further ordered to another end, either to activity, or to the product which one attains by means of activity. Hence habit implies not only an ordering relevant to the very nature of the thing but also, consequently, to its activity insofar as this is the end of the nature, or is conducive to the end. Hence it is said in the definition of habit that it is "a disposition according to which that which is disposed

---

[45] *On the Soul* III, 4 (429b 6).   [46] Cf. Aristotle, *Metaphysics* V, 12 (1019a 15).
[47] *On the Conjugal Good* XXI.
[48] Averroes, *Commentary on "On the Soul"* III, 18. Averroes was an Arabian twelfth-century commentator on Aristotle.

is either well or ill disposed, either in itself," that is, its nature, "or in regard to something," [49] that is, in regard to an end.

But there are some habits which, even on the part of the subject in which they are, imply primarily and principally an ordering toward act. For, as we have said, habit primarily and per se implies a characteristic condition relevant to the nature of the thing. If, then, the nature of the thing in which habit is, consists in this ordering toward act, it follows that habit principally implies an ordering toward act. Now it is clear that it is of the nature and notion of a power that it be the principle of an act. Hence every habit which is in a power as in a subject principally implies an ordering toward act.

Reply to 1: Habit is an act insofar as it is a quality, and in this respect it can be a principle of activity. But it is potential with respect to activity. Hence habit is called *first act* and activity *second act.*[50]

Reply to 2: It is not of the essence of habit to be related to a power, but to the nature of the thing. And since the nature precedes action, to which the power is related, habit is prior to power as a species of quality.

Reply to 3: Health is called a habit, or a habitual disposition, with regard to the nature of the thing, as we have said.[51] Nevertheless, insofar as the nature is a principle of action, it implies, as a consequence, an ordering toward act. Hence the Philosopher says that man—or any of his members—is said to be healthy "when he can perform the operation of a healthy man." [52] The same applies to other habits.

Fourth Article

ARE HABITS NECESSARY?

It seems that habits are not necessary.

1. We are well or ill disposed to something through habits, as has been said.[53] But a thing is well or ill disposed by its form, for according to its form, a thing is good, as well as a being. Therefore there is no necessity for habits.

2. Habit implies an ordering toward act. But power sufficiently implies a principle of act, for natural powers without habits are principles of acts. Therefore it was not necessary that there should be habits.

3. Just as a power is related to good and evil, so also is habit, and just as a power is not always acting, so neither is a habit. Given, then, the existence of powers, habits are superfluous.

---

[49] Aristotle, *Metaphysics* V, 20 (1022b 10).

[50] Cf. Aristotle, *On the Soul* II, 1 (412a 22). First act. for example, is the possession of knowledge which, as science, is a habit. Second act is the employment or exercise of the knowledge or science.

[51] Article 2, reply to 1.

[52] *The History of Animals* X, 1 (633b 23).   [53] Article 2.

On the contrary: Habits are perfections.[54] But perfection is most of all necessary for a thing, since it is in the nature of an end. Therefore it was necessary that there should be habits.

Response: As we have said,[55] habit implies a disposition relevant to the nature of the thing and to its activity or end, whereby the thing is well or ill disposed thereto. Now there are three conditions for a thing's needing to be disposed to something. First, that which is disposed must be distinct from that to which it is disposed, and thus related to it as potentiality to act. Hence if there is something whose nature is not composed of potency and act, whose substance is its operation, and which exists for itself, there is no place for habit or disposition in such a thing. This is evidently the case with God.

Secondly, that which is in potency to something must be able to be determined in several ways and to different things. Hence if a thing is disposed to something in such a way that it is in potency only to that, there is no need of a disposition and habit, for such a subject of its very nature has a disposition sufficient for such an act. Therefore, if a heavenly body is composed of matter and form, since such matter is not in potency to another form, as we have said,[56] there is no place for a disposition or habit toward form, or even activity, because the nature of a heavenly body is only in potency to one fixed movement.

Thirdly, several things, capable of being proportioned in various ways, must concur in order to dispose the subject to one of the things to which it is in potency, so as to dispose it well or ill to its form or its activity. Hence the simple qualities of elements, which are adapted in one determinate way to the natures of elements, are not called dispositions or habits, but *simple qualities*. But we do call health, beauty, and the like, dispositions or habits, for they imply a certain proportion of several things which can vary in their relative proportioning. The Philosopher says, for this reason, that "habit is a disposition," [57] and disposition is "the order of that which has parts either of place or of potency or of kind," [58] as we have said.[59]

Accordingly, since there are many beings for whose nature and activity several things must concur which may vary in their relative proportioning, it follows that habit is necessary.

Reply to 1: The nature of the thing is made complete by the form, but the subject must be disposed to the form by some disposition. The form itself, however, is further ordered to activity, which is either an end or a means to the end. And if the form is restricted to only one determinate activity, no other disposition is required for the activity except the form itself. But if the form is such that it can act in diverse ways, as is the

---

[54] Cf. Aristotle, *Physics* VII, 3 (246a 11).   [55] Articles 2 and 3.
[56] I, question 66, article 2.   [57] *Metaphysics* V, 20 (1022b 10).
[58] *Op. cit.*, 19 (1022b 1).   [59] Article 1, reply to 3.

case with the soul, it must be disposed for its activities by certain habits.

Reply to 2: Powers are sometimes related to many things, and consequently need determining by something else. But if a power is not related to many things, it does not need determining by habit, as we have pointed out.[60] For this reason, natural forces do not perform their acts by means of habits, for they are determined of themselves to one way of acting.

Reply to 3: The same habit is not related to good and evil, as we shall make clear later.[61] But the same power is related to good and evil. Hence habits are necessary to determine the powers to good activity.

---

[60] In the body of this article.   [61] Question 54, article 3.

The Subject of Habits

(*In Six Articles*)

IS THERE ANY HABIT IN THE BODY?

It seems that there is not any habit in the body.

1. The Commentator says that "habit is that whereby we act as we will." [1] But bodily actions are not subject to the will, since they are natural. [2] Therefore there cannot be any habit in the body.

2. All bodily dispositions change easily. But habit is a quality difficult to change. Therefore no bodily disposition can be a habit.

3. All bodily dispositions are subject to alteration. But alteration is found only in the third species of quality, which is distinguished from habit. [3] Therefore no habit is in the body.

On the contrary: The Philosopher says that health of body or indispositions of long standing are called habits. [4]

Response: As we have said, [5] habit is a disposition of a subject which is in potentiality either to form or to activity. Hence, inasmuch as habit implies a disposition to activity, no habit can be principally in the body as in a subject. For every activity of the body is due either to a natural quality of the body or to the soul moving the body. Consequently, as far as activities which are due to nature are concerned, the body is not dis·posed by a habit, for natural powers are determined to one way of acting; and as we have already said, [6] it is when the subject is in potentiality to many things that a habitual disposition is required. But activities which are from the soul by means of the body belong principally to the soul and secondarily to the body. Now habits are proportionate to actions, and hence "from acts of a certain kind, habits of that kind are formed." [7] For this reason, the dispositions to such activities are found principally in the soul. But secondarily they can be in the body insofar as the body is

---

[1] Averroes, *Commentary on "On the Soul"* III, 18.

[2] I.e., natural as distinct from voluntary.

[3] Habit is in the first species of quality. For a description of the four species of quality, see note 37 of the preceding question.

[4] *Categories*, 6 (9a 1).   [5] Question 49, article 2.   [6] Question 49, article 4.

[7] Aristotle, *Nicomachean Ethics* II, 1 (1103b 21).

disposed and conditioned to be readily subject to these activities of the soul.

But if we are talking about the disposition of the subject to form, then a habitual disposition can be in the body, which is compared to the soul as subject to form. It is in this sense that health, beauty, and the like, are called habitual dispositions. They do not, however, realize completely the notion of habit because their causes, of their very nature, are easily changeable.

On the other hand, as Simplicius reports,[8] Alexander denied that habits and dispositions of the first species of quality are in any way in the body; he maintained, rather, that the first species of quality pertained to the soul alone. And he held that Aristotle cites health and sickness in the *Categories*, not as belonging to the first species of quality, but by way of example.[9] The meaning of the text would then be that just as health and sickness can be changed easily or with difficulty so likewise the qualities of the first species, which are called habit and disposition. But clearly this view is contrary to the intention of Aristotle, both because he uses health and sickness as examples in the same way as virtue and science, and because elsewhere he explicitly places beauty and health among habits.[10]

Reply to 1: This objection argues from habit as a disposition for activity and from bodily actions which are due to nature, but not from actions which proceed from the soul, whose principle is the will.

Reply to 2: Because of the changeable character of bodily causes, bodily dispositions are not, absolutely, difficult to change. They may, however, be difficult to change relative to such and such a subject, for as long as such a subject endures they cannot be removed; or because, relative to other dispositions, they are changeable with difficulty. But qualities of the soul are, absolutely, difficult to change, because their subject is immobile. Hence Aristotle does not say that health, when difficult to change, is a habit absolutely, but that it is *like a habit,* as the Greek indicates.[11]

Reply to 3: The bodily dispositions which are in the first species of quality, as some maintained,[12] differ from the qualities of the third species in that the latter are present by way of a becoming and a movement, and hence are called passions or passive qualities. But when they have come to perfection—to a perfection of species, as it were—they are then in the first species of quality. Simplicius, however, rejects this position,[13] for in such a view becoming warm would be in the third species

---

[8] *On the Categories,* 8. Alexander of Aphrodisias was a Greek commentator on Aristotle, writing at the beginning of the third century.
[9] Cf. *Categories,* 8 (8b 36).   [10] *Physics* VII, 3 (246b 4).   [11] *Categories,* 8 (9a 3).
[12] Cf. Simplicius, *On the Categories,* 8.   [13] *Ibid.*

of quality and warmness in the first, whereas Aristotle puts warmness in the third.

Consequently Porphyry, as Simplicius reports,[14] says that passion or passive quality, and habit and disposition differ in bodies by way of intensity and remission. For when something receives warmth so slightly as to be warm but not so as to be able to give warmth, then there is passivity if transitory, and a passive quality if lasting. But when a thing is brought to the point of being able to warm something else, then there is a disposition, and if, further, it becomes so stabilized that it is difficult to change, then it will be a habit. Thus disposition is a sort of intensity, that is, a perfection of passivity or passive quality, and habit an intensity, or perfection of disposition. But Simplicius also rejects this, because such intensity and remission do not imply a diversity coming from the form itself, but from diverse participation in it by the subject. There would thus be no diversity among the species of quality.

We must therefore answer otherwise. As we have said,[15] the proportioning of passive qualities in accord with their suitability to the nature is reckoned as a disposition, and hence when an alteration occurs in these passive qualities—heat and cold, moisture and dryness—there results an alteration as to sickness and health. But alteration does not occur, primarily and directly, with respect to habits and dispositions of this kind.

Second Article

IS THE SUBJECT OF HABIT IN THE ESSENCE OF THE SOUL OR IN ITS POWERS?

It seems that habits are in the essence of the soul rather than in its powers.

1. We speak of dispositions and habits in relation to the nature of a thing, as we have said.[16] But nature refers more to the essence of soul than to its powers, for to be the nature of such a body,[17] and the form of it, pertains to the essence of soul. Therefore habits are in the essence of the soul and not in its powers.

2. One accident is not the subject of another accident. Now habit is an accident. But the powers of the soul belong to the genus of accident, as we have said.[18] Therefore habit is not in the soul by reason of its powers.

3. The subject is prior to what is in the subject. But habit, since it be-

---

[14] *Ibid.* Porphyry was a third century Greek commentator on Aristotle. He is the author of the renowned *Isagoge*, an introduction to Aristotle's *Categories.*

[15] Question 49, article 2, reply to 1.   [16] Question 49, article 2.

[17] I.e., a physical, organic body constituted by various operative powers serving as instruments.

[18] I, question 77, article 1, reply to 5.

longs to the first species of quality, is prior to power, which belongs to the second species. Therefore a habit is not in a power of the soul as in a subject.

On the contrary: The Philosopher places different habits in different parts of the soul.[19]

Response: As we have said,[20] habit implies a certain disposition in relation to a thing's nature or its activity. Accordingly, if we take habit as having relation to the nature, habit cannot be in the soul—at least, if we are speaking of human nature—for the soul is the form that renders human nature complete. In this respect, then, habit or disposition can be found rather in the body by reason of its ordering to the soul than in the soul by reason of its ordering to the body. But if we are speaking of a higher nature, of which man can be a participator (according to *II Peter, 1:4:* "that we may become partakers of the divine nature"), nothing prevents a habit, namely grace, from being in the essence of the soul as in a subject, as we shall say later on.[21]

If, however, we consider habit in relation to activity, habits are most especially found in the soul, inasmuch as the soul is not determined to one operation, but is related to many, which is a condition for a habit, as we have said.[22] And since the soul is the principle of operation through its powers, consequently habits are in the soul according to its powers.

Reply to 1: The essence of soul pertains to human nature, not as a subject needing disposing to something else, but as the form and nature to which someone is disposed.

Reply to 2: An accident by itself cannot be the subject of another accident. But because there is an order among accidents, the subject as it is under one accident is conceived as the subject of another accident. Accordingly, we say one accident is the subject of another; for example, surface is the subject of color. In this way a power can be the subject of habit.

Reply to 3: Habit, as it implies disposition to the nature, is prior to power; and power always implies a relation to operation, which is posterior, since the nature is the principle of operation. On the other hand, the habit whose subject is the power does not imply relation to the nature, but to operation; hence it is posterior to the power. Or we

---

[19] *Nicomachean Ethics* I, 13 (1103a 3).   [20] Question 49, articles 2 and 3.

[21] Question 110, article 4. In this article St. Thomas makes the following point: "Just as grace is prior to virtue so it has a subject prior to the powers of the soul such that grace is in the essence of the soul. For just as man by his intellectual power participates in divine knowledge through the virtue of faith, and by his power of will participates in divine love through the virtue of charity, so likewise through the nature of the soul he participates in the divine nature by a certain similitude, through a sort of regeneration or another creation [a re-creation]."

[22] Question 49, article 4. The soul by nature being indeterminate in relation to its operations, habits are needed to help develop ordered, regular operations.

can say that habit is prior to power as the complete is prior to the incomplete, and act is prior to potentiality. For act is naturally prior, although potentiality is prior in the order of time and generation.[23]

Third Article

CAN THERE BE ANY HABIT IN THE SENSE POWERS?[24]

It seems that there cannot be any habit in the sense powers.

1. Just as a nutritive power is an irrational part of the soul, so is a sense power. But no habit is posited in the powers of the nutritive part of the soul. Therefore we should not posit any habit in the powers of the sense part of the soul.

2. Sense powers are common to us and to the other animals. But there are no habits in the other animals, for there is no will in them, which is included in the definition of habit, as stated above.[25] Therefore there are no habits in the sense powers.

3. The habits of the soul are sciences and virtues, and just as science is referred to the knowing power so virtue is referred to the appetitive power. But there are no sciences in the sense powers, since science deals with universals which the sense powers cannot grasp. Therefore neither can there be habits of virtue in the sense powers.

On the contrary: The Philosopher says that "some virtues," namely, temperance and fortitude, "belong to the irrational parts of the soul." [26]

Response: Sense powers can be considered in two ways; in one way, as operating from natural instinct, in another, as operating at the command of reason. Now as operating from natural instinct, they are ordered to one thing, just as nature is. Hence, just as there are no habits in natural powers, so likewise there is none in sense powers insofar as they operate from natural instinct. But as operating at the command of reason, they can be ordered to various things; and thus there can be habits in them whereby they are well or ill disposed in regard to something.

Reply to 1: The powers of the nutritive part of the soul do not have an innate aptitude for obeying the command of reason, and hence there are no habits in them. But the sense powers do have an innate aptitude to obey the command of reason, and hence there can be habits in them, for insofar as they follow reason they are said to be rational in a certain respect.[27]

Reply to 2: The sense powers in irrational animals do not function

---

[23] Cf. Aristotle, *Metaphysics* VII, 3 (1029a 5); IX, 8 (1049b 4).

[24] More literally, the question reads: "Can there be any habit in the powers of the sense part of the soul?"

[25] Question 49, article 3.   [26] *Nicomachean Ethics* III, 10 (1117b 23).

[27] Cf. Aristotle, *op. cit.,* I, 13 (1102b 25; b 13).

at the command of reason. But if left to themselves, such animals act from natural instinct, and so there are in them no habits regulating their actions. There are in them, however, some dispositions in relation to nature, such as health and beauty. But because animals are disposed through a certain conditioning from man's reason to act in this way or that, to this extent habits can in some sense be admitted in the animals. Hence Augustine says, "We find the most untamed beasts restrained, through fear of pain, from that in which they find the most pleasure, and when this has become customary to them, we say that they are tame and gentle." [28] Nevertheless, in them something essential to habit is absent, that is, exercise of the will, for they do not have dominion over using or not using, which seems to belong to the notion of habit. Consequently, strictly speaking, there can be no habits in them.

Reply to 3: Sense appetite has an innate aptitude to be moved by rational appetite.[29] Rational powers of knowing, on the other hand, have an innate aptitude to receive from the senses. Hence it is more suitable that habits be in appetitive sense powers than in knowing sense powers, since habits are not engendered in the appetitive sense powers except insofar as they function under the command of reason. Nonetheless we can maintain that there are some habits even in the interior sense-knowing powers whereby man is adept at remembering, cogitating, or imagining. Hence the Philosopher says that "custom contributes much to a good memory," [30] for these powers also are moved to action at the command of reason. External powers of knowing, however, such as sight, hearing, and the like, are not subject to habits, for they are ordered to their own determinate acts by the disposition of their nature, just as the bodily members are, which have no habits in them, but rather in the powers commanding their movement.

Fourth Article

IS THERE ANY HABIT IN THE INTELLECT?

It seems that there is no habit in the intellect.

1. Habits are formed by actions, as we have said.[31] But the actions of man are common to the soul and body.[32] Therefore habits also are. But understanding is not the act of the body.[33] Therefore the intellect is not the subject of any habit.

2. Whatever is in something is in it according to the mode of that in which it is. But anything that is form without matter is act only, whereas whatever is composed of form and matter has potentiality and

---

[28] *Book of Eighty-Three Questions,* q. 36.

[29] Cf. Aristotle, *On the Soul* III, 11 (434a 12).

[30] *On Memory and Reminiscence,* 2 (452a 28).   [31] Article 1.

[32] Cf. Aristotle, *On the Soul* I, 1 (403a 8); 4 (408b 8).   [33] *Op. cit.,* III, 4 (429a 24).

act simultaneously. Therefore, in whatever is form only there can be nothing simultaneously in potentiality and in act; this happens only in that which is composed of matter and form. But the intellect is form without matter. Therefore habit, which has potentiality simultaneously with act, as a sort of intermediate between the two, cannot be in the intellect but only in the composite formed from soul and body.

3. Habit is "a disposition whereby one is well or ill disposed to something." [34] But for someone to be well or ill disposed to the act of the intellect derives from some disposition of the body. Hence, "we notice that men who are soft in flesh are gifted in mind." [35] Therefore habits of knowledge are not in the intellect, which is separate, but in a power which is the act of some part of the body.

On the contrary: The Philosopher puts wisdom and science and understanding (which is the habit of first principles) in the intellectual part of the soul.[36]

Response: There have been various opinions concerning the cognitive habits. Those maintaining the possible intellect[37] to be a single intellect in all men were forced to hold that the habits of knowledge are not in the intellect itself, but in the interior sense powers.[38] For it is evident that men differ in their habits; hence the habits of knowledge cannot be put directly in that which, being only one, is common to all men. So if there were but a single possible intellect for all men, the habits of sciences, which make men different from one another, would not be in the possible intellect as in a subject, but in the interior sense powers, which are different in different men.

Now this position, first of all, is contrary to what Aristotle intended to express. For clearly the sense powers are not essentially rational but are so only by participation,[39] yet the Philosopher puts the intellectual virtues—wisdom, science, and understanding—in that which is essentially rational.[40] Hence they are not in the sense powers, but in the intellect itself. Moreover, he says expressly that "once the possible intellect thus becomes each thing," that is, when it is brought to act with respect to singulars through intelligible species, "then it is in act in the way in which a knower is said to be in act, which happens when he is now able to exercise the act of himself," that is, by considering what he knows. "Even then the intellect in a sense is in potency, but not in the same way as before learning and discovering." [41] Therefore the possible intellect itself is the subject of the habit of science whereby one, even

---

[34] Aristotle. *Metaphysics* V, 20 (1022b 10).   [35] Aristotle, *On the Soul* II, 9 (421a 26).
[36] *Nicomachean Ethics* VI, 3 (1139b 16).
[37] The possible intellect is the power of becoming in an intentional manner, through concepts, the forms of other things.
[38] Averroes held this position; cf. his commentary *On the Soul* III, 5.
[39] Cf. Aristotle, *Nicomachean Ethics* I, 13 (1139b 16).   [40] *Op. cit.,* VI, 3 (1139b 16).
[41] Aristotle, *On the Soul* III, 4 (429b 6).

though not actually considering what he knows, is able to consider it.

Secondly, that position is contrary to truth. For just as an activity belongs to that to which the power of activity belongs, so habit belongs to that to which the activity belongs. But to know and to consider what one knows is characteristic of the act of the intellect. Therefore the habit by which one considers what one knows is also properly in the intellect.

Reply to 1: Some have said, as Simplicius reports,[42] that because every activity of man in some way is a joint activity of soul and body, as the Philosopher says,[43] then no habit is in the soul alone, but in the composite. From this it would follow that no habit is in the intellect, since the intellect is something separate, according to the argument advanced.[44] But this argument is not cogent. For habit is not a disposition of the object to the power, but rather a disposition of the power to the object. Hence habit must be in that power which is the principle of the act, and not in that which is compared to the power as its object. Now the act of understanding is not said to be common to soul and body except by reason of the phantasm.[45] But clearly the phantasm is related to the possible intellect as an object.[46] Hence it follows that an intellectual habit is principally on the part of the intellect itself, and not on the part of the phantasm, which is common to soul and body. Therefore it must be said that the possible intellect is the subject of habit, for that is capable of being the subject of habit which is in potency to many things, and this most of all belongs to the possible intellect. Hence the possible intellect is the subject of intellectual habits.

Reply to 2: Just as potentiality to being sensed belongs to corporeal matter, so potentiality to being intelligible belongs to the possible intellect. Hence nothing prevents habit, which is midway between pure potency and complete act, from being in the possible intellect.

Reply to 3: Because it is the interior sense powers that prepare for the possible intellect its proper object, hence it is from the good disposition of these powers, in which a good bodily disposition cooperates, that man is made apt in understanding. And thus intellectual habit can be in these powers in a secondary way. Principally, however, it is in the possible intellect.

Fifth Article

IS THERE ANY HABIT IN THE WILL?

It seems that there is no habit in the will.

1. The habits that are in the intellect are intelligible species,[47] by

---

[42] *On the Categories,* 8.   [43] *On the Soul* I, 1 (403a 8); 4 (408b 8).
[44] Cf. Simplicius, *On the Categories,* 8.   [45] Cf. Aristotle, *On the Soul* I, 1 (403a 5).
[46] *Op. cit.,* III, 7 (431a 14).   [47] I.e., concepts.

means of which the intellect actually knows. But the will does not operate by means of species. Therefore the will is not the subject of any
habit.

2. No habit is assigned to the active intellect, as there is to the possible
intellect, because the former is an active power. But the will most of all
is an active power, for it moves all powers to their acts, as has been
said.[48] Therefore there is no habit in it.

3. There is no habit in natural powers because by their nature they
are determined to something one. But the will by its nature is disposed
to tend to the good that reason prescribes. Therefore no habit is in the
will.

On the contrary: Justice is a habit. But justice is in the will, for it is
"a habit by which one wills and does what is just." [49] Therefore the
will is a subject of habit.

Response: Every power which can be diversely ordered to acting needs
a habit by which it is well disposed to its act. Now since the will is a
rational power, it can be diversely ordered as far as its act is concerned.
Hence we must assign to the will a habit whereby it is well disposed to
its act. It may also be gathered from the very notion of habit that it is
principally ordered to the will insofar as habit is "that which one makes
use of whenever he wills," as was noted above.[50]

Reply to 1: Just as there is in the intellect a species which is a likeness
of the object known, so in the will, and in any appetitive power, there
must be something which inclines the power to its object, since the act
of such a power is nothing but a certain inclination, as we have said.[51]
Now for those things to which it is sufficiently inclined by the nature of
the power itself, the power needs no quality to incline it. But since it
is necessary in relation to what human life is ordered to, that the appetitive power be inclined to something determinate, to which it is not
inclined by its nature—being related to many and diverse things—there
must be in the will and in other appetitive powers some inclining
qualities called habits.

Reply to 2: The active intellect is active only, and in no way passive.
But the will, and any appetitive power, is both mover and moved.[52]
Hence the comparison made between them does not hold, for to be
susceptible to a habit belongs to that which in some way is in potentiality.

Reply to 3: The will, by the very nature of the power, inclines to the
good of reason. But because this good is diversified in various ways, the
will needs to be inclined by a habit to a good determined by reason in
order that action may follow more promptly.

---

[48] Question 9, article 1.   [49] Aristotle, *Nicomachean Ethics* V, 1 (1129a 7).
[50] Article 1, arg. 1; question 49, article 3, *On the contrary.*   [51] Question 6, article 4.
[52] Cf. Aristotle, *On the Soul* III, 10 (433b 16).

Sixth Article

ARE THERE HABITS IN THE ANGELS?

It seems that there are no habits in the angels.

1. Maximus, a commentator on Dionysius, says: "It is not proper to think there are intellectual"—that is, spiritual—"virtues in divine intelligences," namely, in the angels, "in the manner of accidents, as there are in us, as though one were in the other as in a subject, for every kind of accident is foreign to them." [53] But every habit is an accident.[54] Therefore there are no habits in the angels.

2. As Dionysius says, "The holy dispositions of the celestial essences participate more than all other things in God's goodness." [55] But that which exists of itself is always prior to and more powerful than that which exists by means of something else. Therefore the essences of the angels are perfect of themselves in consequence of their conformity with God, and hence not through habits. This also seems to be the reasoning of Maximus who, in the passage already quoted, adds: "For if this were the case, [that is, if there were accidents in the angels as in us] certainly their essence would not continue to be one that is in itself, nor would it have had the power to be, as far as was possible, deified of itself."

3. A habit is a disposition.[56] But a disposition is "the order of that which has parts." [57] Since the angels are simple substances, it therefore seems that in them there are no dispositions and habits.

On the contrary: Dionysius says that the angels of the first hierarchy "are named *Fire-Bearers, Thrones,* and *Outpouring of Wisdom,* with the names evincing the godlike nature of their habits." [58]

Response: Some have maintained that in the angels there are no habits, and that whatever is said of them is said essentially. Hence Maximus says, after the passage quoted above,[59] "Their habits, and the powers which are in them, are essential because in them there is no matter." Simplicius says the same: "The wisdom in the soul is a habit, but the wisdom which is in the intellect is its substance. For all things that are divine are both sufficient of themselves and existent in themselves." [60]

This position is in part true and in part false. Now it is clear from what has been said,[61] that only a being in potentiality is the subject of

---

[53] *Commentary on "On the Celestial Hierarchy"* VII, 1. Maximus the Confessor lived from 580 to 662. The author of *On the Celestial Hierarchy* is actually unknown, and hence is usually referred to as Pseudo-Dionysius.

[54] In the predicamental or categorical sense of the term, and hence as opposed to substance. See note 12 of question 49.

[55] *On the Celestial Hierarchy* IV, 2.   [56] Cf. Aristotle, *Metaphysics* V, 20 (1022b 10).

[57] Aristotle, *op. cit.,* V, 19 (1022b 1).   [58] *On the Celestial Hierarchy* VII, 1.

[59] Cf. note 53.   [60] *Commentary on the Categories,* 8.   [61] Question 49, article 4.

habit. Hence the commentators mentioned above, considering that angels are immaterial substances and that there is not in them the potentiality of matter, for this reason excluded habit and all accidents from them. But although there is no potentiality of matter in the angels, nevertheless there is some potentiality in them (for to be pure act is proper to God), and hence insofar as potentiality is found in them, to that extent habits can be found in them. Because, however, the potentiality of matter and the potentiality of an intellectual substance are not of the same kind, neither are the respective habits. Hence Simplicius says, "The habits of an intellectual substance are not like the habits we have been talking about; rather, they are like simple and immaterial species which the substance contains within itself." [62]

However, the angelic intellect and the human intellect are constituted differently with respect to this kind of habit. The human intellect, since it is lowest in the order of intellects, is in potentiality with respect to all intelligible things, just as prime matter is in potentiality with respect to all sensible forms; therefore, for all intellectual knowing the intellect needs some habit. But the angelic intellect is not like a pure potentiality in respect to intelligible things. It is, rather, like a certain act—not pure act, for this belongs to God alone—but with the accompanying presence of some potentiality, and the less potentiality it has the more superior the intellect. Hence, as we have said,[63] insofar as the angelic intellect is in potentiality, it needs to be habitually perfected for its particular operation by means of intelligible species. But insofar as it is in act, it has the power to understand some things through its own essence, at least itself, and other things by way of its own substance.[64] Accordingly, the more perfect the intellect is the more perfectly will it know.

Nevertheless, because no angel achieves the perfection of God, but is infinitely distant from Him, for this reason, in order to come in contact with God Himself through intellect and will, an angel needs some habits since the angel is in potentiality with respect to that pure act. Hence Dionysius says in the same place,[65] "their habits are godlike," that is, by them they are made like unto God. But those habits which are dispositions to natural [66] being are not in angels, for angels are immaterial.

---

[62] *Commentary on the Categories,* 8.   [63] I, question 55, article 1.
[64] Cf. Dionysius, *Book of Causes,* VIII. The intellectual power of the angels extends to the understanding of all things, yet the angels do not know all things by their own essences. All things are in God's essence perfectly and according to their own natures. Hence only God has a proper knowledge of all things by His own essence. The angelic intellect must be perfected by some species in order to know, and especially to know God, which admits of some potentiality and hence the basis for some habits. See I, question 55, article 1.
[65] *On the Celestial Hierarchy* VII, 1.   [66] Natural in the sense of physical.

Reply to 1: Maximus is to be understood as speaking of material habits and accidents.

Reply to 2: With respect to what belongs to them by their essence, angels do not need a habit. But they are not beings of themselves to such an extent as not to participate in divine wisdom and goodness, hence insofar as they need to participate in something from without, to that extent there must be habits in them.

Reply to 3: There are not essential parts in the angels, but there are potential parts insofar as their intellect is perfected by several species and their will is related to several things.

The Cause of the Formation of Habits

(In Four Articles)

IS ANY HABIT FROM NATURE?

It seems that no habit comes from nature.

1. The activation[1] of what arises from nature is not subject to man's will. But habit "is that which one activates when he wills." [2] Therefore habit does not come from nature.

2. Nature does not do through two things what can be done by one. Now the powers of the soul are from nature. Accordingly, if the habits of powers were from nature, habit and power would be one.

3. Nature does not fail with respect to what is necessary. But habits are necessary in order to act well, as we have said.[3] If, accordingly, any habits were from nature, it seems that nature would not fail to cause all habits that are necessary. But this is clearly false. Therefore habits are not from nature.

On the contrary: Included among the various habits is the understanding of principles,[4] and this habit is from nature; and this is the reason that first principles are said to be naturally known.

Response: Something can be natural to a thing in two ways: first, in a way consistent with the nature of the species, as it is natural to man to be capable of laughter and for fire to rise upwards; secondly, in a way consistent with the individual nature, as it is natural to Socrates or Plato to be sickly or healthy, according to their respective physical constitutions. Further, with respect to each nature, something can be called natural in two additional ways: first, because the whole of it is from nature; secondly, because it is partly from nature and partly from an exterior principle. For example, when a man recovers his health with no extrinsic help, his health is entirely from nature, but when he is healed by the help of medicine, his health is partly from nature and partly from an exterior principle.

---

[1] The Latin for "activation" is *usus,* but a translation into "use" would be misleading in this argument.

[2] Averroes, *In De Anima* III, comm. 18.   [3] Question 49, article 4.

[4] Cf. Aristotle, *Nicomachean Ethics* VI, 6 (1141a 5).

If, then, we are speaking of habit as the disposition of the subject in relation to a form or nature, habit may be natural in any of the foregoing ways. For there is a natural disposition which is proper to the human species, which no man is without, and this is natural with respect to the nature of the species. But since such a disposition has a certain latitude, different gradations of this disposition can belong to different men according to their individual nature. And this sort of disposition can be either wholly from nature, or partly from nature and partly from an exterior principle, as we have said in regard to those who are healed by art.

But the habit which is a disposition for operation, whose subject, as we have said,[5] is the power of the soul, can be natural both with respect to the nature of the species and the individual nature—as regards the nature of the species, on the part of the soul which, as the form of the body, is the specific principle; as regards the individual nature, on the part of the body, which is the material principle. Nevertheless, in neither way is it possible that these habits in men be natural to such an extent that they are wholly from nature. This indeed does happen in the angels, for they are naturally endowed with intelligible species, but this is not the case with the human soul, as we have said.[6]

There are, therefore, in man some habits that are natural, which owe their existence partly to nature and partly to an extrinsic principle—in one way, in the powers of knowing and in another way in the appetitive powers. In the knowing powers, there can be a natural habit by way of a beginning, both with respect to the nature of the species and to the nature of the individual. In regard to the nature of the species, this takes place on the part of the soul; as the understanding of principles, for instance, is said to be a natural habit. For it is owing to the very nature of the intellectual soul that man, as soon as he grasps what a whole is and what a part is, at once knows that every [quantitative] whole is greater than its part, and so with other instances. But what a whole is and what a part is he cannot know except by means of intelligible species taken from phantasms;[7] and because of this the Philosopher shows that knowledge of principles comes to us via the senses.[8] In regard to the individual nature, a habit of knowing is natural by way of a beginning insofar as one man, by organic disposition, is more apt than another to understand well, inasmuch as we need sense powers for the operation of our intellect.

In appetitive powers, however, no habit is natural as to its beginning on the part of the soul itself, as far as the substance of habit is concerned,

---

[5] Question 50, article 2.   [6] I, question 55, article 2; question 84, article 3.

[7] That is, the human intellect abstracts what a whole is and what a part is from the sense-knowing of individual instances, and so forms an intelligible species or concept.

[8] *Posterior Analytics* II, 19 (100a 5).

but only as far as certain of its principles are concerned; as the principles of common law, for instance, are said to be "seeds of virtues." And this is because the inclination to proper objects, which seems to be the beginning of habit, does not belong to the habit but rather to the very nature of the powers. But on the part of the body, as regards the individual nature, there are some appetitive habits by way of natural beginnings. For some persons are disposed by their bodily temperament to chastity or to gentleness, or something of this kind.

Reply to 1: This argument takes nature as divided against reason and will; but nonetheless reason and will belong to man's nature.

Reply to 2: Something can be added to a power even naturally and yet not belong to the power itself. For example, it is not within the angel's intellectual power by itself to know all things, because it would have to be the act of all things and this belongs to God alone. For that by which something is known must be an actual likeness of that which is known, and hence if the power of the angel of itself knew all things, it would follow that it was the likeness and the act of all things. Consequently, some intelligible species which are likenesses of the things understood have to be added to an angel's intellectual power since it is by participation in divine wisdom, and not through their own essence, that intellects of angels can actually be the things they understand. Clearly, then, some things that belong to a natural habit may not belong to the power.

Reply to 3: Nature is not uniformly capable of causing all the different kinds of habits, for some can be caused by nature and some not, as we have said.[9] Hence it does not follow that if some habits are natural, all are natural.

Second Article

IS A HABIT CAUSED BY ACTS?

It seems that no habit can be caused by acts.

1. Habit is a quality, as we have said.[10] But every quality is caused in a subject insofar as the subject receives something. Since, then, an agent, inasmuch as it acts, does not receive but rather dispenses something, it seems that habit cannot be caused in an agent by its own acts.

2. The thing in which a quality is caused is moved toward that quality, as is evident in something being heated or cooled, while the thing which produces the act causing the quality is the mover, as is evident in that which does the heating or cooling. If, then, a habit were caused in something by its own act, it would follow that the same thing would be mover and moved, active and passive, which is impossible.[11]

---

[9] In the body of this article.   [10] Question 49, article 1.
[11] Cf. Aristotle, *Physics* VII, 1 (241b 24).

3. An effect cannot be superior to its cause. But a habit is superior to the act which precedes the habit; this is evident from the fact that habit makes an act more perfect. Therefore a habit cannot be caused by an act which precedes the habit.

On the contrary: The Philosopher maintains that the habits of virtue or vice are caused by acts.[12]

Response: Sometimes in an agent there is only an active principle of its acts; for example, in fire there is only the active principle of heating. In such an agent a habit cannot be caused by its own act; this is why natural things cannot become habituated or unhabituated to something.[13] But there is an agent in which there is an active and passive principle of its act. Clearly this is the case in human acts, for the acts of the appetitive power proceed from that power according as it is moved by the knowing power presenting the object; further, the intellectual power, as it is reasoning to conclusions, has as its active principle a proposition known in itself. Hence, from such acts habits can be caused in their agents, not with regard to the first active principle, but with regard to the principle of the act, which is a mover that is moved. For everything that is passive and moved by another is disposed through the act of the agent. Hence by repeated acts, a quality is formed in the passive and moved power, and this quality is called a habit. For example, habits of moral virtue are caused in appetitive powers as they are moved by reason, and habits of science are caused in the intellect according as it is moved by primary propositions.

Reply to 1: An agent as agent is not receiving something. But insofar as it is acting as moved by another, it is receiving something from that which moves it, and thus a habit is caused.

Reply to 2: The same thing, in the same respect, cannot be mover and moved. But nothing prevents a thing from being moved by itself in different respects.[14]

Reply to 3: The act that precedes a habit, insofar as it proceeds from an active principle, proceeds from a principle superior to the habit which it causes. For example, reason is a principle superior to the habit of moral virtue produced in an appetitive power by repeated acts, and the understanding of primary principles is superior to the knowledge of conclusions.

Third Article

CAN A HABIT BE PRODUCED BY ONE ACT?

It seems that a habit can be produced by one act.

1. Demonstration is an act of reasoning. But science, the habit by

---

[12] *Nicomachean Ethics* II, 1 (1103a 31).   [13] Cf. Aristotle, *op. cit.,* (1103a 19).
[14] Cf. Aristotle, *Physics* VIII, 5 (257a 31).

which reason moves determinately to a conclusion, is caused by one demonstration. Therefore a habit can be caused by one act.

2. Just as it is possible for act to grow by multiplication, so it is possible for act to increase by intensity. But when acts are repeated, a habit is formed. Therefore, if an act is very intense, it can be the formative cause of a habit.

3. Health and sickness are habits. But from one act a man may become healthy or sick. Therefore one act can cause a habit.

On the contrary: The Philosopher says that "one swallow does not make spring, nor does one day; and so, also, one day, or a short time, does not make a man blessed and happy." [15] But "happiness is activity in conformity with the most perfect virtue." [16] Therefore the habit of a virtue, and for the same reason any other habit, is not caused by one act.

Response: As we have said,[17] a habit is produced by act insofar as a passive power is moved by an active principle. But in order that some quality be caused in what is passive, the active principle must wholly dominate the passive. Hence we see that because fire cannot totally dominate an inflammable substance, it does not immediately set it on fire, but gradually expels contrary dispositions so that thus overcoming it entirely, it may impress its likeness upon it.

Now obviously reason, which is an active principle, cannot wholly dominate an appetitive power in one act. For the appetitive power is inclined in different ways and to many things, whereas reason judges in a single act that this should be willed for these reasons and in these circumstances. Consequently, the appetitive power is not at once wholly controlled so as to be inclined like nature to the same thing for the most part, which is proper to a habit of virtue. Hence a habit of virtue cannot be caused by one act, but only by many.

In the powers of apprehending, however, we must take into account that there are two passive principles. One is the possible intellect itself; the other is what Aristotle calls the passive intellect,[18] which is the particular reason, that is, the cogitative power in association with memory and imagination.[19] In regard to the first passive principle, there can be an active principle which, by one act, can overcome entirely the power of its own passive principle; for example, one self-evident proposition convinces the intellect to assent firmly to a conclusion. This a probable proposition cannot do; hence many acts are needed to cause a habit of opinion even as regards the possible intellect, whereas a scientific habit can be caused

---

[15] *Nicomachean Ethics* I, 7 (1098a 18).   [16] *Ibid.,* (1098a 16).   [17] Article 3.
[18] *On the Soul* III, 5 (430a 24).
[19] Hence this passive principle refers to an interior sense power of knowing, not properly to the intellect itself. The human intellect is called the *possible intellect* because it is in potency to intelligible things.

by a single act of reason as far as the possible intellect is concerned.

With regard to the lower powers of apprehending, it is necessary that the same acts be repeated many times so that something may be impressed firmly on the memory. Hence the Philosopher says that "'frequent contemplation of something as a likeness, and not as out of relation, preserves one's memory." [20] Bodily habits, however, may be caused by one act, if the active principle is of great power; for example, sometimes a powerful medicine immediately brings about a healthy condition.

The replies to the arguments initially given are clear from what has been said.

Fourth Article

ARE ANY HABITS INFUSED IN MAN BY GOD?

It seems that no habits are infused in man by God.

1. God treats all men equally. Hence, if He infused habits in some men, He would infuse them in all, which is clearly false.

2. God works in all things in a way appropriate to their nature, for "it belongs to divine providence to preserve nature," as Dionysius says.[21] But in man habits are caused naturally by acts, as we have said.[22] Therefore God does not cause any habits in man except by acts.

3. If a habit is infused by God, by that habit man can produce many acts. But "from acts of a certain kind, like habits are caused." [23] It follows, then, that there would be two habits of the same kind in the same man, one acquired and the other infused. This seems to be impossible, for two forms of the same species cannot be in the same subject. Therefore no habit is infused in man by God.

On the contrary: "God filled him with the spirit of wisdom and understanding" (*Ecclesiasticus 15:5*). But wisdom and understanding are habits. Therefore some habits are infused in man by God.

Response: Some habits are infused in man by God, which can be shown by two arguments. The first is that there are some habits which dispose man well with respect to an end exceeding the power of human nature, this end being the ultimate and perfect happiness of man, as we have said.[24] Now, since habits must be proportionate to what a man is disposed to by them, it follows that the habits disposing man to such an end must also exceed the power of human nature. Consequently, such habits can never be in man except by infusion from God, as is the case with all virtues gratuitously given.

The second argument is based on the fact that God can produce the effects of secondary causes without the secondary causes themselves, as

---

[20] *On Memory and Reminiscence,* 1 (451a 12).   [21] *The Divine Names* III, 33.
[22] Article 2.   [23] Aristotle, *Nicomachean Ethics* II, 1 (1103b 21).
[24] Question 5, article 5.

we have pointed out.[25] Consequently, just as God, in order to manifest His power, sometimes produces health without a natural cause even though it could be caused by nature, so also to manifest His power, He sometimes infuses into man habits which can be caused by a natural power. For example, He gave to the Apostles the knowledge of the Scriptures and of various tongues, which men can acquire by study or custom, though not so perfectly.

Reply to 1: God, with respect to His nature, is related equally to all, but according to the order of His wisdom, and for some determined reason, He gives certain things to some which He does not give to others.

Reply to 2: The fact that God works in all things in a way appropriate to their nature does not prevent His doing what nature cannot do; but it follows from this that He does nothing adverse to what is fitting to nature.

Reply to 3: Acts produced by an infused habit do not cause a habit, but strengthen the habit already existing, just as medicinal treatment given to a man who is naturally healthy does not cause a healthy condition, but invigorates the health he already has.

---

[25] I, question 105, article 6.

The Increase of Habits

(In Three Articles)

CAN HABITS INCREASE?

It seems that habits cannot increase.

1. Growth or increase has reference to quantity.[1] Habits, however, are not in the genus of quantity, but in the genus of quality. Therefore habits cannot grow.

2. Habit is a perfection.[2] But since perfection implies an end and a boundary, it seems that it cannot be subject to more and less. Therefore a habit cannot increase.

3. Alteration is possible in things subject to more and less, for when something less hot becomes more hot we say it is altered. But there is no alteration in habits, as is proved in the *Physics.*[3] Therefore habits cannot increase.

On the contrary: Faith is a habit, and yet it increases. Hence the disciples said to our Lord: "Increase our faith" (*Luke 17:5*). Therefore habits increase.

Response: Increase, like other things having reference to quantity, is transferred from corporeal quantities to spiritual and intellectual things because of the connaturality of our intellect for corporeal things, which fall within the imagination. Now in regard to corporeal quantity, something is called great insofar as it attains a due perfection of quantity, and hence a certain quantity is regarded as great in a human being which is not regarded as great in an elephant. So also, in regard to forms, we say that something is great because it is perfect. And since the good is conceived as a perfection, therefore "in those things which are not great in bulk, to be greater is the same as to be better." [4]

Now perfection of form can be looked at in two ways: first, from the viewpoint of form itself; second, from the viewpoint of the subject's participation in the form. When we have in mind the perfection of a form, intending the form itself, we say it is *little* or *great;* for example, little or great health or science. But when we have in mind the perfection

---

[1] Cf. Aristotle, *Physics* V, 2 (226a 30).   [2] Cf. Aristotle, *op. cit.,* VII, 3 (246a 13).
[3] *Ibid.*   [4] Augustine, *The Trinity* VI, 8.

of a form, intending the subject's participation in it, we say it is *more* or *less;* for example, more or less white or healthy. This distinction is not to be taken as implying that the form exists outside of its matter or subject, but rather that the consideration of a form as to its kind is one thing and the participation of the subject in it is another.

Accordingly, there were four opinions among philosophers about the intensity and remission of habits and forms.[5] Plotinus and other Platonists held that qualities and habits themselves admitted of more and less because they were material, and hence had a certain lack of determination because of the infinity of matter. Others, on the contrary, held that qualities and habits of themselves were not subject to more and less, but that the things having such qualities are said to be more or less, according to their diverse participation in them; for example, that justice is not said to be more or less, but a just action or thing is. Aristotle touches upon this opinion in the *Categories*.[6] The third opinion was that of the Stoics, which is midway between these two. They held that some habits of themselves are subject to more and less, such as the arts; others are not, such as the virtues. A fourth opinion was held by those who said that immaterial qualities and forms are not subject to more and less, but material ones are.

In order to make the truth of this matter evident, we must note that that from which a thing takes its species must be fixed and constant, and in a way indivisible; for whatever attains to that is contained under the species and whatever recedes from that, whether more or less, belongs to another species, either a more perfect or a more imperfect one. Hence the Philosopher says that the species of things are like numbers, in which addition or subtraction varies the species.[7] If therefore any form, or anything whatever, either as to itself or as to something belonging to it, takes on the notion of species, it must, considered in itself, have a determinate nature which can be neither more nor less. Such are hotness, whiteness, and other such qualities which are not said in relation to something else; and much more so substance, which is a being per se.

But things which receive their species from something to which they are ordered can be diversified, in themselves, according to more and less; nonetheless, they remain the same in species because of the unity of that to which they are ordered and by which they are specified. For example, a movement as such increases or decreases, but it still remains the same species of movement because of the oneness of the term by which it is specified. The same point can be noted about health, for the body attains a healthy condition to the extent that it has a disposition suitable to the animal's nature, for which various dispositions are suitable; hence a disposition can be varied more or less with the body still remaining in a

[5] Cf. Simplicius, *Commentary on the Categories,* VIII.   [6] *Categories,* 8 (10b 30).
[7] *Metaphysics* VIII, 3 (1043b 33).

healthy condition. Thus the Philosopher says, "Health itself is susceptible of more or less, for the proportion is not the same in all things, nor is it always the same in one and the same thing, for it may diminish down to a certain point and the health still remain." [8] These varying dispositions or proportions of health are by way of excess and defect. Hence if the name *health* were imposed only for the most perfect proportion, then health itself could not be called greater or less. It is thus evident how a quality or a form can of itself increase or diminish and how it cannot.

Now if we regard a quality or a form in terms of the subject's participation in it, again we find that some qualities and forms are susceptible of more or less and some are not. Simplicius gives as the cause of this diversity the fact that substance in itself cannot be subject to more and less because it is a being per se.[9] Hence every form in which a subject participates substantially has no increase and decrease, and accordingly in the genus of substance nothing is said by way of more and less. And because quantity is close to substance, and shape follows upon quantity, hence in neither of these is anything said by way of more or less. As a consequence, the Philosopher says that when something receives form and shape, this is not spoken of as an alteration but rather as a becoming.[10] But other qualities, which are more removed from substance and connected with passions and actions, are susceptible of more and less according to the subject's participation.

The reason for this diversity, however, can be made more explicit. As we have said, that from which a thing has its species must remain fixed and constant in an indivisible way. Hence there are two ways in which it can happen that a form is not participated in more or less. First, because the species of the participant is coincident with that form. Thus it is that no substantial form is more or less participated in. This is the reason the Philosopher says, "just as number does not admit of the more or less, so neither does substance in the sense of species," that is, as far as participation of the specific form is concerned, "but if the substance involves matter," that is, when material dispositions are involved, "more or less is found in substance." [11]

Secondly, this can happen because of the fact that indivisibility is of the very notion of the form. This being so, it follows that if something participates in that form, it must participate in it with regard to its indivisibility. This is why we do not speak of the species of number as varying in respect to more or less seeing that each species of number is formed by means of an indivisible unity. This same point applies to the species of continuous quantity, which are denominated from numbers, such as two feet long and three feet long; and to relations of quantity, such as double and triple; and to figures, such as triangle and square.

---

[8] *Nicomachean Ethics* X, 3 (1173a 24).   [9] Cf. Simplicius, *op. cit.*, VIII.
[10] Cf. *Physics* VII, 3 (246a 1).   [11] *Metaphysics* VIII, 3 (1044a 10).

The same point is made by Aristotle in the *Categories* when, explaining why figures are not susceptible of more or less, he says, "Those things which are given the definition of triangle or circle are all equally triangles and circles," [12] because indivisibility belongs to their very notion; hence whatever participates in their notion must participate in it indivisibly.

Accordngly it is evident, since we speak of habits and dispositions in terms of an ordering to something,[13] that increase and decrease in habits and dispositions can be considered in two ways. In one way, in regard to the habit itself—as health is said to be greater or less, or knowledge greater or less, which is extended to more or fewer things. In another way, according to the subject's participation; thus, an equal degree of knowledge or health is received in one person more than in another because of a differing aptitude, either from nature or from custom. For habit and disposition do not give species to a subject, nor does either in its notion include indivisibility.

We shall speak subsequently about the relation of this to virtue.[14]

Reply to 1: Just as the name *magnitude* is derived from corporeal quantities and applied to the intelligible perfections of forms, so also is the name *growth,* whose term is something great.

Reply to 2: Habit is a certain perfection, but not the perfection which is terminal in respect to its subject, namely, one that gives specific being to it. Nor does habit include a term in its notion as do the species of number. Hence there is nothing to prevent a habit from being subject to more and less.

Reply to 3: It is true that alteration is in the third species of quality primarily. But there can be alteration in the first species of quality, though secondarily, for once there is an alteration with respect to hot and cold, an alteration in the animal with respect to health and sickness results. Likewise, when there is an alteration with respect to passions of the sense appetite, or the powers of sense apprehension, an alteration with respect to sciences and virtues results.[15]

Second Article

DOES A HABIT INCREASE THROUGH ADDITION?

It seems that habits increase through addition.

1. The name *increase,* as we have said,[16] is transferred from corporeal

---

[12] *Categories,* 8 (11a 7).   [13] Cf. Aristotle, *Physics* VII, 3 (246b 3; 247a 1).

[14] Question 66, article 1. The general conclusion reached through the foregoing extended and highly developed treatment may be summarized as follows. In the last analysis, we have to recognize that a habit is understood with reference to something else, not being substantial in nature. Consequently, whether considered in itself or as participated in by the subject, a habit admits of increase or decrease, and can be strengthened or weakened.

[15] Cf. Aristotle, *Physics* VII, 3 (247a 6; 248a 6).   [16] Article 1.

quantities to forms. But in corporeal quantities there is no increase without addition, and hence it is said that "an increase is an addition to an already existing magnitude." [17] Therefore there is also no increase in habit except by addition.

2. A habit does not increase except by means of some agent. But every agent produces something in the receiving subject; for instance, that which heats causes heat in what is heated. Therefore there cannot be increase without some addition.

3. Just as that which is not white is in potency to be white, so that which is less white is in potency to be more white. But that which is not white does not become white except by the addition of whiteness. Therefore that which is less white does not become more white except by the adding of more whiteness.

On the contrary: "It is the same material which from being hot becomes still hotter; there is nothing in the material which, when it was less hot, was something nonhot, and which thereupon becomes hot." [18] With equal reason, therefore, there is not any addition in other forms which are increased.

Response: The solution to this question depends upon what we have already said.[19] For we said that increase and decrease in the forms which are enlarged or diminished occurs, in one way, not in point of the form considered in itself, but through the diverse participation of the subject. Therefore such an increase of habits and other forms is not caused by the addition of a form to a form, but by the subject's participating more or less perfectly in one and the same form. And just as, through an agent which is in act, something is made actually hot, beginning anew, as it were, to participate in that form—not that a new form is caused, as is proved in the *Metaphysics*[20]—so by an intense action of the agent it is made more hot, as though it were participating more perfectly in the form, not as though something were added to the form.

For if such an increase in forms were understood to be by way of addition, this could only be either on the part of the form itself or on the part of the subject. But if it were on the part of the form itself, we have already noted [21] that such an addition or subtraction would change the species, as the species of color is changed when someone becomes tan from being white. But if the addition were understood on the part of the subject, this could only be either because a part of the subject receives a form which it did not have previously—for example, we could say that cold increases in a man who previously was cold in one part of his body and now is cold in several parts—or because there is the addition of some other subject that is a participant in the same form, as when one

---

[17] Aristotle, *On Generation and Corruption* I, 5 (320b 30).
[18] Aristotle, *Physics* IV, 9 (217a 34).   [19] In the preceding article.
[20] *Metaphysics* VII, 8 (1033b 5); 9 (1034b 7).   [21] Article 1.

hot thing is joined to another, or one white thing to another. But with respect to either of these two, we do not speak of a more white or hot thing, but of a greater white or hot thing.

Since, however, there are certain accidents which are in themselves subject to increase, as we have said,[22] in some of these there may be increase by addition. For movement increases by an addition either to the time it lasts or to the course it follows; but it remains the same species of movement because of the oneness of the term. A movement increases in intensity as well, according to the participation of its subject, namely, inasmuch as the same movement is more or less readily or quickly executed. In a similar manner, a science can be increased in itself by addition; for example, when someone learns many conclusions of geometry, the habit of a science that is the same in species increases in him. A science, however, also increases in intensity according to the subject's participation, namely, inasmuch as one man is quicker and more discerning than another in considering the same conclusions.

In corporeal habits, however, there does not seem to be much increase by addition. For an animal is not called healthy unqualifiedly, or beautiful, unless it be such as to all of its parts. And if it is brought to a more perfect proportion, this occurs through a change of simple qualities, which are not increased except according to intensity on the part of the participating subject.

We shall show how this relates to the virtues subsequently.[23]

Reply to 1: Even in bodily magnitude there can be an increase in two ways. First, by the addition of a subject to a subject, as in the increase of living things. Second, by intensity alone, without any addition, as in things subject to rarefaction.[24]

Reply to 2: A cause which increases a habit does produce something in the subject, but not a new form. What it does, rather, is make the subject participate more perfectly in a form already existing, or it makes the form extend further.

Reply to 3: What is not yet white is in potency to white as not yet having that form, and hence the agent causes a new form in the subject. But what is less hot or less white is not in potency to the form since it already actually has that form, but it is in potency to participating in it in a more perfect way. And this results from the action of an agent.

Third Article

DOES EVERY ACT INCREASE A HABIT?

It seems that every act increases a habit.

1. When a cause is multiplied the effect is multiplied. But acts are

---

[22] *Ibid.*   [23] Question 66, article 1.   [24] Cf. Aristotle, *Physics* IV, 7 (214b 2); 9 (217b 8).

the causes of some habits, as we have said.[25] Therefore a habit is increased by multiplying its acts.

2. A like judgment should be formed about similar things. But all acts proceeding from the same habit are similar.[26] Therefore, if some acts increase a habit, every act will increase it.

3. Like is increased by its like. But any act is like the habit from which it proceeds. Therefore every act increases its habit.

On the contrary: The same thing is not the cause of contrary effects. But some acts proceeding from a habit diminish the habit, for example, when done carelessly.[27] Therefore not every act increases a habit.

Response: "Like acts cause like habits." [28] But things are judged like or unlike not only according to sameness or diversity of quality, but also according to sameness or diversity in their mode of participation. For not only is black unlike white, but less white is unlike more white, for there is also movement from less white to more white, which is similar to movement from one opposite to another.[29]

Now since the use of habits depends upon man's will, as we have shown,[30] just as someone who has a habit may not use it or may even do an act contrary to it, so he may use the habit in an act not corresponding proportionally to the intensity of the habit. If, then, the intensity of the act is proportionally equal to the intensity of the habit, or even exceeds it, such acts either increase the habit or dispose it to an increase, bearing in mind that we are speaking of the increase of habits as analogous to the increase of an animal. For not every portion of food actually increases an animal in size, just as not every drop of water hollows out a stone, but when there is a repeated intake of food an increase in size finally takes place. So also, with repeated acts, a habit grows. But if the intensity of the act falls short of the intensity of the habit, such an act does not dispose a habit to increase, but rather to decrease.

The replies to the opening arguments are clear from the response.

---

[25] Question 51, article 2.   [26] Cf. Aristotle, *Nicomachean Ethics* II, 2 (1104a 29).
[27] Cf. Aristotle, *op. cit.*, II, 2 (1104a 18).   [28] Aristotle, *op. cit.*, II, 1 (1103b 21).
[29] Cf. Aristotle, *Physics* V, 5 (229b 14).
[30] Question 49, article 3, *On the contrary;* question 50, article 5.

The Corruption and Diminishing of Habits
(In Three Articles)

CAN HABITS BE CORRUPTED?

It seems that habits cannot be corrupted.

1. A habit is present in its subject as a kind of nature; this is the reason it is enjoyable to act from habit. But as long as a thing exists, its nature is not corrupted. Therefore neither can a habit be corrupted as long as its subject remains.

2. Corruption of a form is caused either through the corruption of its subject or by the contrary form; for example, sickness disappears with the death of the animal or the return of health. But science, which is a habit, cannot be corrupted through the corruption of its subject because the intellect, which is its subject, "is like an incorruptible substance." [1] Nor can it be corrupted by a contrary, for intelligible species[2] are not contrary to each other.[3] Therefore the habit of science can in no way be corrupted.

3. All corruption is by means of some movement. But the habit of science, which is in the soul, cannot be corrupted by movement of the soul itself directly, for the soul itself does not move; rather, it is moved incidentally by movement of the body. Now no bodily change seems able to corrupt the intelligible species existing in the intellect since the intellect is the immediate and independent locus of the species; this is the reason habits are not lost through either age or death. Therefore science cannot be corrupted and, consequently, neither can the habit of virtue, which also is in the rational soul; in fact, as the Philosopher says, "virtues are even more lasting than sciences." [4]

On the contrary: The Philosopher says that "science is lost by forgetfulness and deception." [5] Furthermore, some habits of virtue are lost by sinning. And finally, virtues come into being and are lost through contrary acts.[6]

---

[1] Aristotle, *On the Soul* I, 4 (408b 18).   [2] I.e., concepts.
[3] Cf. Aristotle, *Metaphysics* VII, 7 (1032b 2).   [4] *Nicomachean Ethics* I, 10 (1100b 14).
[5] *On the Length and Shortness of Life*, 2 (465a 23).
[6] Cf. Aristotle, *Nicomachean Ethics* II, 1 (1103b 7); 3 (1105a 15).

Response: A form is said to be directly corrupted by its contrary, but accidentally by the corruption of its subject. If therefore there should be some habit whose subject is corruptible and whose cause has a contrary, then the habit could be corrupted in either way, as is evident with bodily habits, such as sickness and health. Those habits whose subject is incorruptible, however, cannot be corrupted accidentally. But there are some habits which, though existing principally in an incorruptible subject, nevertheless exist secondarily in a corruptible subject; this is the case with the habit of science, which is principally in the possible intellect,[7] but secondarily in the sense-knowing powers, as we have said.[8] Consequently, on the part of the possible intellect, the habit of science cannot be corrupted accidentally; it can only be corrupted accidentally on the part of the lower sense powers.

We have to consider, then, whether habits of this kind can be directly corrupted. If there should be a habit which has a contrary either in regard to itself or in regard to its cause, it could be directly corrupted; if it does not have a contrary, however, it cannot be directly corrupted. Now clearly an intelligible species[9] existing in the possible intellect does not have any contrary; nor can anything be contrary to the agent intellect,[10] which is the cause of the species. Hence if in the possible intellect there is a habit caused immediately by the agent intellect, such a habit cannot be corrupted either directly or accidentally. Such habits are the understanding of first principles, both speculative and practical, which can never be lost by forgetfulness or deception, as the Philosopher says of prudence: "it is not lost through being forgotten." [11]

There is, however, a habit in the possible intellect that is caused by reason; it is the habit of arriving determinately at conclusions, and is called science. Now something can be contrary to the cause of this habit in two ways. In one way, on the part of the very propositions from which the reasoning process begins, for a proposition such as *A good is not good* is contrary to *A good is good.*[12] In a second way, on the part of the process of reasoning itself, and thus a sophistic syllogism is opposed to a dialectical or a demonstrative syllogism. It is evident, therefore, that spurious reasoning can corrupt the habit of true opinion, or even of science. Hence the Philosopher says that "science is lost through deception," as we have noted above.[13]

---

[7] The possible intellect is distinguished from the active or agent intellect. The act of the agent intellect is to abstract what is intelligible from what is perceived by the senses. The act of the possible intellect is the production of a concept from the object made ready to be known by the agent intellect. The agent intellect and the possible intellect are therefore two distinct powers of the human soul, but both combine to produce the act of understanding.

[8] Question 50, article 3, reply to 3.   [9] See note 2 above.   [10] See note 7 above.

[11] *Nicomachean Ethics* VI, 5 (1140b 29).

[12] Cf. Aristotle, *On Interpretation,* 14 (24a 2).   [13] This article; *On the contrary.*

Now some virtues are intellectual and exist in reason itself, as Aristotle points out;[14] and what we have said about science and opinion applies to these. Others, however, the moral virtues, are in the appetitive part of the soul, as are also their contraries, the vices. Now habits are caused in the appetitive part by the fact that reason has a natural aptitude to move the appetitive part. Consequently, a habit of virtue or vice is corrupted by the judgment of reason whenever it moves contrary to such virtue or vice, whether through ignorance or passion or even deliberate choice.

Reply to 1: A habit is like a nature, and yet it falls short of being a nature.[15] Consequently, while the nature of a thing can in no way be removed from that thing, a habit can be removed, though with difficulty.

Reply to 2: Although there is no contrary to intelligible species, nevertheless there can be a contrary to propositions and to the process of reasoning, as we have indicated.[16]

Reply to 3: Science is not removed by bodily change as far as the root of the habit is concerned, but bodily change may be an obstacle to its functioning inasmuch as the intellect in its act needs the sense powers, which are impeded by bodily change. But the intellectual movement of reason can corrupt a habit of science, even in regard to its very root. In a similar way, a habit of virtue can be corrupted. Even so, the remark "virtues are more lasting than sciences," [17] must be understood, not of the subject or the cause, but of the act, for the use of virtue continues throughout the whole of life, but not the use of learning.

Second Article

CAN A HABIT BE DIMINISHED?

It seems that a habit cannot be diminished.

1. A habit is a quality and a simple form. Now what is simple is either possessed wholly or wholly lost. Therefore a habit, although it can be wholly lost, cannot be diminished.

2. Everything belonging to an accident belongs to the accident as such or by reason of its subject. Now a habit as such does not intensify or diminish, otherwise it would follow that a species could be predicated more or less of the individuals of the species. And if a habit can be diminished through the subject's participation, it follows that something characteristic happens to a habit which is not common to the habit and its subject. Now whenever something characteristic belongs to a form over and beyond the subject in which it is, such a form is separable from

---

[14] *Nicomachean Ethics* VI, 1 (1139a 1); 2 (1139b 12).
[15] Cf. Aristotle, *op. cit.,* VII, 10 (1152a 31).   [16] In the body of this article.
[17] Aristotle, *Nicomachean Ethics* VII, 10 (1152a 31).

its subject.[18] It would follow then that a habit is a separable form, which is impossible.

3. The very notion and nature of a habit, as of any accident, consists in being united with a subject, and hence any accident is defined with reference to its subject. If, then, a habit as such does not intensify or diminish, neither can it diminish by being united with a subject. Thus in no way is a habit diminished.

On the contrary: Contraries are naturally apt to happen with respect to the same thing. Now increasing and diminishing are contraries. Since a habit can increase, it therefore seems that it can also diminish.

Response: Habits diminish as well as increase in two ways, as is evident from what we have said above.[19] And just as they are increased through the same cause that generates them so they are diminished through the same cause that corrupts them, for the diminishing of a habit is the means to its corruption just as, conversely, the generation of a habit is the foundation for its increase.

Reply to 1: A habit, considered in itself, is a simple form, and in this respect it does not diminish. It does diminish according to the different ways the subject participates in it. This is because the potentiality of the subject is indeterminate and thus able to participate in one form in various ways or extend to more or fewer things.

Reply to 2: The argument given would stand if the essence of the habit could in no way be diminished. We do not hold this; rather, we maintain that a certain diminishing of the essence of the habit originates, not from the habit, but from the subject participating in it.

Reply to 3: However an accident is signified, its very notion involves dependence upon a subject, though in different ways. If an accident is signified in the abstract, it implies a relationship to the subject which begins with the accident and terminates in the subject, for *whiteness* designates *that by which a thing is white.* Hence in defining an abstract accident, the subject is not stated as the first part of the definition, which is the genus, but as the second part, which is the difference, for we say that *snubness* is a *curvature of the nose.* But in an accident signified concretely, the relationship begins with the subject and terminates in the accident, for *white* denotes *that which has whiteness.* Accordingly, in defining such an accident, the subject is stated as the genus, which is the first part of the definition, for we say that a snub [nose] is a *nose that is curved.* Thus what belongs to accidents apropos of the subject, but is not of the very essence of the accident, is attributed to the concrete accident but not to the abstract one. Now increasing and diminishing are like this, in some accidents. Hence we do not say *more* or *less* of whiteness, but we do of white. The same holds for habits and other qualities, except

---

[18] Cf. Aristotle, *On the Soul* I, 1 (403a 10).   [19] Question 52, article 1.

that some habits increase or diminish by a kind of addition, as we have already explained.[20]

Third Article

IS A HABIT CORRUPTED OR DIMINISHED BY MERE CESSATION OF ACT?

It seems that a habit is not corrupted or diminished by mere cessation of act.

1. Habits are more permanent than passive qualities, as we have said.[21] But passive qualities are not corrupted nor diminished by a cessation of act, for whiteness is not diminished if it is not affecting the sight nor is heat diminished if it is not making something hot. Therefore habits are not corrupted nor diminished by cessation of act.

2. Corruption and diminishing are changes. But nothing is changed without some moving cause. Hence, since cessation of act does not imply a moving cause, it does not seem that a habit can be corrupted or diminished by cessation of act.

3. The habits of science and virtue are in the intellectual soul, which is above time. But things which are above time are neither corrupted nor diminished by the passage of time. Therefore habits are not corrupted or diminished by the passage of time even if one should not exercise them for a long time.

On the contrary: The Philosopher says that "science is lost not only by deception, but also by forgetfulness." [22] He also says that "lack of communication dissolves many friendships." [23] Similarly, other virtuous habits are diminished or lost by a cessation of act.

Response: A thing can cause movement in two ways.[24] First, directly, as in the case of a thing that causes movement by reason of its own form; for example, fire causes heat. Second, accidentally, when something removes an obstacle. It is in this latter way that cessation of act causes the corruption or diminishing of habits, insofar as the act is not exercised which restrains the causes that corrupt or diminish the habit. For, as we have said,[25] habits are directly corrupted or diminished by the action of a contrary. Hence, all habits that are in time subject to being undetermined by contraries (which need counteracting by an act proceeding from the habit) are diminished or even wholly destroyed by a long cessation from act, as is evident in both science and virtue. For clearly a habit of moral virtue makes a man disposed to choose the mean in actions and passions. However, when someone does not make use of the virtuous habit to mod-

---

[20] Question 52, article 2.   [21] Question 49, article 2, reply to 3; question 50, article 1.
[22] *On the Length and Shortness of Life,* 2 (465a 23).
[23] *Nicomachean Ethics* VIII, 5 (1157b 13).   [24] Cf. Aristotle, *Physics* VIII, 4 (254b 7).
[25] Article 1.

erate his passions or actions, the necessary consequence is that many of his passions and actions fail to observe the mean of virtue because of the inclination of sense appetite and other external influences. Hence the virtue is corrupted or diminished by cessation from act.

The same holds on the part of intellectual habits, which dispose a man to judge rightly about things represented in the imagination. Hence when a man ceases to make use of his intellectual habit, strange images arise, sometimes moving him to the contrary of a right judgment; so that unless these illusory images are in some way cut off and curbed by frequent use of his intellectual habit, a man is rendered less apt to judge rightly and sometimes is inclined wholly to the opposite of a right judgment. This is the way intellectual habit is diminished or even destroyed by cessation of act.

Reply to 1: Heat also would be destroyed through ceasing to heat if by this, cold, which is destructive of heat, were to increase.

Reply to 2: Cessation of act is a moving cause leading to corruption or diminution, inasmuch as it removes the restraints thereto, as we have said.[26]

Reply to 3: The intellectual part of the soul of itself is above time; but the sense part is subject to time, and hence by the passage of time is changed in regard to passions of the appetitive part and even in regard to its apprehensive powers. The Philosopher accordingly says that time is the cause of our forgetting.[27]

---

[26] In the body of this article.   [27] Cf. *Physics* IV, 12 (221a 32); 13 (222b 16).

The Distinction of Habits

(In Four Articles)

CAN MANY HABITS BE IN ONE POWER?

It seems that there cannot be many habits in one power.

1. When things are distinguished with reference to the same thing, then if one is multiplied so also is the other. But powers and habits are distinguished with reference to the same thing, that is, their acts and objects. They are therefore multiplied in a similar way. Consequently, there cannot be many habits in one power.

2. A power is a kind of simple aptitude. But in one simple subject there cannot be a diversity of accidents, for the subject is the cause of an accident, and from one simple cause only one effect proceeds. Therefore many habits cannot be in one power.

3. Just as a body is given form by figure so a power is given form by a habit. But one body cannot be formed with different shapes simultaneously. Therefore neither can one power simultaneously be formed by different habits. Consequently, many habits cannot be in one power at the same time.

On the contrary: The intellect is one power, and yet there are habits of different sciences in it.

Response: As we have said,[1] habits are dispositions of some subject which is in potentiality in regard to something, either in regard to a thing's nature, or to its operation, which is the end of its nature. With respect to those habits which are dispositions in regard to a thing's nature, it is clear that there can be many habits in one subject inasmuch as the parts of one subject can be considered in various ways; and depending on the disposition of these parts there are various habits. For example, if we consider the humors[2] as parts of the human body, then according as they are disposed in proportion to human nature, there is

---

[1] Question 49, article 4.

[2] The humors of the body are understood here as fluids. In this understanding of physiology, there were four fluids: blood, phlegm, choler (a yellow bile), and melancholy (a black bile). These fluids were conceived as determining a person's health and also his temperament which, respectively, would be sanguine, phlegmatic, choleric, or melancholic.

the habit or disposition of health. If, however, we take parts that are alike, such as nerves, bones, and flesh, their disposition in relation to the nature is called the habit of strength or weakness. Finally, if we take the members of the body, such as hands, feet, and the like, the disposition of these in proportion to human nature is called beauty. And thus there are many habits or dispositions in the same subject.

But if we are concerned with habits which are dispositions for operation and belong properly to powers, then again there may be many habits in one power. This is because the subject of a habit is a passive power, as we have said,[3] for it is only an active power that is not the subject of a habit, as is clear from what has been said.[4] Now a passive power is compared to the determinate act of one specific kind as matter is to form, in that just as matter is determined to one form through an agent, so too a passive power by the nature of one active object is determined to an act that is one in species. Hence, just as many objects can move one passive power, so one passive power can be the subject of acts or perfections that are diverse in species. Now habits are certain qualities or forms inherent in a power, inclining the power to acts of a determinate kind. Hence many habits that differ specifically can belong to one power, as can also many acts.

Reply to 1: Just as in natural things diversity of species is due to form and diversity of genus is due to the matter,[5] (for those things are diverse in genus whose matter is diverse) so also a generic difference of objects gives rise to a distinction of powers (and hence the Philosopher says that "when objects are different in genus, the parts of the soul corresponding to them are also different"[6]); while a specific difference of objects entails a specific difference of acts, and consequently also of habits. Now everything that differs in genus differs in species, but not conversely. Hence the acts of the various powers are specifically different, and also the habits, but it does not follow that habits that are diverse are in different powers, for many habits can be in one power. And just as there are many genera in one genus, and many species in one species, so there may be various species of habits and of powers.

Reply to 2: A power, even though it is simple as to essence, is multiple in capacity, inasmuch as it admits of many specifically different acts. Consequently, there is nothing to preclude there being many specifically different habits in one power.

Reply to 3: A body is given form by figure as a kind of specific termination of it, whereas a habit is not a termination of a power, but is a disposition for act as its ultimate term. Hence there cannot simultaneously be many acts of one power except perhaps insofar as one is

---

[3] Question 51, article 2.   [4] *Ibid.*
[5] Cf. Aristotle, *Metaphysics* V, 28 (1024b 9); IX, 3 (1054b 26).
[6] *Nicomachean Ethics* VI, 1 (1139a 8).

though extending to many things. For a habit does not extend to many things except as related to one, from which it has its unity.

Reply to 1: A habit is not formed successively because one part is formed after another but because the subject does not acquire at once a disposition that is stable and difficult to change; and also because the habit begins by being in the subject imperfectly and is developed gradually. The same holds for the other qualities.

Reply to 2: The parts which are assigned to the various cardinal virtues are not integral parts from which a whole is composed, but subjective or potential parts,[24] as we shall explain later.[25]

Reply to 3: One who acquires demonstrative knowledge of a conclusion in some science does indeed have the habit, but imperfectly. And when he acquires demonstrative knowledge of another conclusion, another habit is not developed in him, but the habit which was in him before is now perfected more inasmuch as it is extended to more things. For the conclusions and demonstrations of one science are so ordered to each other that one is derived from the other.

---

[24] A whole formed from integral parts is one having parts which, taken together, constitute a whole with respect to the functioning of the whole. A government, as a whole, has as integral parts, the executive, legislative, and judiciary parts. A whole formed from subjective parts is a whole as related to its essential parts or kinds, for example, animal as related to its essential kinds, man and brute. A whole formed from potential parts has parts virtually contained in the whole, where the form of the whole is the principle of operation of the virtual parts, as a principal virtue is related to secondary virtues subordinated to it. See the following note for references explaining how virtues are wholes in the latter two senses and not properly in the first sense of having integral parts.

[25] Question 57, article 6; reply to 4; II-II, question 48.

QUESTION LV

The Essence of Virtue

(In Four Articles)

Now we need to consider habits in particular. And since habits are distinguished in terms of good and evil, as we have said,[1] we shall first speak of the good habits, which are virtues, and of the other things connected with them, namely, the gifts, beatitudes, and fruits.[2] Secondly, we shall treat the bad habits, namely, vices and sins.[3] Five general points will be considered with respect to the virtues: (1) the essence of virtue, (2) the subject of virtue,[4] (3) the division of virtues,[5] (4) the cause of virtue,[6] and (5) certain properties of virtues.[7]

First Article

IS HUMAN VIRTUE A HABIT?

It seems that human virtue is not a habit.

1. Virtue is the maximum of a power.[8] But the maximum of anything is reducible to that genus of which it is the maximum, as a point is reducible to the genus of line. Therefore virtue is reducible to the genus of power, and not to that of habit.

2. Augustine says that "virtue is the good use of free choice."[9] But the use of free choice is an act. Therefore virtue is not a habit, but an act.

3. We merit by acts, not by habits, otherwise a man would merit continuously, even when sleeping. But we do merit by virtues. Therefore virtues are not habits, but acts.

4. Augustine says that "virtue is the ordering of love,"[10] and that "the ordination which is called virtue consists in enjoying what we should enjoy and using what we should use."[11] Now an ordering, or ordination, designates either an act or a relation. Therefore virtue is not a habit, but an act or a relation.

5. Just as there are human virtues so there are natural virtues.[12] But

---

[1] Question 54, article 3.   [2] Question 68.   [3] Question 71.   [4] Question 56.
[5] Question 57.   [6] Question 63.   [7] Question 64.
[8] Cf. Aristotle, *On the Heavens* I, 11 (281a 15).
[9] *On Free Will* II, 19. The point is made more expressly in *Retractions* I, 9.
[10] *On the Morals of the Catholic Church* I, 15.
[11] *Book of Eighty-Three Questions*, q. 30.
[12] "Natural virtue" is taken here in the sense of a natural active power, for example, the natural power of strength one has.

natural virtues are not habits, but certain powers. Therefore neither are human virtues habits.

On the contrary: The Philosopher maintains that science and virtue are habits.[13]

Response: Virtue designates a certain kind of perfection of a power. Now the perfection of a thing is considered especially in relation to its end. But act is the end of a power. Hence a power is said to be perfect according as it is determined to its act.

Now some powers are of themselves determined to their acts, for instance, active natural powers. Hence these natural powers are in themselves called virtues. But the rational powers, which are proper to man, are not determined to some one thing, but are related indeterminately to many, and they are determined to their acts by habits, as we have said.[14] Therefore human habits are virtues.

Reply to 1: We sometimes give the name of virtue to that to which the virtue is directed, either to its object or to its act. For example, the name *faith* sometimes stands for that which is believed, sometimes for the act itself of believing, and sometimes for the habit by which one believes. Hence, when virtue is said to be the maximum of a power, virtue is taken for the object of virtue. For the maximum of which a power is capable is said to be its virtue; for example, if someone can carry a hundred pounds and no more, his virtue[15] is determined according to a hundred pounds, and not according to sixty pounds. The objection proceeds as though the essence of virtue were maximum of power.

Reply to 2: Good use of free choice is said to be virtue for the reason already given, namely, because it is that to which virtue is ordered as its proper act. For the act of virtue is simply the good use of free choice.

Reply to 3: We are said to merit by something in two ways. In one way, by the merit itself, as we are said to run by running, and this is the way we merit by acts. In another way, we are said to merit by something as it is a principle of meriting, as we are said to run by the power of moving, and this is the sense in which we are said to merit by virtues and habits.

Reply to 4: Virtue is called an ordering or ordination of love with respect to the end to which virtue is ordered, for love in us is set in order by virtue.

Reply to 5: Natural powers are of themselves determined to something one, but not rational powers. Hence the comparison between the two does not hold, as we have pointed out in this article.

---

[13] *Categories,* 8 (8b 29).   [14] Question 49, article 4.   [15] Cf. n. 12 above.

Second Article

IS HUMAN VIRTUE AN OPERATIVE HABIT?

It does not seem that being an operative habit belongs to the notion of human virtue.

1. Cicero says that as health and beauty are to the body, so is virtue to the soul.[16] But health and beauty are not operative habits, and therefore neither is virtue.

2. In natural things there is found not only virtue in respect to act but also in respect to being, as is evident from Aristotle,[17] since some things have the virtue to be always while others have not the virtue to be always, but in some determinate time. But as natural virtue is in natural beings, so is human virtue in rational beings. Therefore human virtue is not only in respect to act, but also in respect to being.

3. The Philosopher says that virtue is "the disposition of what is perfect to what is best for it [i.e., to the end or operation] in accord with nature." [18] But the best thing, to which man must be disposed by virtue, is God Himself, as Augustine proves,[19] to whom the soul is disposed by being made like to Him. It therefore seems that virtue should be called a quality of the soul ordered to God, as likened to Him, but not as ordered to operation. Hence virtue is not an operative habit.

On the contrary: The Philosopher says that "the virtue of a thing is that which makes its work be done well." [20]

Response: Virtue, from the very meaning of the name, implies a certain perfection of power. Now since power is twofold, power in regard to being and power in regard to acting, the perfection of each is called virtue. But power in regard to being is on the part of matter, which is potential being, while power in regard to acting is on the part of form, which is the principle of acting in that anything acts insofar as it is in act.

Now in the nature of man the body is considered as matter and the soul as form. With respect to his body, man has this in common with the other animals; the same holds also for the powers which are common to the soul and the body. Only those powers which are proper to the soul itself, the rational powers, belong to man alone. Hence human virtue, which we are speaking of now, cannot pertain to the body, but only to that which is proper to the soul. Accordingly, human virtue does not imply an ordering to being, but rather to act. It therefore belongs to the very notion of human virtue that it be an operative habit.

---

[16] Cf. *Tusc. Disp.*, IV, 13.

[17] *On the Heavens* I, 12 (281a 15). Throughout this sentence, "virtue" means "capacity."

[18] *Physics* VII, 3 (246a 13).   [19] *On the Morals of the Catholic Church* II, 3.

[20] *Nicomachean Ethics* II, 6 (1106a 15).

Reply to 1: The way of acting conforms to the disposition of the one acting, for as a thing is, so does it act. Consequently, since virtue is a principle of some kind of operation, a disposition adapted to the virtue must exist beforehand in the one who acts. But virtue produces an ordered operation. Hence virtue itself is an ordered disposition of the soul, according as the powers of the soul are ordered in some way to each other and to what is external. Hence virtue, inasmuch as it is the befitting disposition of the soul, is likened to health and beauty, which are harmonious dispositions of the body. Nonetheless, this does not exclude virtue's being also a principle of operation.

Reply to 2: The virtue in regard to being is not proper to man, but only the virtue in regard to works of reason, which are proper to man.

Reply to 3: Since the substance of God is His action, the greatest likeness of man to God is in respect to some operation. Therefore, as we have said,[21] happiness or beatitude, by which man most of all is conformed to God and which is the end of human life, consists in an operation.

Third Article

IS HUMAN VIRTUE A GOOD HABIT?

It does not seem essential to virtue that it be a good habit.

1. Sin is always taken as something evil. But there is some virtue even with respect to sin, for "the virtue[22] of sin is the Law" (*I Corinthians 15:56*). Therefore virtue is not always a good habit.

2. The virtue corresponds to the power. But a power has to do not only with good, but also with evil, for as Scripture says, "Woe to you that are mighty to drink wine, and stout men at drunkenness" (*Isaias 5:22*). Therefore virtue also has to do with both good and evil.

3. According to the Apostle, "virtue[23] is made perfect in weakness" (*II Corinthians 12:9*). But weakness is an evil. Therefore virtue has to do with evil as well as good.

On the contrary: Augustine says, "No one has doubted that virtue makes the soul exceedingly good." [24] And the Philosopher says that "virtue is that which makes the one who has it good and the work which he does good." [25]

Response: As we have said,[26] virtue implies a perfection of a power, and hence the virtue of anything is determined by the maximum of

---

[21] Question 3, article 2.

[22] The translation in the *Confraternity of Christian Doctrine of the New Testament* has "power" instead of "virtue." *Virtus* in Latin can mean either "power" or "virtue."

[23] *The Confraternity of Christian Doctrine* version has "strength" for "virtue."

[24] *On the Morals of the Catholic Church* I, 6.   [25] *Nicomachean Ethics* II, 6 (1106a 15).

[26] Article 1.

which its power is capable.[27] Now the maximum of any power must be what is good, for all evil implies a defect; hence Dionysius says that every evil is a weakness.[28] For this reason, the virtue of a thing must be expressed in terms of the good. Hence human virtue, which is an operative habit, is a good habit and productive of good works.

Reply to 1: Just as "perfect" is said metaphorically about evil things, so is "good," for we speak of a perfect thief or robber and a good thief or robber, as the Philosopher notes.[29] In this way, therefore, even "virtue" is said metaphorically about evil things. And thus "the virtue of sin" is said to be the Law inasmuch as occasionally sin is increased through law and in a way attains the maximum of its power.

Reply to 2: The evil of drunkenness and excessive drink consists in departing from the order of reason. But it can happen that, along with this departing from reason, some lower power remains perfect with respect to what belongs to itself, even with the aversion or turning away from reason. But the perfection of such a power, since it accompanies a turning away from reason, cannot be called a human virtue.

Reply to 3: Reason is shown to be more perfect in proportion as it is able to overcome or bear with weaknesses of the body and of the lower powers. Hence human virtue, which is attributed to reason, is said "to be made perfect in weakness," not indeed a weakness of the reason, but of the body and the lower powers.

Fourth Article

IS VIRTUE APPROPRIATELY DEFINED?

It seems that the definition usually given of virtue is not appropriate: "Virtue is a good quality of the mind, by which we live rightly, of which no one can make bad use, which God works in us without us." [30]

1. Virtue is the goodness of man, for virtue is that which makes its possessor good. But goodness is not good, just as whiteness is not white. Hence it seems unfitting to say that virtue is "a good quality."

2. No difference is more universal than its genus, for it divides the genus. But good is more universal than quality, since good is convertible with being. Therefore *good* should not be put in the definition of virtue as the difference of *quality*.

3. Augustine says, "When we come upon something which is not common to us and the beasts of the field, this is something belonging to the mind." [31] But there are virtues even of the irrational parts of man, as the Philosopher says.[32] Therefore not every virtue is a good quality "of the mind."

---

[27] Cf. Aristotle, *On the Heavens* I, 11 (281a 15).   [28] *The Divine Names* IV, 32.
[29] *Metaphysics* V, 16 (1021b 17).   [30] Cf. Peter Lombard, *Sentences* II, d. 27, 5.
[31] *The Trinity* XII, 8.   [32] *Nicomachean Ethics* III, 9 (1117b 23).

4. What is right seems to belong to justice, and hence what is right is called just. But justice is one kind of virtue. Therefore it is inappropriate to use "rightly" in the definition of virtue, in the part "by which we live rightly."

5. Whoever is proud of a thing makes bad use of it. But many are proud of their virtue, for Augustine says in his *Rule* that "pride lies in wait for good works, so that they may perish." [33] It is therefore false that no one can make bad use of virtue.

6. Man is justified by virtue. But Augustine says, in commenting on *John* 14:12 ("greater than these he shall do"), "He who created thee without thee, will not justify thee without thee." [34] Therefore it is improper to say that "God works in us without us."

On the contrary: We have the authority of Augustine, from whose words the definition is gathered, especially in his treatise *On Free Will*.[35]

Response: This definition expresses perfectly the whole nature of virtue, for the complete notion of a thing is gathered from all its causes. Now the definition given above comprises all the causes of virtue. For the formal cause of virtue, as of anything, is taken from its genus and difference, when it is defined as "a good quality," for the genus of virtue is *quality* and the difference is *good*. But the definition would be more appropriate if in place of quality, we use *habit*, which is a more proximate genus.

Now virtue does not have matter *out of which* it comes to be, as neither do other accidents, but it does have matter *about which* it is concerned, and matter *in which* it is, namely, a subject. The matter *about which* virtue is concerned is the object of virtue, but this could not be stated in the definition because by its object virtue is determined to a particular species, and here we are presenting the definition of virtue in general. Hence the subject is given in place of the material cause when it is said that a virtue is a good quality *of the mind*.

Now the end of virtue, since it is an operative habit, is operation. But we must note that some operative habits are always related to evil, as in the case of habits of vice; others are related to what is good and at other times to what is evil, as opinion, which is related to both the true and the false; but virtue is a habit which is always related to the good. Consequently, in order to distinguish virtue from habits which always relate to evil, "by which we live rightly" is stated in the definition; and the distinction of virtue from habits which are related sometimes to good and at other times to evil is expressed by "of which no one can make bad use."

The efficient cause of infused virtue, which is the virtue defined here, is God. The definition therefore says, "which God works in us without us." If this last part of the definition is omitted, the rest of it is common to all virtues, both acquired and infused.

---

[33] *Epist.* 211.   [34] *Serm.* 169, 11.   [35] Book II, 19.

Reply to 1: That which first falls under the intellect is being, and hence whatever we apprehend we refer to it as being, and consequently as one and good, which are convertible with being. We therefore say that essence is being, and is one, and is good, and of oneness that it is and is one and is good, and likewise of goodness. But this does not hold in the case of specific forms, such as whiteness and health, for we do not grasp everything we apprehend under the notion of white and of health. Yet we must note that, just as accidents and nonsubsistent forms are called beings, not that they have being themselves but because something is by them, so also they are called good or one, not by some distinct goodness or oneness, but because by them something is good or one. This is the way, then, that virtue is called good, because by it something is good.

Reply to 2: The good which is stated in the definition of virtue is not the universal good, which is convertible with being and more universal than quality. It is, rather, the good according to reason, with respect to which Dionysius says that "the good of the soul is to be in accord with reason." [36]

Reply to 3: Virtue can be in the irrational part of the soul only insofar as this participates in reason.[37] Hence reason, or mind, is the proper subject of human virtue.

Reply to 4: The rightness which is proper to justice concerns those external things which come into human use, which constitute the proper matter of justice, as we shall show later on.[38] But the rightness which implies an ordering to an appropriate end and to the divine law, which is the rule for the human will, as we have said,[39] is common to all virtue.

Reply to 5: One can make bad use of virtue by treating it as an object, for example, by thinking evil about it, by hating it or being proud about it. But one cannot make bad use of virtue as a principle of action so that an act of virtue be evil.

Reply to 6: Infused virtue is caused in us by God without action on our part, but not without our consent.[40] The expression "which God works in us without us" is to be understood in that way. As to actions done by us, God causes them in us but not without action on our part, for God works in every will and nature.

---

[36] *The Divine Names* IV, 32.
[37] Cf. Aristotle, *Nicomachean Ethics* I, 13 (1102b 13; 1103a 3).
[38] Question 60, article 2; II-II, question 58, article 8.   [39] Question 19, article 4.
[40] The theological virtues of faith, hope, and charity, which are infused virtues, are treated in question 62.

The Subject of Virtue

(In Six Articles)

IS A POWER OF THE SOUL THE SUBJECT OF VIRTUE?

It seems that a power of the soul is not the subject of virtue.

1. Augustine says that "virtue is that by which we live rightly." [1] But we are alive, not by reason of a power of the soul, but by reason of its essence. Therefore virtue is not in a power of the soul, but in its essence.

2. The Philosopher says that "virtue is that which makes the one who has it good and the work he does good." [2] But as a work is achieved through a power, so having virtue is achieved through the essence of the soul. Therefore virtue does not belong any more to a power of the soul than to its essence.

3. Power is in the second species of quality. [3] But virtue is also a quality, as we have said, [4] and there is not a quality in a quality. Therefore virtue is not in a power of the soul as in a subject.

On the contrary: "Virtue is the maximum of a power." [5] But the maximum is in that of which it is the maximum. Therefore virtue is in a power of the soul.

Response: It can be shown in three ways that virtue belongs to a power of the soul. First, because of the very notion of virtue, which implies the perfection of a power, and a perfection is in that of which it is a perfection. Second, from the fact that virtue is an operative habit, as we have said, [6] and every operation comes from the soul through some power. Third, from the fact that virtue disposes to what is best, and the best is the end, which is either a thing's operation or something acquired by an operation proceeding from the power. Hence human virtue is in a power of the soul as in a subject.

Reply to 1: "To live" has two meanings. Sometimes it is said of the very being of a living thing; in this sense it concerns the essence of the

---

[1] *On Free Will* II, 19.   [2] *Nicomachean Ethics* II, 6 (1106a 15).

[3] The four species of the category of quality are (1) Habit and disposition, (2) Potency (Power), (3) Sense quality, and (4) Figure and form. Virtue, as a quality, belongs to the first species. Cf. Aristotle, *Categories*, 8.

[4] Question 55, article 4.   [5] Aristotle, *On the Heavens* I, 11 (281a 15).

[6] Question 55, article 2.

soul, which is the principle of existence in the living being. At other times it is said of the operation of a living being, and in this sense we live rightly by virtue, inasmuch as through virtue we act rightly.

Reply to 2: Good is said of the end or of something referred to the end. Hence, since the good of the worker consists in the work, this fact also, that virtue makes the worker good, is referred to the work and, consequently, to the power.

Reply to 3: One accident is said to be in another as in a subject, not because an accident by itself can sustain another accident, but because one accident inheres in a substance by means of another; thus, color is in a body by means of surface, and hence surface is said to be the subject of color. In the same way a power of the soul is said to be the subject of virtue.

Second Article

CAN ONE VIRTUE BE IN MANY POWERS?

It seems that one virtue can be in many powers.

1. Habits are known through acts. But one act proceeds in a different way from various powers. For example, walking proceeds from reason as directing, from the will as moving, and from the power of locomotion as carrying it out. Therefore one habit of a virtue can be in several powers.

2. The Philosopher says that three things are required for virtue: "to know, to will, and to act steadfastly." [7] But knowing belongs to the intellect, willing to the will. Therefore virtue can be in many powers.

3. Prudence is in reason, since it is "right reasoning about what is to be done." [8] It is also in the will, for there cannot be prudence with a bad will, as is also said.[9] Therefore one virtue can be in two powers.

On the contrary: Virtue is in a power of the soul as in a subject. But one and the same accident cannot be in many subjects. Therefore one virtue cannot be in several powers of the soul.

Response: There are two ways in which something can be in two subjects. In one way, so that it is equally in either. It is impossible for one virtue to be in two powers in this way, for diversity of powers concerns general conditions of objects while diversity of habits concerns specific conditions; hence whenever there is a diversity of powers there is a diversity of habits, but not conversely.

In another way, something can be in two or more subjects, not equally, but in a certain order, and thus one virtue can belong to several powers. It is then in one principally and extended to others by way of diffusion,

---

[7] *Nicomachean Ethics* II, 4 (1105a 31).

[8] Aristotle, *op. cit.*, VI, 5 (1140b 4; b 20); 13 (1144b 27).

[9] *Op. cit.*, VI, 12 (1144a 36).

or by way of disposition, according as one power is moved by another and one power receives something from another.

Reply to 1: The same act cannot belong to different powers equally and in the same degree, but it can according to different viewpoints and in different degrees.

Reply to 2: Knowledge is required for moral virtue insofar as moral virtue is operation in conformity with right reason. But moral virtue is essentially in the appetite or desire.

Reply to 3: Prudence is really in reason as in a subject, but it presupposes rectitude of the will as a principle, as we shall say shortly.[10]

Third Article

CAN THE INTELLECT BE THE SUBJECT OF VIRTUE?

It seems that the intellect is not a subject of virtue.

1. Augustine says that all virtue is love.[11] The subject of love, however, is not the intellect but an appetitive power alone. Therefore no virtue is in the intellect.

2. Virtue is ordered to the good, as is evident from what has been said.[12] Good, however, is not the object of the intellect, but of an appetitive power. Therefore the subject of virtue is not the intellect, but an appetitive power.

3. "Virtue is that which makes the one who has it good," as the Philosopher says.[13] But a habit which perfects the intellect does not make the one having it good, for man is not called good because of knowledge or art. Therefore the intellect is not the subject of virtue.

On the contrary: The mind especially is called intellect. But the subject of virtue is the mind, as is evident from the definition of virtue already given.[14] Therefore the intellect is the subject of virtue.

Response: As we have said,[15] virtue is a habit by which we perform well. Now a habit is ordered to a good act in two ways. In one way, insofar as by such habit man acquires the facility to do a good act; for example, through the habit of grammar man has an aptitude to speak correctly. But the habit of grammar does not make a man always speak correctly, for one who is competent in grammar can commit a barbarism or a solecism. The same holds for the other sciences and arts. In another way, habit not only induces an aptitude to act well, but also its right use; for example, justice not only gives a man readiness of will to do what is just, but also makes him act justly.

Now since a thing is not said simply to be good, or to be, according to

---

[10] Article 3; question 57, article 4.   [11] *On the Morals of the Catholic Church* I, 15.
[12] Question 55, article 3.   [13] *Nicomachean Ethics* II, 6 (1106a 15).
[14] Question 55, article 4.   [15] Question 55, article 3.

what it is potentially but according to what it is actually, therefore from habits of the latter kind man is said simply to do good and to be good; for instance, because he is just or temperate, and the same holds for other virtues like these. And because virtue is that which makes the one who has it good and his work good, habits of this kind are called virtues simply, because they make the work actually good and make the one having such virtues good simply. But habits of the former kind are not called virtues simply, for they do not make the action good except in regard to a certain aptitude, nor do they make the one possessing them good simply. For because a man is learned or an artist, he is not said to be good simply, but good only in a qualified sense, for example, a good grammarian or a good builder. For this reason, science and art are frequently divided off from virtue, while at other times they are called virtues.[16]

Accordingly, the intellect—not only the practical but also the speculative intellect—can be the subject of a habit that is said to be a virtue in a qualified sense, and without any ordering to the will. In such a way, the Philosopher holds that science, wisdom, and understanding, and also art, are intellectual virtues.[17] But the subject of a habit which is called virtue simply can only be the will, or some power as moved by the will. This is because the will moves to their acts all other powers that are in some way rational, as we have said.[18] Hence if a man actually acts well, this is a result of his having a good will. Therefore, the virtue which makes a man actually act well, not merely have the ability to act well, must be in the will or in some power as it is moved by the will.

Now it happens that the intellect is moved by the will, as are also the other powers; for a man actually considers something because he wills to do so. Hence the intellect, inasmuch as it has an ordering to the will, can be the subject of virtue in the absolute sense. And in this way the speculative intellect, or reason, is the subject of the virtue of faith; for the intellect is moved to assent to what is of faith by the command of the will, for "no one believes unless he wills to do so." [19] The practical intellect, however, is the subject of prudence. For, since prudence is right reasoning about what is to be done, it is required for prudence that a man be well ordered to the principles involved in reasoning about things to be done, that is, in regard to their ends, and man is well ordered to these through rectitude of will, just as man is rightly ordered to the principles of speculative truth through the natural light of the agent intellect. Consequently, just as the subject of science, which is right reasoning about speculative matters, is the speculative intellect in its ordering

---

[16] Cf. Aristotle, *Nicomachean Ethics* VI, 3 (1139b 16); 2 (1139b 13).
[17] *Op. cit.*, VI, 3 (1139b 16).
[18] Question 9, article 1; question 17, articles 1 and 5; I, question 82, article 4.
[19] Augustine, *Commentary on John* VI, 44.

to the agent intellect, so the subject of prudence is the practical intellect in its ordering to right will.

Reply to 1: What Augustine says applies to virtue taken absolutely— not that every such virtue is love simply—but that it depends in some way on love insofar as it depends on the will, whose first inclination is to love, as we have said.[20]

Reply to 2: The good of anything is its end, and hence, since truth is the end of the intellect, to know what is true is the good act of the intellect. Hence the habit perfecting the intellect with respect to knowing truth, either speculative or practical, is called a virtue.

Reply to 3: The argument given proceeds from virtue taken absolutely.

Fourth Article

ARE THE IRASCIBLE AND CONCUPISCIBLE
POWERS SUBJECTS OF VIRTUE?[21]

It seems that the irascible and concupiscible powers cannot be subjects of virtue.

1. These powers are common to us and irrational animals. But we are speaking now of virtue as it is proper to man, for in terms of this it is called human virtue. The irascible and concupiscible powers, therefore, which are parts of the sense appetite, as we have said,[22] cannot be subjects of human virtue.

2. The sense appetite is a power using a corporeal organ. But the good of virtue cannot be in the human body, for the Apostle says, "For I know that in me, that is, in my flesh, no good dwells" (*Romans 7:18*). Therefore sense appetite cannot be a subject of virtue.

3. Augustine proves that "virtue is not in the body but in the soul because the body is ruled by the soul; hence the good use of the body is due entirely to the soul; for example, if my driver, being obedient to me, guides well the horses he is driving, this is all due to me." [23] But just as the soul rules the body so also does reason rule the sense appetite. Therefore it is due entirely to the rational part of man that the irascible and concupiscible powers are ruled rightly. But "virtue is that by which we live rightly," as we have said.[24] Hence virtue is not in the irascible and concupiscible powers, but only in the rational part of man.

---

[20] Question 25, articles 1, 2, and 3; question 27, article 4; I, question 20, article 1.

[21] Sense appetite is one generic power, divided specifically into the irascible and concupiscible powers. We seek by the concupiscible power what is suitable to the senses and avoid what is injurious. We resist by the irascible power attacks that hinder what is suitable and inflict harm.

[22] I, question 81, article 2.   [23] *On the Morals of the Catholic Church* I, 5.

[24] Question 55, article 4.

4. "The principal act of moral virtue is choice." [25] But choice is not an act of the irascible or of the concupiscible power, but of reason, as we have said.[26] Therefore moral virtue is not in the irascible and concupiscible powers, but in reason.

On the contrary: Fortitude is attributed to the irascible power and temperance to the concupiscible. Hence the Philosopher says that "these virtues belong to the irrational parts of man." [27]

Response: The irascible and concupiscible powers can be considered in two ways. First, in themselves, as they are parts of sense appetite, and in this way they do not qualify as a subject of virtue. Second, they can be considered as participating in reason through their natural aptitude to obey reason. In this way the irascible and concupiscible powers can be the subject of human virtue, for to the extent they participate in reason they are a principle of acts that are human, and to them we must assign virtues. Now it is evident that there are some virtues in the irascible and concupiscible powers. For an act which proceeds from one power as it is moved by another power cannot be perfect unless both powers are well disposed to act; for example, the act of a craftsman cannot be well done unless both the craftsman and his instruments are well disposed to act. Hence in those matters which engage the concupiscible and irascible powers according as they are moved by reason, there must be some habit for effecting good action, not only in reason, but also in the irascible and concupiscible powers. And since the good disposition of the power which moves through being moved depends on its conformity with the power moving it, it follows that the virtue which is in the irascible and concupiscible powers is nothing else but a habitual conformity of these powers to reason.

Reply to 1: The irascible and concupiscible powers, considered in themselves and as parts of sense appetite, are common to us and irrational animals. But to the extent that they are rational by participation, as obedient to reason, they are then proper to man. And in this way they can be the subject of human virtue.

Reply to 2: Just as the flesh of man does not of itself have the good of virtue, yet becomes the instrument of virtuous action, insofar as being moved by reason "we yield our members to serve justice" (*Romans 6:19*), so also the irascible and concupiscible powers of themselves do not have the good of virtue, but rather the infection of unruly desire;[28] yet insofar as they are conformed to reason, the good of moral virtue is produced in them.

Reply to 3: The body is ruled by the soul in a different way than the irascible and concupiscible powers are ruled by reason. The body spontaneously obeys the soul without resistance in those things in which it is

---

[25] Aristotle, *Nicomachean Ethics* VIII, 13 (1163a 22).   [26] Question 13, article 2.
[27] *Nicomachean Ethics* III, 10 (1117b 23).   [28] *infectio fomitis.*

natural for it to be moved by the soul. Hence the Philosopher says that "the soul rules the body with despotic power," [29] that is, as a master rules a servant, and therefore the whole motion of the body is referred to the soul; and for this reason virtue is not in the body, but in the soul. But the irascible and concupiscible powers do not spontaneously obey reason; on the contrary, they have their own movement which at times goes against reason. Hence the Philosopher says that reason rules the irascible and concupiscible powers by "political rule," [30] in the manner in which free men are ruled who exercise their own will in regard to some things. For this reason, there must be virtues in the irascible and concupiscible powers by which they are disposed to act well.

Reply to 4: Two things are involved in choice, the intending of the end, which pertains to moral virtue, and the previous acceptance of the means to the end, which pertains to prudence.[31] Now having the right intention of the end regarding the passions of the soul comes from the good disposition of the irascible and concupiscible powers. Hence the moral virtues concerned with the passions are in the irascible and concupiscible appetite, but prudence is in reason.

Fifth Article

ARE SENSE POWERS OF KNOWING THE SUBJECT OF VIRTUE?

It seems possible for some virtue to be in the internal sense powers of knowing.

1. Sense appetite can be the subject of virtue insofar as it obeys reason. But the internal sense powers of knowing obey reason, for the powers of imagination, cogitation, and memory act at the command of reason. Therefore virtue can be in these powers.

2. Just as rational appetite, which is the will, can be hindered or helped in its act by sense appetite, so also intellect or reason can be hindered or helped by the forementioned powers. Therefore, just as there can be virtue in the sense appetitive powers, so also in the sense knowing powers.

3. Prudence is a virtue, a part of which Cicero says is memory.[32] Therefore there can also be a virtue in the memory, and for the same reason in other internal sense powers of knowing.

On the contrary: All virtues are either intellectual or moral.[33] Now all moral virtues are in the appetitive part of the soul while intellectual virtues are in the intellect or reason.[34] Therefore there is no virtue in the internal sense powers of knowing.

Response: Some have claimed that there are some habits in the internal

[29] *Politics* I, 2 (1254b 4).   [30] *Ibid.* (1254b 5).
[31] Cf. Aristotle, *Nicomachean Ethics* VI, 12 (1144a 6).   [32] *Rhetoric* II, 53.
[33] Cf. Aristotle, *Nicomachean Ethics* II, 1 (1103a 14).
[34] Cf. Aristotle, *op. cit.,* VI, 1 (1138b 35).

sense powers of knowing. The principal evidence for this view is the statement of the Philosopher that "by the effect of custom we tend to remember one thing after another, and custom is a sort of nature." [35] Now a customary habit is nothing other than a conditioning acquired by custom, which is like a second nature. Hence Cicero says about virtue that it is "a habit like a nature in harmony with reason." [36] In man, however, what he acquires by custom in his memory and in the other internal sense powers of knowing is not strictly a habit, but something annexed to habits of the intellectual part of the soul, as we have said.[37]

But even if in fact there are habits in such powers, they cannot be called virtues. For virtue is a perfect habit by which only something good is done, and hence virtue must be in a power which brings a good work to completion. Now the knowing of truth is not brought to completion in the sense powers of knowing, for such powers prepare the way for intellectual knowing. Hence in such powers there are none of the virtues by which we know what is true; they are, rather, in the intellect or reason.

Reply to 1: Sense appetite is related to the will, which is rational appetite, through being moved by it. Therefore the work of an appetitive virtue is fulfilled in the sense appetite, and because of this, sense appetite is a subject of virtue. But sense powers of knowing are related to the intellect more as moving it, for phantasms are related to the intellective soul like colors to sight.[38] Consequently, the work of cognition is terminated in the intellect, and for this reason the cognitive virtues are in the intellect itself, or reason.

Reply to 2: The solution is evident from what has been said.

Reply to 3: Memory is not asserted to be a part of prudence as a species is a part of a genus, and as though memory in itself were a virtue. It is a part of prudence because one of the things needed for prudence is good memory, and hence memory is related to prudence in the manner of an integral part.[39]

Sixth Article

CAN THE WILL BE THE SUBJECT OF VIRTUE?

It seems that the will cannot be the subject of a virtue.

1. A habit is not required for anything that belongs to a power by reason of its very nature. But it is of the nature of the will, since it is in reason,[40] to tend to what is good according to reason. Now every virtue

---

[35] *On Memory*, II (451b 29; 452a 27).   [36] *Rhetoric* II, 53.

[37] Question 50, article 4, reply to 3.   [38] Cf. Aristotle, *On the Soul* III, 7 (431a 14).

[39] An integral part is that sort of part which is needed for the complete functioning of the whole, as the legislative part of a government is needed for the complete functioning of government. See note 24 of question 54.

[40] Cf. Aristotle, *On the Soul* III, 9 (432b 5).

is ordered to this good, since everything naturally desires its own good; for virtue, as Cicero says, "is a habit like a nature in harmony with reason." [41] Therefore the will is not a subject of virtue.

2. All virtue is either intellectual or moral.[42] But intellectual virtue is in intellect and reason as in a subject, and not in the will, while moral virtue has for its subject the irascible and concupiscible powers, which are rational by participation. Therefore no virtue is in the will as in a subject.

3. All human acts, to which the virtues are ordered, are voluntary. If, then, in regard to some human acts there is a virtue in the will, with equal reason there will be a virtue in the will in regard to all human acts. Consequently, either there will be no virtue in any other power or there will be two virtues ordered to the same act, which does not seem reasonable. The will therefore cannot be the subject of virtue.

On the contrary: Greater perfection is required in the mover than in the moved. But the will moves the irascible and concupiscible powers. Therefore, much more should there be virtue in the will than in the irascible and concupiscible powers.

Response: Since habits perfect powers in regard to acting, then, in order to act well a power needs perfecting by a habit (and such a habit is a virtue) when the power's own nature is not equal to this. Now the proper nature of a power is seen in terms of its object. Since, then, the object of the will is a good of reason proportionate to the will, in regard to this the will does not need a virtue perfecting it, as we have said.[43] But if man's will is intent upon a good which exceeds what is proportionate to it, whether this be as far as all mankind is concerned, such as the divine good, which transcends the limits of human nature, or as far as the individual is concerned, such as the good of one's neighbor, then the will needs virtue. Therefore the virtues which order the love of man to God or to his neighbor, such as charity, justice, and the like, are in the will as in a subject.

Reply to 1: This argument is acceptable in respect to the virtue which is ordered to the proper good of the one who wills, such as temperance and fortitude, which have to do with human passions, and others like these, as is clear from what we have said.[44]

Reply to 2: Not only are the irascible and concupiscible powers rational by participation, but the appetitive powers entirely, that is, universally.[45] Now the will is included under the appetitive power. There-

---

[41] *Rhetoric* II, 53.

[42] Cf. Aristotle, *Nicomachean Ethics* I, 13 (1103a 4); II, 1 (1103a 14).

[43] Question 19, article 3.

[44] Question 25, article 6, reply to 3; I, question 21, article 1, reply to 1; question 59, article 4, reply to 3.

[45] Cf. Aristotle, *Nicomachean Ethics* I, 13 (1102b 30).

fore, any virtue in the will must be a moral virtue, unless it be a theological virtue, as will be evident later.[46]

Reply to 3: Some virtues are ordered to moderated passion as a good, which is the proper good of this or that man. In respect to these, it is not necessary that there be a virtue in the will since the nature of the power suffices for this sort of good. The necessity arises only in regard to those virtues which are ordered to an external good.

---

[46] Question 58, article 3, reply to 3; question 62, article 3.

The Distinction of the Intellectual Virtues

(*In Six Articles*)

We must now consider the distinction of the virtues; first, the intellectual virtues, second the moral virtues,[1] third, the theological virtues.[2]

First Article

ARE SPECULATIVE INTELLECTUAL HABITS VIRTUES?

It seems that the speculative[3] habits of the intellect are not virtues.

1. Virtue is an operative habit, as we have already pointed out.[4] But speculative habits are not operative, for the speculative is distinguished from the practical, which is operative. Therefore speculative habits are not virtues.

2. Virtue concerns those things through which man is made happy or blessed, for "happiness is the reward of virtue." [5] But intellectual habits do not regard human acts or other human goods by which man acquires happiness; rather, they regard things pertaining to nature and to God. Therefore such habits cannot be called virtues.

3. Science is a speculative habit. But science and virtue are distinguished as diverse genera without either being placed under the other, as the Philosopher points out.[6] Therefore speculative habits are not virtues.

On the contrary: Only speculative habits are concerned with necessary things, which cannot be otherwise than they are. But the Philosopher puts certain intellectual virtues in that part of the soul which considers necessary things, which cannot be otherwise than they are.[7] Therefore speculative intellectual habits are virtues.

---

[1] Question 58.   [2] Question 62.

[3] The word "speculative," translated literally from the Latin *speculativus*, signifies theoretical knowledge, or knowledge sought for its own sake. It is distinguished from practical knowledge, which is always ordered to some activity beyond knowledge. In this context, "speculative" is wholly distinct from the current meaning it has in English of a calculated guess or an opinion or a risk.

[4] Question 55, article 2. An *operative* habit disposes a human power to perform readily some work or activity. It is distinguished from an *entitative* habit, a derived meaning of "habit," which signifies some relatively permanent disposition of the very substance of a being; for example, health is such a disposition on the part of the body.

[5] Aristotle, *Nicomachean Ethics* I, 9 (1099b 16).   [6] *Topics* IV, 2 (121b 34).

[7] *Nicomachean Ethics* VI, 1 (1139a 7).

Response: Since every virtue is said with reference to what is good, as we have said,[8] a habit is called a virtue for two reasons, as noted above.[9] The first reason is that a habit gives an aptitude to act well; the second is that it induces good use of it. The latter, as we have said,[10] pertains only to those habits which concern the appetitive part of the soul, for it is the appetitive power of the soul which commits to use all the powers and habits.

Now since the speculative intellectual habits do not perfect the appetitive part nor concern it in any way, but only have regard to the intellectual part, they may be called virtues insofar as they confer an aptitude for good operation, namely, for considering truth, for truth is the good work of the intellect; however, they are not called virtues in the second way as though they made a power or a habit be used well. For it is not from the fact that one has a speculative scientific habit that he is inclined to its use, but only that he is rendered able to investigate truth in those matters of which he has scientific knowledge; that he use it comes from the movement of his will. Consequently, a virtue which perfects the will, such as charity or justice, brings about the good use of these speculative habits. And in this way too there can be merit in the acts of these habits, if done out of charity; thus Gregory says that the "contemplative life has greater merit than the active life." [11]

Reply to 1: A work is of two kinds, external and internal. Now practical or operative activity, which is distinguished from speculative, is concerned with an external work. A speculative habit is not ordered to an external work, but to an internal work of the intellect, the investigation of truth. It is in this way that it is an operative habit.

Reply to 2: Virtue is about certain things in two ways. In one way, virtue is about objects, and thus speculative virtues are not about the things by which man is made happy, unless perhaps the expression "by which" signifies the efficient cause or the object of complete happiness, which is God, who is the highest object of contemplation. In another way, virtue is about acts, and in this way intellectual virtues are about things which make man happy, both because the acts of these virtues can be meritorious, as we have said,[12] and also because they are a kind of beginning of perfect happiness, which consists in the contemplation of truth, as we have also said.[13]

Reply to 3: Science is distinguished from virtue taken in the second sense, which pertains to the appetitive power.

---

[8] Question 55, article 3.   [9] Question 56, article 3.   [10] *Ibid.*
[11] Gregory the Great, *Moral.*, VI, 37.   [12] In the body of this article.
[13] Question 3, article 8.

Second Article

ARE THERE ONLY THREE SPECULATIVE INTELLECTUAL HABITS, WISDOM, SCIENCE, AND UNDERSTANDING?

It seems inappropriate to distinguish three speculative intellectual virtues: wisdom, science, and understanding.

1. A species should not be codivided with its genus.[14] But "wisdom is a science." [15] Therefore wisdom should not be codivided with science in the enumeration of the intellectual virtues.

2. When distinguishing powers, habits, and acts in terms of objects, we base the distinction principally on their formal aspect as objects, as we have said.[16] Therefore diverse habits should not be distinguished according to a material object, but according to a formal aspect of the object itself. Now the principle of a demonstration is the formal aspect under which conclusions are known. Therefore the understanding of principles should not be given as a habit or virtue different from knowledge of conclusions.

3. We call that an intellectual virtue which is in an essentially rational power. But even speculative reason uses a dialectical syllogism in arguing, just as it uses a demonstrative syllogism.[17] Therefore just as science, which is caused by a demonstrative syllogism, is held to be an intellectual virtue, so also should opinion be.

On the contrary: Aristotle holds that there are only three intellectual virtues: wisdom, science, and understanding.[18]

Response: As we have said,[19] an intellectual virtue is one that perfects the speculative intellect for knowing truth, for knowing truth is its good work. Now truth can be considered in two ways: first, as known in itself; second, as known by means of something else. What is known in itself is like a principle and is grasped at once by the intellect, and the habit perfecting the intellect for such consideration of truth is called *understanding,* which is the habit of knowing principles.

Now a truth which is known by means of something else is not understood by the intellect immediately but through an inquiry of reason, and is like a limit. This can happen in two ways: first, as it is ultimate in some particular genus; second, as it is ultimate with respect to all human

---

[14] A species, for example, man, should be a dividing member under its genus, animal, and not codivided with animal as though parallel with it, under some other genus.

[15] Aristotle, *Nicomachean Ethics* VI, 7 (1141a 19).

[16] Question 54, article 2, reply to 1.

[17] In other words, it is by the same power of knowing that we reason sometimes to a conclusion necessarily true and certain, and other times to a conclusion that is only probably true, thereby reaching opinion.

[18] Cf. *Nicomachean Ethics* VI, 7 (1141a 19); 3 (1139b 16).   [19] In the preceding article.

knowledge. And since "things which subsequently are intelligible to us are prior and more intelligible in their nature," [20] therefore that which is ultimate in regard to all human knowledge is first and most knowable as to its nature. *Wisdom* is about such things, for it "considers the highest causes." [21] It is proper, therefore, that wisdom judge all things and set them in order, because perfect and universal judgment can be had only by resolving things to their primary causes. But in regard to that which is ultimate in this or that genus of knowable things, it is *science* that perfects the intellect. Consequently, there are different habits of science according to the different kinds of knowable things, whereas wisdom is only one in kind.

Reply to 1: Wisdom is a science to the extent it has what is common to all sciences, namely, it demonstrates conclusions from principles. Because, however, it has something distinctive over and beyond the other sciences, inasmuch as it judges all other sciences not only as to their conclusions, but also as to their principles, it is therefore a more perfect virtue than science.

Reply to 2: When the formal aspect of the object is referred to the power or habit in the same act, then habits or powers are not distinguished in respect to the formal aspect and material object; for example, it belongs to the same power of sight to see color and to see light, which is the aspect under which color is seen, and is seen at the same time as the color. But the principles of demonstration can be considered by themselves apart from any consideration of the conclusions. They can also be considered along with the conclusions inasmuch as conclusions are deduced from the principles. To consider principles in the second way belongs to science, which also considers the conclusions; but to consider the principles in themselves belongs to understanding.

Hence if the matter is considered rightly, these three virtues are not distinguished as though they were all equal, but according to a certain order. The same thing is observed in potential wholes,[22] one part of which is more perfect than another, as the rational soul is more perfect than the sensitive soul, and the sensitive soul more perfect than the vegetative soul. It is in this way that science depends upon understanding as upon something higher, and both depend upon wisdom as upon

---

[20] Aristotle, *Physics* I, 1 (184a 18).   [21] Aristotle, *Metaphysics* I, 1 (981b 28); 2 (982b 9).

[22] A whole can be divided into quantitative, essential, or potential parts. The division into quantitative parts is the most obvious, for example, the division of a line into parts. An example of a division into essential parts is the division of animal into man and brute. The division of a whole into potential parts is a division into the powers belonging to the whole. Thus the rational soul, having more perfect powers, is a more perfect living thing than the sensitive soul, and the latter more perfect than the vegetative soul.

something highest, which includes under it both understanding and science by judging the conclusions of science and the principles on which they are based.

Reply to 3: As we have said,[23] the habits of virtues are related determinately to good and in no way to evil. Now the good of the intellect is what is true, and the evil what is false. Consequently, only those habits are called intellectual virtues by which what is true is said and never what is false. But there can be opinion and suspicion of what is true or what is false, and hence they are not intellectual virtues.[24]

Third Article

IS THE INTELLECTUAL HABIT OF ART A VIRTUE?

It seems that art is not an intellectual virtue.[25]

1. Augustine says that "no one makes bad use of a virtue." [26] But one can make bad use of an art, for a craftsman can work badly according to the knowledge of his art. Therefore art is not a virtue.

2. There is no virtue of a virtue. But there is some virtue in art.[27] Therefore art is not a virtue.

3. The liberal arts are more excellent than the mechanical arts. But the mechanical arts are practical while the liberal arts are speculative. Therefore, if art were an intellectual virtue it would have to be acknowledged as a speculative virtue.

On the contrary: The Philosopher maintains that art is a virtue, yet he does not include it among the speculative virtues, whose subject, he asserts, is the scientific part of the soul.[28]

Response: Art is nothing other than *right reasoning about certain works to be made.* The good of these things, however, does not consist in man's appetite being disposed in some way but in the very work produced being good. For praise is bestowed upon the craftsman as craftsman not for the will with which he does the work, but for the quality of his work. Art, therefore, properly speaking, is an operative habit.

But art does have something in common with speculative habits, for how the thing is known which the speculative habits consider, affects

---

[23] Question 55, articles 3 and 4.   [24] Cf. Aristotle, *Nicomachean Ethics* VI, 3 (1139b 17).

[25] This treatment of art as an intellectual virtue, in this article and the following one, is in the context of a practical art, such as carpentry or engineering, and a liberal art, such as logic and mathematics. St. Thomas is not expressly thinking of fine art, and while what is said in these articles would apply in a common way to fine art also, nevertheless some important qualifications and distinctions would also have to be made. The word "art" is not univocal in meaning, nor is "virtue," as we shall see in the next question.

[26] *On Free Will* II, 18, 19.   [27] Cf. Aristotle, *Nicomachean Ethics* VI, 5 (1140b 22).

[28] *Nicomachean Ethics* VI, 3 (1139b 16); 7 (1141a 19).

them, but not how the human appetite is related to the object. For as long as a geometer demonstrates what is true, it does not matter how he is disposed as far as his appetitive part is concerned, whether he be joyful or angry, just as it does not matter in the case of the craftsman, as we have noted. Consequently, art has the nature of virtue in the same way as speculative habits, that is, insofar as neither art nor a speculative habit effects a good work in regard to the use of the habit—which is characteristic of a virtue that perfects the appetite[29]—but only in regard to the aptitude to work well.[30]

Reply to 1: When someone having an art produces a bad work, the result is not a work of art and, moreover, is contrary to art, just as one who lies when he knows the truth does not speak in accord with his knowledge but contrary to it. Hence, just as science is always related to a good, as we have said,[31] so also is art, and in this respect is called a virtue. Art falls short of being a perfect virtue, however, in that it does not confer good use on the part of the one who has art. Something else is required for good use,[32] although there cannot be good use without the art.

Reply to 2: In order that a man use his art well, a good will is required, which is achieved through moral virtue. Hence the Philosopher says that there is virtue in art, namely, moral virtue, insofar as its good use requires moral virtue. For clearly the builder is inclined by justice, which makes the will right, to do his work faithfully.

Reply to 3: Even in speculative matters there is something by way of a work, for example, the construction of a syllogism, an appropriate vocal expression, or the work of enumerating or measuring. Accordingly, those speculative habits which are ordered to such works of reason are called arts by a certain likeness, namely, liberal arts, in order to distinguish them from the arts which are ordered to works done by bodily activity, which are in a fashion servile, inasmuch as the body serves the soul whereas man according to the soul is free.[33] But those sciences which in no way are ordered to a work of this kind are called sciences unqualifiedly, and not arts. It does not follow, on the other hand, that if the liberal arts are

---

[29] Namely, a moral virtue.

[30] In other words, an intellectual virtue, whether a speculative virtue like science or a practical one like art, does not require goodness in the use to which the virtue is put, which is required in moral virtue, but only good activity of the intellectual power itself. The will, upon which use depends, remains extrinsic to the good of intellectual virtue, but is intrinsic to moral virtue. See the following question, especially article 3.

[31] Article 2, reply to 3.

[32] Rectitude of appetite, or a good will, is further required, which depends on having moral virtue, whose role is to perfect man's appetite.

[33] The Latin word is *liber*, thus indicating the derivation of the word "liberal" in liberal arts. It is relevant to note that the Latin *liber* also signifies "book," which is also intimately connected with liberal art.

more excellent than other arts that the notion of art applies primarily to them.[34]

Fourth Article

IS PRUDENCE A VIRTUE DISTINCT FROM ART?

It seems that prudence is not a virtue distinct from art.

1. Art is right reasoning about certain works. But a diversity in kinds of works does not result in any loss of the nature of art, for the different arts concern widely different works. But since prudence is a kind of right reasoning about works, it seems that prudence also should be called an art.

2. Prudence agrees more with art than with a speculative habit, for both concern the contingent, which can be otherwise than it is.[35] But some speculative habits are called arts. Therefore much more should prudence be called an art.

3. "It belongs to prudence to deliberate well." [36] But deliberation also takes place in some of the arts,[37] for example, in the military, governing, and medical arts. Therefore prudence is not distinct from art.

On the contrary: The Philosopher distinguishes prudence from art.[38]

Response: Where there is a difference in the nature of virtue then virtues must be distinguished. Now we have already said[39] that some habits have the nature of virtue solely from inducing an aptitude to do a good work, while other habits are virtues not only from conferring an aptitude for a good work but also its use. Now art gives only the ability for good work since it does not have reference to appetite, while prudence not only gives the ability of achieving a good work but the use of it as well, for prudence has reference to appetite since it presupposes rectitude of appetite.

The reason for this difference is that art is *right reasoning about what is to be made* whereas prudence is *right reasoning about what is to be done.* Now *making* and *doing* differ in that *making* is an activity having an effect on exterior matter, such as building, sawing, and the like, while *doing* is an activity remaining within the agent, such as seeing, willing, and the like.[40] Accordingly, prudence is related to such human arts, that is, the exercise of powers and habits, as art is related to external works, for each is perfect reasoning about the things with which it is concerned. But perfection and rightness of reasoning in speculative

---

[34] The liberal arts are more perfect with respect to the work produced, but with respect to what the name "art" first means, servile or manual art is primary.

[35] Cf. Aristotle, *Nicomachean Ethics* VI, 6 (1140b 35).

[36] Aristotle, *op. cit.,* VI, 5 (1140a 25).   [37] Cf. Aristotle, *op. cit.,* III, 3 (1112b 3).

[38] *Op. cit.,* VI, 3 (1139b 16).   [39] Article 1; question 56, article 3.

[40] Cf. Aristotle, *Metaphysics* IX, 8 (1050a 30).

matters depends upon the principles from which the reasoning proceeds, for, as we have said,[41] science depends upon understanding, which is the habit of principles, and science presupposes such understanding. Now in human acts, ends stand in the same relation as principles do in speculative matters.[42] Consequently, for prudence, which is right reasoning about what is to be done, it is required that man be well disposed in regard to ends, and this depends on right appetite. Hence for prudence, one must have moral virtue, which rectifies the appetite.

Now the good of artifacts is not the good of the human appetite, but the good of the works of art themselves, and consequently art does not presuppose rectitude of appetite. It follows from this that more praise is given to a craftsman who wittingly does something amiss than to one who does so unwittingly whereas, on the other hand, it is more contrary to prudence to do something amiss wittingly than unwittingly since rectitude of the will belongs to the nature of prudence, but not to the nature of art. Clearly, then, prudence is a virtue distinct from art.

Reply to 1: The different kinds of things made by art are all extrinsic to man, and hence they do not cause a different kind of virtue. But prudence is right reasoning about human acts themselves, and consequently it is a different kind of virtue from art, as we have said.[43]

Reply to 2: With respect to its subject and matter, prudence resembles art more than it does a speculative habit, for both are in the opinionative part of the soul and are about things that can be otherwise than they are. But if we consider them as virtues, art resembles the speculative habits more than it does prudence, as we have pointed out.[44]

Reply to 3: Through prudence we deliberate well about matters pertaining to the whole of human life and the ultimate end of human life. But the deliberation found in some of the arts is about matters pertaining to the proper ends of those arts. Hence, those who deliberate well about matters of war or seamanship are called prudent officers or pilots, but not prudent unqualifiedly. Only those who deliberate well about matters concerning the whole of human life are called prudent without qualification.

Fifth Article

IS PRUDENCE A VIRTUE THAT IS NECESSARY FOR MAN?

It seems that prudence is not a virtue necessary for leading the good life.

1. Just as art is related to things to be made, and about which there is right reasoning, so prudence is related to things which are to be done,

---

[41] Article 2, reply to 2.   [42] Cf. Aristotle, *Nicomachean Ethics* VII, 8 (1151a 16).
[43] In the body of this article.   [44] Article 3.

with respect to which human life is judged, since prudence is right reasoning about such matters, as Aristotle says.[45] But art is necessary for things which are to be made only in order to bring them into being, but it is not necessary after they are made. Therefore prudence is not necessary for man in order to lead a good life after he has become virtuous, but perhaps only in order that he may become virtuous.

2. "It is by means of prudence that we deliberate well." [46] But a man can act not only from his own good deliberation but also by taking another's counsel. Therefore it is not necessary for leading the good life that a man himself have prudence, for it is enough if he follow the counsel of some prudent man.

3. An intellectual virtue is one by which it is possible to say always what is true and never what is false. But this does not seem possible with regard to prudence, for it is not human never to err in deliberating about what is to be done, since human actions are contingent and can turn out otherwise. Accordingly, it is written in Scripture: "The thoughts of mortal men are fearful, and our counsels uncertain" (*Wisdom 9:14*). Therefore it does not seem that prudence should be regarded as an intellectual virtue.

On the contrary: Prudence is included among the virtues necessary for human life when it is written in Scripture concerning divine wisdom that "She teaches temperance and prudence and justice and fortitude, which are such things as man can have nothing more profitable in life" (*Wisdom 8:7*).

Response: Prudence is a virtue that is most necessary for human life, for a good life consists in good deeds. Now doing good deeds not only involves *what* a man does but also *how* he does them, namely, that he does them from right choice and not merely out of impulse or passion. And since choice has to do with matters which are for the sake of an end, rightness of choice requires two things: a due end and something suitably ordered to that end. Now man is suitably disposed to his due end through virtue, which perfects the part of the soul that is appetitive, the object of which is the good and the end. But for that which is suitably ordered to the due end, man must be rightly disposed by a habit in his reason, for to deliberate and to choose (which are about things ordered to the end) are acts of reason.[47] Consequently, an intellectual virtue is needed in

---

[45] *Nicomachean Ethics* VI, 5 (1140b 3).

[46] Aristotle, *op. cit.*, VI, 5 (1140a 25); 7 (1141b 9).

[47] Choice may be considered, in different respects, as an act of reason and an act of the will. Thus in question 13, article 1, of this part of the *Summa*, St. Thomas says: "The word 'choice' implies something belonging to reason or intellect and something belonging to the will. . . . Now it is clear that reason precedes the will in a certain way and orders its act to the extent that the will tends to its object according to the order of reason, for the power of knowing presents the appetite with its object. There-

man's reason which perfects reason so that it is suitably disposed toward the things that are for the end, and this virtue is prudence. Hence prudence is a virtue that is necessary in order to lead a good life.

Reply to 1: The good of art is to be found, not in the craftsman, but rather in the product of art, since art is right reasoning about things to be made; for making, as having an effect on exterior matter, is not a perfection of the maker but of the thing made, just as movement is the act of what is moved. Now art is about things to be made. The good of prudence, on the other hand, is found in the agent himself, whose doing is his perfection, for prudence is right reasoning about things to be done, as we have said.[48] Therefore art does not require of the craftsman that he do a good act, but that he make a good work.[49] It would be required, rather, that the thing made act well, for example, that a knife should carve well or a saw cut well, if it were proper for such things to act rather than to be acted upon, for they do not have control over their own acts. Hence art is needed by the craftsman, not in order to lead a good life, but only in order to produce good works of art and to preserve them. Prudence, however, is necessary to man in order to lead a good life and not only for his becoming good.

Reply to 2: As long as a man does a good action, not by the deliberation of his own reason, but as moved by the counsel of another, his action is not wholly perfect as regards reason's direction and his will's movement. Consequently, if he does a good act, he still does not do a good act simply, which is required in order that he lead a good life.

Reply to 3: The truth of the practical intellect is not the same as the truth of the speculative intellect, as Aristotle points out.[50] Truth in the speculative intellect depends on the conformity of thought with thing. And since the intellect cannot be infallibly in conformity with contingent things, but only with necessary things, hence no speculative habit about contingent things is an intellectual virtue, but only one about necessary things. Truth in the practical intellect, however, depends on conformity with a right appetite. Such a conformity has no place in necessary matters, which do not come about by human will, but only in contingent matters which can originate in us, whether they be matters of interior action or products of exterior work. Hence it is solely in regard to contingent

---

fore, the act whereby the will tends to something proposed as good, from the fact that it is ordered to an end by reason, is materially an act of the will and formally an act of reason."

[48] Article 4.

[49] In other words, the act of the maker need not be a good act in the moral sense since it is not, as such, a moral act, whereas his work must be good in the artistic sense, that is, according to the nature and requirements of art.

[50] *Nicomachean Ethics* VI, 2 (1139a 26).

matters that we ascribe virtue to the practical intellect, art in regard to things to be made, and prudence in regard to things to be done.

Sixth Article

ARE GOOD DELIBERATION, SAGACITY, AND EQUITABLE JUDGMENT VIRTUES ANNEXED TO PRUDENCE? [51]

It seems that it is unsuitable to adjoin good deliberation, sagacity, and equitable judgment to prudence.

1. Good deliberation is "the habit by which we weigh the options correctly." [52] But to weigh the options correctly belongs to prudence, as Aristotle says. [53] Therefore good deliberation is not a virtue joined to prudence, but rather is prudence itself.

2. It pertains to the higher to judge of the lower. The highest virtue would therefore seem to be one whose act it is to judge. Now sagacity enables one to judge well. Therefore sagacity is not a virtue joined to prudence but, rather, is the principal virtue itself.

3. Just as there are different things on which to pass judgment, so also there are different options to weigh. But there is one virtue, good deliberation, for all weighing of options. Therefore, for making a good judgment about what is to be done, there is no need to posit, besides sagacity, the virtue of equitable judgment.

4. Cicero lists three other parts of prudence: "memory of the past, understanding of the present, and foresight in regard to the future." [54] Macrobius also gives some other parts of prudence, such as caution, docility, and the like. [55] Therefore it does not seem that the virtues mentioned above are the only ones connected with prudence.

On the contrary: The Philosopher holds that the virtues listed above are the three which are adjoined to prudence. [56]

Response: Whenever there are powers subordinate to one another, the more principal power is that which is ordered to the more principal act.

---

[51] The Latin words for good deliberation, sagacity, and equitable judgment are, respectively, *eubulia, synesis,* and *gnome.* These Latin words are simply transliterations of the Greek words εὐβουλία, σύνεσις, γνώμη. English equivalents of these words are not easy to find, and the words used in this translation are offered as approximations. The development of this article by St. Thomas will clarify more what these associated virtues of prudence mean and the role they play in man's moral life. For a fuller treatment of them, upon which the analysis of St. Thomas is based, see Aristotle, *Nicomachean Ethics* VI, 9-11.

[52] Aristotle, *Nicomachean Ethics* VI, 9 (1142b 16; b 20; b 33).

[53] *Op. cit.,* VI, 5 (1140a 25); 7 (1141b 9).   [54] *On Rhetorical Discovery* II, 53.

[55] *Commentary on the Dream of Scipio* I, 8. Macrobius was a fourth century author, influenced by Plato and Plotinus.

[56] *Nicomachean Ethics* VI, 11 (1143a 25).

Now there are three acts of reason in respect to actions done by man; the first is deliberation, the second judgment, and the third command. The first two correspond to acts of the speculative intellect, namely, inquiry and judgment, for to deliberate is to make a kind of inquiry. The third act, however, is proper to the practical intellect insofar as it is productive, for reason is not such that it can command those things man cannot do. Now it is clear that in regard to things which are done by man, the principal act is command, to which the other acts are ordered. Consequently prudence, as the virtue which commands what is good, and is therefore the more principal power, has joined to it the secondary virtues of good deliberation, sagacity, and equitable judgment. The latter two are the parts of prudence related to judgment, and we shall shortly distinguish between them.[57]

Reply to 1: Prudence makes us deliberate correctly, not as though its immediate act is to deliberate correctly, but because prudence brings about this act by means of a virtue subordinate to it, which is the virtue of good deliberation.

Reply to 2: A judgment about what is to be done is ordered to something further, for a man may make a good judgment as to what is to be done and still not carry it out rightly. The final result is achieved when reason has commanded rightly in point of what has to be done.

Reply to 3: A judgment about anything is made in terms of the proper principles of that thing. But inquiry is not yet in terms of the proper principles, for if we had these we would no longer be inquiring, since the matter would already be resolved. Consequently, only one virtue is ordered to good deliberation, whereas there are two virtues for judging well, because there is not a distinction in common principles, but there is in proper principles. Hence even in theoretical knowledge, there is one kind of dialectic for inquiring about all things, whereas demonstrative sciences, which resolve matters by judgment, are diverse sciences about different things. Accordingly, sagacity and equitable judgment are distinguished according to different rules by which they judge. Sagacity judges of actions according to common law; equitable judgment is based upon natural reason itself, in the cases where common law fails to apply, as we shall make evident later.[58]

Reply to 4: Memory, intelligence, and foresight, as well as caution, docility, and the like, are not virtues distinct from prudence but are in a certain way connected with prudence as integral parts, insofar as they are all required for the perfection of prudence. Furthermore, there are the subjective parts or species of prudence, such as domestic and political

---

[57] Reply to 3 of this article.   [58] II-II, question 51, article 4.

prudence, and so on. But the first three mentioned are, after a fashion, potential parts of prudence, because they are ordered to prudence as what is secondary to what is principal.[59] We shall treat of them in a subsequent section.[60]

---

[59] On the distinction of integral, subjective, and potential parts, see note 24 of question 54, article 4, reply to 2.

[60] II-II, question 48.

The Distinction between Moral and Intellectual Virtues

(*In Five Articles*)

We must now consider the moral virtues. First, we shall examine the distinction between them and intellectual virtues; second, the distinction of moral virtues from each other;[1] third, the distinction between the cardinal virtues and other virtues.[2]

First Article

IS EVERY VIRTUE A MORAL VIRTUE?

It seems that every virtue is a moral virtue.

1. Moral virtue is so named from the Latin *mos, moris,* that is, from a word signifying custom. Now we can accustom ourselves to acts of all virtues. Therefore every virtue is a moral virtue.

2. The Philosopher says that "moral virtue is the habit of choosing the mean as determined by reason." [3] But every virtue appears to be a habit of choosing because the acts of any virtue can be done from choice and, furthermore, all virtue consists somehow in following a mean of reason, as we shall show subsequently.[4] Therefore every virtue is a moral virtue.

3. Cicero says that "virtue as a habit is like a second nature, in accord with reason." [5] But since every human virtue is ordered to the goodness of man, it must be in accord with reason, for "man's goodness is to be in accord with reason." [6] Therefore every virtue is a moral virtue.

On the contrary: The Philosopher says, "In speaking about one's character, we do not say that he is wise or intelligent but that he is kind or temperate." [7] Now wisdom and understanding are not moral virtues, and yet they are virtues, as we have shown.[8] Not every virtue, therefore, is a moral virtue.

Response: By way of giving a clear answer, we must consider what the Latin word *mos* means, for in this way we can come to know what *moral* virtue is. Now the word *mos* signifies two things. Sometimes it signifies

---

[1] Question 59. [2] Question 61. [3] *Nicomachean Ethics* II, 6 (1106b 36).
[4] Question 64, articles 2, 3 and 4. [5] *On Rhetorical Discovery* II, 53.
[6] Dionysius, *On the Divine Names* IV, 32. [7] *Nicomachean Ethics* I, 13 (1103a 7).
[8] Question 57, article 2.

custom, and so in Scripture we read, "Unless you be circumcised after the manner [i.e., *custom*] of Moses, you cannot be saved" (*Acts 15:1*). Sometimes it signifies a certain natural or quasinatural inclination to do something, and in this sense even irrational animals are said to act in a customary way. Thus we read again in Scripture that "rushing violently upon the enemy like lions [i.e., according to the custom of lions], they slew them" (*II Machabees 11:11*), and also when it is said, "Who maketh men of one manner [i.e., of one custom] to dwell in a house" (*Psalms 67:7*). In Latin, the same word has these two meanings, but in Greek there are different words, for *ethos*, which signifies the same as the Latin word *mos*, sometimes has a long *e* and then is written with the Greek letter η, and other times has a short *e* and then is written with the Greek letter ε.

Now *moral* virtue is named from the Latin word *mos*, as it signifies a certain natural or quasinatural inclination for doing some particular action. The other meaning of *mos*, that is, custom, is close to this meaning, for custom in a certain way turns into nature and produces an inclination similar to a natural one. Now it is clear that the inclination to an action belongs properly to an appetitive power, whose function is to move all powers to act, as we have said.[9] Consequently, not every virtue is called a moral virtue, but only those that are in an appetitive power.

Reply to 1: The argument is based on the Latin word *mos* as signifying custom.

Reply to 2: Every act of virtue can be done from choice, but only the virtue which is in the appetitive part of the soul makes us choose rightly, for, as we have said,[10] choice is an act of an appetitive power. Hence a habit of choosing, which is the principle by which we choose, is a habit which perfects only the appetitive power, although the acts of other habits may fall under choice.

Reply to 3: "Nature is the principle of motion."[11] But to move to action is the proper function of the appetitive power. Consequently, to become like nature by consenting to reason is proper to the virtues which are in an appetitive power.

Second Article

DOES MORAL VIRTUE DIFFER FROM INTELLECTUAL VIRTUE?

It seems that moral virtue is not distinguished from intellectual virtue.

1. Augustine says that "virtue is the art of right living."[12] But art is an intellectual virtue. Therefore moral virtue does not differ from intellectual virtue.

2. A number of authors place science in the definition of moral virtue.

---

[9] Question 9, article 1.   [10] Question 13, article 1.
[11] Aristotle, *Physics* II, 1 (192b 21).   [12] *The City of God* IV, 21.

For example, some define perseverance as "a science or habit about matters that we should continue in or not continue in," and sanctity as "a science making those who render what is owed to God faithful and obedient." [13] Now science is an intellectual virtue. Therefore moral virtue should not be distinguished from intellectual virtue.

3. Augustine says that "virtue is sound and perfect reasoning." [14] But this pertains to intellectual virtue.[15] Therefore moral virtue does not differ from intellectual virtue.

4. Nothing is distinguished except by what is included in its definition. But intellectual virtue is placed in the definition of moral virtue, for the Philosopher says that "moral virtue is the habit of choosing the mean decided upon by reason as a prudent man would decide it." [16] Now this right reason determining the mean of moral virtue pertains to intellectual virtue.[17] Therefore moral virtue does not differ from intellectual virtue.

On the contrary: "Virtue is distinguished into two kinds, for we call some virtues intellectual and others moral." [18]

Response: Reason is the first principle of all human acts, and whatever other principles of human acts may be found, they obey reason in a certain fashion but in different ways. Some follow reason at once and without any opposition whatever, such as the bodily members, if they are in good condition; thus, at the command of reason, the foot immediately begins to function. Hence the Philosopher says that "the soul rules the body despotically," [19] that is, like a master rules a servant who does not have the right of opposing his master. Some accordingly held that all the active principles in man are so related to reason. If this position were true, for man to act well it would suffice that his reason be perfected; consequently, since virtue is the habit by which we are perfected in regard to acting well, it would follow that virtue would only be in reason and that there would be none but intellectual virtues. This was the opinion of Socrates, who said that "all virtues are forms of prudence." [20] Hence he maintained that when a man possessed knowledge he could not sin, and that anyone who sinned, did so because of ignorance.[21]

Such a view is based on a false supposition. For the appetitive part in man does not just obey reason spontaneously, but with a certain power of opposition. Hence the Philosopher says that "reason commands the ap-

---

[13] The definition of perseverance is quoted again by St. Thomas in II-II, question 137, article 1, *On the contrary.* The definitions given in the text are attributed to Andronicus of Rhodes, who edited the works of Aristotle in the 1st century B.C.

[14] *Soliloquies* I, 6.   [15] Cf. Aristotle, *Nicomachean Ethics* VI, 13 (1144b 21).

[16] *Nicomachean Ethics* II, 6 (1106b 36).   [17] Cf. *Nicomachean Ethics* VI, 13 (1144b 21).

[18] Aristotle, *op. cit.,* I, 13 (1103a 3).   [19] *Politics* I, 2 (1254b 4).

[20] As quoted by Aristotle, *Nicomachean Ethics* VI, 13 (1144b 19).

[21] Cf. Aristotle, *op. cit.,* VII, 2 (1145b 23). Cf. also Plato, *Protagoras* (352 B; 355 A; 357 B).

petitive principle by political rule," [22] namely, that by which one rules over free men who have a certain right of opposition. Thus Augustine says that "sometimes the intellect leads the way, and the desire follows belatedly or not at all," [23] inasmuch as sometimes the passions or habits of the appetitive powers act in such a way that they impede the use of reason in a particular act. In this sense, there is something true in the remark of Socrates that when a man possesses knowledge he does not sin, provided this knowledge extends even to the use of reason in this individual act of choice.

Therefore, in order that man's actions be good, not only must his reason be well disposed by a habit of intellectual virtue but also his appetitive power by a habit of moral virtue. Accordingly, just as appetite is distinguished from reason so moral virtue is distinguished from intellectual virtue. And hence just as the appetite is the principle of human acts insofar as it participates in reason in some way, so moral habit is considered a human virtue inasmuch as it is in conformity with reason.

Reply to 1: Augustine generally takes art as any sort of right reasoning, and in this sense even prudence is included under art, for prudence is right reasoning about what is to be done just as art is right reasoning about what is to be made. Accordingly, when he says that virtue is the art of right living, this applies to prudence essentially and to the other virtues by participation insofar as they are directed by prudence.

Reply to 2: Such definitions, by whomever given, follow the Socratic opinion and are to be explained in the way art was explained in the preceding reply.

Reply to 3: The same applies to this argument as well.

Reply to 4: Right reason, which corresponds to prudence, is placed in the definition of moral virtue, not as part of the essence of moral virtue, but as something shared in by all the moral virtues insofar as they are all under the direction of prudence.

Third Article

IS THE DIVISION OF VIRTUE INTO MORAL AND INTELLECTUAL ADEQUATE?

It seems that the division of human virtue[24] into moral and intellectual is not adequate.

1. Prudence appears to be a mean between moral and intellectual virtue, for it is included among the intellectual virtues,[25] and is also generally included among the four cardinal virtues, which are moral

---

[22] *Politics* I, 5 (1254b 4).   [23] *Exposition of the Psalms,* Sermon 8; *Psalms* 118:20.
[24] See note 30 below.   [25] Cf. Aristotle, *Nicomachean Ethics* VI, 3 and 5.

virtues, as will be made evident later.[26] Therefore virtue is not divided adequately into intellectual and moral as though there were nothing intermediate between them.

2. Continence, perseverance, and even patience are not counted among the intellectual virtues nor, on the other hand, are they moral virtues since they do not preserve a mean in the passions; rather, there is a superabundance of passions in connection with them. Therefore virtue is not adequately divided into moral and intellectual.

3. Faith, hope, and charity are virtues, yet they are not intellectual virtues, for there are only five intellectual virtues: science, wisdom, understanding, prudence, and art, as we have already stated.[27] Nor are they moral virtues, for they do not have to do with passions, which is the principal concern of moral virtue. Therefore virtue is not adequately divided into moral and intellectual.

On the contrary: The Philosopher says that virtue is "of two kinds, intellectual and moral." [28]

Response: Human virtue is a habit perfecting man so that he may do good actions. Now in man there are only two principles of human action: intellect or reason, and appetite, for these are the two moving principles in man.[29] Hence every human virtue must perfect one of these principles. If the virtue perfects the speculative or practical intellect in order that a man's act may be good, then the virtue is intellectual; if it perfects the appetitive part, the virtue is moral. It follows, therefore, that every human virtue[30] is intellectual or moral.

Reply to 1: Prudence in essence is an intellectual virtue, but as regards its matter it has something in common with the moral virtues, for it is "right reasoning *about things to be done,*" as we have said.[31] In this respect it is included among moral virtues.

Reply to 2: Continence and perseverance are not perfections of the sense appetitive power. This is evident from the fact that inordinate passion can abound in one who is continent and in one who perseveres, which would not be the case if the sense appetite were perfected by a habit making it conform to reason. Continence and perseverance, however, are a perfection of the rational part of man, which resists the passions in order that reason may not be seduced. They fall short of being virtues, however, for intellectual virtue, which makes reason rightly disposed with regard to moral matters, presupposes right desire of the end,

---

[26] Question 61, article 1.   [27] Question 57, articles 2, 3 and 4.
[28] Cf. *Nicomachean Ethics* II, 1 (1103a 14).
[29] Cf. Aristotle, *On the Soul* III, 10 (433a 9).
[30] The word "human" needs stressing here since, properly speaking, the theological virtues of faith, hope, and charity are not intellectual or moral, nor are they human virtues either. This point is referred to in the reply to 3.
[31] Question 57, article 4.

so that reason may hold itself rightly in respect to principles, that is, the ends, from which it reasons; and this is lacking with regard to continence and perseverance. Furthermore, a perfect act cannot proceed from two powers unless each power is perfected by a habit adequate to the act; thus, however perfect the principal agent using an instrument may be, a perfect action will not ensue if the instrument is not well disposed. Hence if sense appetite, which is moved by the rational part of man, is not perfect, however perfect the rational part may be, the ensuing action will not be perfect, and consequently the principle of that action will not be a virtue.[32] And on that account, continence with respect to pleasure, and perseverance with respect to pain and sorrow, are not virtues, but something less than virtues, as the Philosopher points out.[33]

Reply to 3: Faith, hope, and charity are more than human virtues; they are virtues of man insofar as he is a partaker of divine grace.

Fourth Article

CAN THERE BE MORAL VIRTUE WITHOUT INTELLECTUAL VIRTUE?

It seems that moral virtue can exist without intellectual virtue.

1. Cicero says that moral virtue "is a habit like a second nature in accord with reason." [34] But though a nature may be in accord with some superior reason that moves it, this reason does not need to be joined to the nature in that subject, as is evident in the natural things which lack knowledge. Therefore there can be moral virtue in man like to nature, inclining him to consent to reason, even though his reason is not perfected by intellectual virtue.

2. Through intellectual virtue, man attains perfect use of his reason. But it sometimes happens that some men are virtuous and acceptable to God in whom there is not much active use of reason. Therefore it seems that there can be moral virtue without intellectual virtue.

---

[32] This remark points up an important aspect of virtue, namely, that for *virtuous* action, it is not enough to do what one knows by reason to be right; a man's emotional inclination must also be disposed to what is good and right to do. For example, it will not be a virtuous act, though still a good act, to know that it is right not to indulge the enjoyment of food and therefore not indulge oneself; it is a virtuous act when the sense desire as well as reason delights in doing the act. In this way we see the positive meaning of virtue and that virtuous action of all kinds is human action at its best.

[33] *Nicomachean Ethics* VII, 1 (1145b 1); 9 (1151b 32). While continence is not a virtue, it should be seen as a favorable disposition toward leading the good moral life and hence to the life of virtue. A person is continent when he resists evil desires in the concupiscible appetite for the good of reason. The fact that his sense appetite has not yet realized the order of reason in its movement sets off continence from the perfection of virtue.

[34] *On Rhetorical Discovery* II, 53.

3. Moral virtue brings about an inclination to do good works. But some persons have a natural inclination to do good deeds even without the judgment of reason. Therefore moral virtues can be present without intellectual virtues.

On the contrary: Gregory says that "the other virtues, unless we act prudently with regard to what we desire, can never really be virtues." [35] But prudence is an intellectual virtue, as we have said.[36] Therefore the moral virtues cannot exist without the intellectual virtues.

Response: Moral virtue can exist without some of the intellectual virtues, such as wisdom, science, and art, but not without the virtues of understanding and prudence. It cannot exist without prudence because moral virtue is a habit of choice, that is, a habit making us choose well. Now in order that a choice be good, two things are required. First, one must intend a suitable end, and this comes about through moral virtue, which inclines the appetitive power to a good in accord with reason, that is, to a suitable end. Second, one needs to deal rightly with those things that are for the sake of the end, and this can only come about through reason rightly deliberating, judging, and commanding, which is the function of prudence and the virtues allied with prudence, as we have said.[37] Hence there can be no moral virtue without prudence; and as a consequence there cannot be moral virtue without understanding. For it is by the virtue of understanding that we grasp the principles we come to know naturally,[38] in regard to both speculative and practical matters. Hence, just as right reasoning in speculative matters, insofar as it proceeds from naturally known principles, presupposes the understanding of those principles, so also does prudence, which is right reasoning about things to be done.

Reply to 1: The inclination of nature in things that do not have reason, is without choice, and hence such inclination does not require reason of necessity. But the inclination to moral virtue involves choice, and hence in order that this be perfect it requires that reason be perfected by intellectual virtue.

Reply to 2: A person may be virtuous and still not use his reason actively in regard to everything, provided he does so in regard to those things which should be done virtuously; and in this way all virtuous persons use reason actively. Hence even those who seem simple, in that they lack worldly cleverness, can be prudent, for, as is said in Scripture, "Be therefore wise[39] as serpents, and guileless as doves" (*Matthew 10:16*).

Reply to 3: The natural inclination to the good of virtue is a kind of beginning of virtue, but is not perfect virtue. For the stronger this inclination is the more dangerous it could be unless it is accompanied by

---

[35] Gregory the Great, *Moral.* XXII, 1.   [36] Article 3, reply to 1; question 57, article 4.
[37] Question 57, articles 4, 5 and 6.   [38] That is, with little or no reasoning or discourse.
[39] "Prudentes" in the Latin; hence wise in a practical sense.

right reason, through which right choice is made of means to a suitable end. For example, if a running horse is blind, the faster it runs the more forcefully will it strike something and the more severely will it be injured. Consequently, although moral virtue is not right reason, as Socrates maintained, neither is it only *being in accord with right reason,* inasmuch as it inclines one to what is in accord with right reason, as the Platonists held, but it must also *be present with right reason,* as Aristotle says.[40]

Fifth Article

CAN THERE BE INTELLECTUAL VIRTUE WITHOUT MORAL VIRTUE?

It seems that there can be intellectual virtue without moral virtue.

1. The perfection of what precedes does not depend upon the perfection of what comes after. But reason precedes and moves sense appetite. Therefore intellectual virtue, which is the perfection of reason, does not depend upon moral virtue, which is the perfection of the appetitive part of man; accordingly, it can be without it.

2. Things to be done morally are the matter of prudence just as things to be made are the matter of art. But there can be art without there being proper matter, for example, a blacksmith without iron. Therefore there can be prudence without moral virtues although, of all the intellectual virtues, prudence seems most of all connected with the moral virtues.

3. Prudence is "the virtue by which we deliberate well." [41] But many persons deliberate well who nonetheless lack the moral virtues. Therefore there can be prudence without moral virtue.

On the contrary: Wishing to do evil is directly opposed to moral virtue, but it is not opposed to anything that can be without moral virtue. Now sinning willingly is contrary to prudence, as Aristotle says.[42] Therefore prudence cannot be without moral virtue.

Response: All other intellectual virtues can exist without moral virtue, but there cannot be prudence without moral virtue. The reason for this is that prudence is right reasoning about what is to be done—and this not only in general, but also in particular, in respect to which man acts. Now right reasoning requires principles from which the reasoning proceeds. And reasoning about particulars must proceed not only from universal principles but from particular principles as well. As to universal principles about things to be done, man is rightly disposed by the natural[43] understanding of principles, whereby he recognizes that no evil

---

[40] *Nicomachean Ethics* VI, 13 (1144b 21).
[41] Aristotle, *op. cit.,* VI, 5 (1140a 25); 7 (1141b 10).   [42] *Op. cit.,* VI, 5 (1140b 23).
[43] See note 38 above.

is to be done; or again by some practical science. But this is not enough for right reasoning about particular cases. For it sometimes happens that such a universal principle known by understanding or through some science, is perverted in a particular case by some passion; for example, to a person very desirous of something when the desire overcomes him, the object of it seems good to him, although it is contrary to the universal judgment of his reason.

Consequently, just as man is disposed rightly with regard to universal principles by natural understanding or by the habit of science, so in order to be rightly disposed with regard to the particular principles concerning things to be done, which are ends or goals, he must be perfected by certain habits, so that it becomes connatural, as it were, to him to judge rightly about an end. This comes about through moral virtue, for the virtuous person judges about the end of virtue rightly, since "such as a man is, so does the end seem to him." [44] Hence in order to reason rightly about what is to be done, which is prudence, man must have moral virtue.

Reply to 1: Reason, as apprehending the end, precedes desire for the end, but desire for the end precedes reason's reasoning about the choice of things which are for the sake of the end, which is the concern of prudence; just as in speculative matters, the understanding of principles is the source for reasoning syllogistically.

Reply to 2: The principles of art are not judged by us as good or bad according to the disposition of our appetite, as are ends, which are principles in moral matters. The judgment about the principles of art depends only on reason. Hence art does not require, as prudence does, a virtue perfecting the appetite.

Reply to 3: Prudence not only makes us deliberate well but also enables us to judge well and command well. This is not possible unless the hindrance of the passions, which destroys the judgment and command of prudence, be removed. This is done by moral virtue.

---

[44] Aristotle, *Nicomachean Ethics* III, 5 (1114a 32).

The Relation of Moral Virtue to Passion

(*In Five Articles*)

We must now consider the distinction of moral virtues from each other. And because moral virtues, which are about the passions, are distinguished according to the diversity of passions, we must consider (1) the relation of virtue to passion and (2) the distinction of the moral virtues according to the passions.[1]

First Article

IS MORAL VIRTUE A PASSION?

It seems that moral virtue is a passion.[2]

1. The mean belongs to the same genus as the extremes. But moral virtue is the mean between passions. Therefore moral virtue is a passion.

2. Virtue and vice, being contraries, are in the same genus.[3] But some passions are regarded as vices; for example, envy and anger. Therefore some passions are also virtues.

3. Pity is a passion, for it is sorrow about another's misfortune, as indicated above.[4] Moreover, "Cicero, the famous orator, did not hesitate to call pity a virtue," as Augustine says.[5] Therefore a passion can be a moral virtue.

On the contrary: "The passions are neither virtues nor vices." [6]

Response: Moral virtue cannot be a passion. There are three reasons for this. First, a passion is a sort of movement of the sense appetite, as we have said.[7] Now a moral virtue is not a movement but, rather, being a habit, it is a principle of the appetite's movement. Second, passions in

---

[1] This second consideration is taken up in question 60.

[2] "Passion" is understood here as emotion. An emotion is a movement of the sense appetite consequent upon the sense perception of something as good or evil. It is thus distinguished from a movement of the intellectual appetite, the will, which is consequent upon the intellectual apprehension of something as good or evil. St. Thomas has treated the passions in general and in detail in the treatise immediately preceding the present one on habits and virtues, namely, from questions 22 to 48.

[3] Contraries by definition are those things which differ most from each other within a common genus, as odd and even are contraries of number, white and black of color.

[4] Question 35, article 8.   [5] *The City of God* IX, 5.

[6] Aristotle, *Nicomachean Ethics* II, 5 (1105b 28).   [7] Question 22, article 3.

themselves do not have the character of good or evil, for human good or evil has reference to reason. Consequently, the passions considered in themselves are referable to both good and evil inasmuch as they can be in accord or not with reason. Now nothing of this kind can be a virtue, since virtue is referable only to good, as we have said.[8] Third, granted that a passion is in some way related to good only, or to evil only, nevertheless the movement of passion, as passion, has its beginning in the appetite itself and its term in reason, since the appetite's tendency is to be conformed to reason. The movement of virtue, on the contrary, has its beginning in reason and its term in the appetite, inasmuch as the appetite is moved by reason. Accordingly, it is stated in the definition of moral virtue that "it is a habit of consistently choosing the mean as determined by reason, and as a prudent man would determine it." [9]

Reply to 1: Virtue is not in essence a mean between passions, but it is by way of its effect, for it establishes the mean between passions.

Reply to 2: If by vice we mean a habit of doing evil deeds, then clearly no passion is a vice. But if by vice we mean a sin, which is a vicious act, then nothing prevents a passion from being a vice just as, conversely, nothing prevents a passion from concurring in an act of virtue; for a passion either goes against reason or follows in accordance with reason.

Reply to 3: Pity is said to be a virtue, that is, an act of virtue,[10] inasmuch as "this movement of the soul is obedient to reason, namely, when pity is bestowed so as to preserve justice, as when the needy are helped or when someone who is penitent is forgiven," as Augustine says in the same place.[11] If, however, pity is taken to mean a habit perfecting man so that he bestows pity reasonably, nothing prevents pity or mercy, so understood, from being a virtue. The same reasoning applies to similar passions.

Second Article

CAN THERE BE MORAL VIRTUE TOGETHER WITH PASSION?

It seems that there cannot be moral virtue together with passion.

1. The Philosopher says that "a gentle person is one who does not experience passion, whereas a patient person is one who experiences passion and is not led astray by it." [12] The same argument applies to all moral virtues. Therefore all moral virtue is without passion.

2. A virtue is a certain right disposition of the soul, just as health is a right disposition of the body.[13] Accordingly, "virtue seems to be a sort of health of the soul," as Cicero remarks.[14] But passions of the soul are

---

[8] Question 50, article 3.   [9] Aristotle, *Nicomachean Ethics* II, 6 (1106b 36).
[10] In II-II, question 30, St. Thomas discusses pity or mercy in some detail.
[11] *The City of God* IX, 5.   [12] *Topics* IV, 5 (125b 22).
[13] Cf. Aristotle, *Physics* VII, 3 (246b 2; 247a 2).   [14] *Tusculan Disputations* IV, 13.

called "diseases of the soul," as Cicero also says.[15] Now health is not compatible with disease. Therefore neither is virtue compatible with passion.

3. Moral virtue requires a perfect use of reason, even in regard to particular instances. But the passions are an obstacle to this, for the Philosopher says that "pleasures destroy the judgment of prudence," [16] and Sallust says that "when they," i.e., the passions, "interfere, the mind does not easily grasp what is true." [17] Therefore there cannot be moral virtue along with passion.

On the contrary: Augustine says that "if the will is perverse, the movements," namely, of the passions, "will be perverse also; but if the will is upright, not only are the passions blameless, but also truly praiseworthy." [18] Now moral virtue prevents nothing which is praiseworthy. Therefore moral virtue does not exclude the passions but can be present with them.

Response: The Stoics and the Peripatetics were in disagreement about the relation of moral virtue and passion, as Augustine points out.[19] The Stoics maintained that in a wise or virtuous man there could not be passions of the soul, whereas the Peripatetics, whose school was founded by Aristotle, Augustine says,[20] held that the passions could be actively present along with moral virtue, but as reduced to a mean.

Now this difference between them, as Augustine remarks,[21] was more a matter of words than a divergence of opinion. For the Stoics, because they did not distinguish between intellectual appetite, the will, and sense appetite, which is divided into irascible and concupiscible, accordingly did not distinguish, as the Peripatetics did, the passions of the soul (as being movements of sense appetite) from other human affections, which are not passions of the soul but movements of intellectual appetite, which is called the will; they only considered the passions as being any emotions which go against reason. And they maintained that if these emotions could be aroused deliberately they could not be in a man of practical wisdom or virtue, but if they could arise suddenly, they could be present in the virtuous man. Thus, in the words of Aulus Gallius, as reported by Augustine,[22] "it is not in our power whether visions of the mind which are known as phantasies sometimes occur in the mind; and when they arise from horrible things they necessarily disturb the mind of a wise man so that he is for a moment struck by fear or depressed by sorrow as much as by those passions which prevent the use of reason; and yet he does not therefore approve of or consent to them."

If, then, we mean by the passions inordinate affections, they cannot be in the virtuous man in the sense that after deliberation he consents to

---

[15] *Op. cit.,* IV, 10.   [16] *Nicomachean Ethics* VI, 5 (1140b 12).
[17] *In Coniurat. Catil.,* LI.   [18] *The City of God* XIV, 6.   [19] Cf. *op. cit.,* IX, 4.
[20] *Ibid.*   [21] *Ibid.*   [22] *Ibid.*

them, as the Stoics also maintained. But if by the passions we mean any movement of the sense appetite, then they can be in the virtuous man insofar as they are directed by reason. Hence Aristotle says that "some men do not define the virtues well, when they speak of them as being certain states of impassivity and repose, for they are speaking without qualification;" they should have said that virtue is freedom from those passions which "are not as they should be and when they should not be." [23]

Reply to 1: The Philosopher cites this example, as he often does in his logical works, not as illustrating his own view, but the opinion of others. It was the opinion of the Stoics that virtues were to be without passions of the soul; Aristotle rejects this opinion when he says that "virtues are not states of impassivity." [24] It may be said, however, that when Aristotle says that "a gentle person is one who does not experience passion," the meaning is that he does not experience passion in an inordinate way.

Reply to 2: This argument, and others like them which Cicero gives,[25] takes passions in the sense of inordinate affections.

Reply to 3: When a passion interferes with the judgment of reason so as to prevail upon it to give consent, it hinders the deliberation and judgment of reason. But if a passion follows a judgment of reason as commanded by reason, the passion helps in the carrying out of the command of reason.

Third Article

CAN THERE BE MORAL VIRTUE TOGETHER WITH SORROW?

It seems that there cannot be moral virtue together with sorrow.

1. Virtues are the effects of wisdom, according to Scripture: "She," i.e., divine wisdom, "teacheth temperance, and prudence, and justice, and fortitude" (*Wisdom 8:7*). But, as we read further on, "the conversation of wisdom hath no bitterness" (*v. 16*). Therefore neither can virtues and sorrow exist at the same time.

2. Sorrow is an impediment to action, as the Philosopher notes.[26] But an impediment to good action militates against virtue. Therefore sorrow militates against virtue.

3. Cicero calls sorrow a sort of sickness of the soul.[27] But sickness of soul is contrary to virtue, which is a good condition of the soul. Therefore sorrow is contrary to virtue and cannot exist at the same time with it.

On the contrary: Christ was perfect in virtue. But there was sorrow in Him, for He said: "My soul is sorrowful even unto death" (*Matthew 26:38*).

---

[23] *Nicomachean Ethics* II, 3 (1104b 25).   [24] *Ibid.*   [25] *Tusculan Disputations* IV.

[26] *Nicomachean Ethics* VII, 13 (1153b 2); X, 5 (1175b 17). Aristotle actually speaks of pain as an impediment.

[27] *Tusculan Disputations* III, 7.

Response: As Augustine says,[28] the Stoics maintained that there are in the soul of the wise person three εὐπάθειαι, i.e., three good passions, in place of three disturbances: instead of greed, delight; instead of mirth, joy; instead of fear, caution. But they denied that there could be anything in the soul of a wise person corresponding to sorrow. They gave two reasons for this view.

First, sorrow concerns an evil that is now present, and they maintained that no evil could befall a wise person. For they believed that just as virtue is the only good of man, with no bodily goods being good at all for man, so also man's evil is only what is dishonorable, which cannot exist in a virtuous person. But this is not a reasonable position; for, since man is a composite of body and soul, whatever is conducive to preserving the life of the body is good for man. This, however, is not man's greatest good because he can use this good badly. Accordingly, the evil contrary to this good can exist in a wise person and induce a moderate sorrow. Furthermore, although the virtuous person can be without grievous sin, nevertheless no one manages to lead a life devoid of slight sins, as is said in Scripture: "If we say that we have no sin, we deceive ourselves" (*I John 1:8*). A third reason is that the virtuous person, even though now not in a state of sin, may sometimes have been in the past, and to be sorrowful about this is praiseworthy, as is also said in Scripture: "For the sorrow that is according to God produces repentance that surely tends to salvation" (*II Corinthians 7:10*). Finally, to be sorrowful about the sin of another is commendable. Consequently, moral virtue is compatible with sorrow in the same way as it is compatible with other passions which are moderated by reason.

The second reason the Stoics gave was that sorrow is concerned with a present evil while fear is about a future evil, just as delight is about a present good while desire is for a future good. Hence to enjoy a good possessed, or to wish for a good not yet had, or even to beware of a future evil, can all belong to virtue, but that the soul of man be depressed (which comes from sorrow) by a present evil is altogether contrary to reason, and hence incompatible with virtue. But this view, too, is unreasonable. For an evil can be present to a virtuous person, as we have said,[29] which evil, indeed, reason abhors. Accordingly, the sense appetite follows reason's abhorrence by being sorrowful about such an evil, but moderated according to the judgment of reason. Now it is proper to virtue that the sense appetite be conformed to reason, as we have said.[30] Hence to have a moderated sorrow about things for which there should be sorrow is proper to virtue, as the Philosopher also says.[31] In fact, this is useful for avoiding evil, since, just as we seek a good more readily because of pleasure, so we avoid an evil more steadfastly because of sorrow.

---

[28] *The City of God* XIV, 8.   [29] In the preceding article.   [30] Articles 1 and 2.
[31] *Nicomachean Ethics* II, 6 (1106b 20).

Accordingly, then, we must say that a sorrow about things proper to virtue itself is incompatible with virtue, for virtue delights in what is proper to it. But virtue sorrows moderately for all that obstructs virtue in whatever way.

Reply to 1: What the quotations show is that a wise person does not sorrow about wisdom itself; but he does sorrow about obstacles to wisdom. Consequently, there is no room for sorrow in the blessed,[32] in whom there can be no hindrance to wisdom.

Reply to 2: Sorrow impedes an action that saddens us, but it helps us accomplish more readily whatever banishes sorrow.

Reply to 3: Immoderate sorrow is a sickness of the soul, but a moderated sorrow is compatible with the good condition of the soul, according to our present state of life.

Fourth Article

ARE ALL MORAL VIRTUES ABOUT THE PASSIONS?

It seems that all moral virtues are about the passions.

1. The Philosopher says that "moral virtue is concerned with delight and sorrow."[33] But delight and sorrow are passions, as we have acknowledged.[34] Therefore all moral virtues are about the passions.

2. What is rational by participation is the subject of moral virtue.[35] But the passions are in this part of the soul. Therefore all moral virtues are about the passions.

3. Some passion is found in all moral virtue. Therefore, either all the moral virtues are about the passions or none is. But such moral virtues as fortitude and temperance are about the passions.[36] Therefore all moral virtues are about the passions.

On the contrary: Justice, which is a moral virtue, is not about the passions.[37]

Response: Moral virtue perfects the appetitive part of the soul by directing it to a good of reason. Now a good of reason is that which is directed and moderated according to reason. Hence moral virtue is possible about anything that may be directed or moderated by reason.

---

[32] I.e., in those now in Heaven, enjoying the vision of God.

[33] *Nicomachean Ethics* II, 3 (1104b 9).

[34] Question 23, article 4; question 31, article 1; question 35, articles 1 and 2.

[35] Cf. Aristotle, *Nicomachean Ethics* I, 13 (especially 1102b 29–1103a 3). The passions are said to be "rational by participation" in the sense that they are subject to direction by reason. Reason itself is the rational principle while the will, being the rational appetite, and therefore also rational by participation, tends to follow what is known by reason.

[36] Cf. Aristotle, *Nicomachean Ethics* III, 5 (1115a 6); 10 (1117b 25).

[37] Aristotle makes this point in discussing justice in the *Nicomachean Ethics* V, 1, and in subsequent chapters.

Now reason directs not only the passions of sense appetite but also the operations of the intellectual appetite, that is, the will, which is not a subject of passion, as we have said.[38] Hence not all moral virtues are about the passions; some are about passions while others are about operations.[39]

Reply to 1: Not all moral virtues are about delight and sorrow, as their proper matter, but only insofar as they are something consequent to the proper acts of virtue. For every virtuous person delights in an act of virtue and is saddened by an act contrary to virtue. Hence the Philosopher says shortly after the passage quoted, that "if virtues are about actions and passions, and delight or sorrow follow upon every action and every passion, then by reason of this, virtue will be concerned with delight and sorrow," [40] namely, as they are something consequent to virtue.

Reply to 2: Not only is the sense appetite, which is the subject of the passions, rational by participation, but also the will, in which there are no passions, as we have stated.[41]

Reply to 3: Some virtues have the passions as their proper matter while other virtues do not. Hence the same reasoning does not serve for all moral virtues, as we shall show further on.[42]

Fifth Article

CAN THERE BE MORAL VIRTUE WITHOUT PASSION?

It seems that there can be moral virtue without passion.

1. The more perfect moral virtue is the more it overcomes the passions. In its most perfect state, therefore, moral virtue is wholly without passions.

2. A thing is perfect when it is removed from what is contrary to it and from whatever inclines it to what is contrary. But passions incline us to sin, which is contrary to virtue, and hence they are named "sinful passions" (*Romans 7:5*). Therefore perfect virtue is wholly without passion.

3. By virtue, we are conformed to God, as Augustine shows.[43] But God does all things without passion. Therefore virtue in its most perfect state is without any passion.

On the contrary: "No man is just who does not rejoice in a just act."[44]

---

[38] Question 22, article 3.

[39] Virtues not concerned directly with the passions are treated in the next question, particularly the virtue of justice.

[40] *Nicomachean Ethics* II, 3 (1104b 13-15); in this passage, however, Aristotle actually speaks of pleasure and pain.

[41] In the body of this article; cf. also question 56, article 6, reply to 2.

[42] Question 60, article 2.   [43] *On the Morals of the Catholic Church* I, 6; 11; 13.

[44] Aristotle, *Nicomachean Ethics* I, 8 (1099a 18).

But joy is a passion. Therefore justice cannot be without passion, and much less other virtues.

Response: If by passions we mean inordinate affections, as the Stoics held,[45] then it is clear that perfect virtue is without passions. But if by passions we mean all movements of sense appetite, then it is plain that the moral virtues, which are about the passions as their proper matter, cannot be without the passions. The reason for this is that otherwise it would follow that moral virtue would make the sense appetite wholly inactive. Now it is not the role of virtue to free the powers subject to reason from their own activity, but to make them carry out the commands of reason by exercising their own acts. Hence, just as virtue directs bodily members to their proper external acts, so it directs the sense appetite to its own orderly movements.

Those moral virtues, however, which are not about passions, but about operations, can be without the passions; and justice is a virtue of this kind, for through it the will is applied to its own act, which is not a passion. Nevertheless, joy results from an act of justice, at least in the will, and in this case it is not a passion. And if this joy is intensified by perfection of justice, it flows over into the sense appetite inasmuch as the lower powers attend the movement of higher powers, as we have explained.[46] Hence by reason of this kind of overflow, the more perfect has been the virtue the more passion it causes.

Reply to 1: Virtue overcomes inordinate passions; but it produces orderly passions.

Reply to 2: Inordinate passions incline one to sin, but not moderated ones.

Reply to 3: The good of anything depends upon the condition of its nature. Now there is no sense appetite in God and the angels as there is in man, and hence good operation in God and the angels is wholly without passion, as it also is without a body. Good operation in man, however, is attended by passion, just as it also is attended by the body's service.[47]

---

[45] Cf. article 2.   [46] Question 17, article 7; question 24, article 3.

[47] This remark raises the question of whether the moral virtues remain, after death, in the human soul existing apart from the body. In one sense they do, and in another they do not. On this matter, see question 67, article 1.

The Distinction of Moral Virtues
from Each Other

(In Five Articles)

IS THERE ONLY ONE MORAL VIRTUE?

It seems that there is only one moral virtue.

1. Just as the direction of moral actions belongs to reason, which is the subject of the intellectual virtues, so the inclination to moral action belongs to the appetitive power, which is the subject of the moral virtues. But there is one intellectual virtue, prudence, for directing all moral action. Therefore there is also only one moral virtue inclining one to all moral actions.

2. Habits are not distinguished according to their material objects but according to the formal natures of their objects. Now the formal nature of good, to which moral virtue is ordered, is something one, the measure of reason. Therefore it seems that there is only one moral virtue.

3. Moral actions are specified by their end, as we have said.[1] But the common end of all moral virtue is one, namely, happiness, whereas proper and proximate ends are infinite in number. But the moral virtues are not infinite in number. Therefore it seems that there is only one moral virtue.

On the contrary: One habit cannot be in various powers, as we have pointed out.[2] But the subject of the moral virtues is the appetitive part of the soul, which is distinguished into various powers, as we have said.[3] Therefore there cannot be only one moral virtue.

Response: As we have indicated,[4] moral virtues are certain habits of the appetitive part of the soul. Now habits differ specifically according to the distinctive differences of their objects, as we have said.[5] And the species of an appetible object, as of anything, is determined by its specific form, which it receives from an agent.

Now we must bear in mind that the matter of the receiving subject is related in two ways to the agent. Sometimes it receives a form from

---

[1] Question 1, articles 3 and 5. [2] Question 56, article 2. [3] I, question 81, article 2.
[4] Question 58, article 2. [5] Question 54, article 2.

the agent that is the same in kind as in the agent, as happens with all univocal agents. Hence, if the agent is one in kind, the matter must receive a form of one kind; for example, what is univocally produced by fire must be something in the species of fire. Sometimes, however, the matter receives a form from the agent but not of the same kind as in the agent, as is evident in non-univocal generation; thus, an animal is generated by the sun. In this case, the forms received in the matter from the same agent are not of one kind but are diversified according to the varying disposition of the matter for receiving the influx of the agent. Thus we see that due to the one action of the sun, animals of different kinds are generated by putrefaction, according to the varying disposition of the matter.[6]

Now it is clear that in moral matters, reason is like a commanding and moving agent, whereas the appetitive power is commanded and moved. The appetite, however, does not receive the influence of reason univocally, as it were, because the appetite does not become rational essentially, but only participates in reason.[7] Accordingly, the objects made appetible by the influence of reason are of various kinds according to their different relations to reason. It follows, then, that the moral virtues are different in kind, and not one only.

Reply to 1: The object of reason is what is true. But there is one kind of truth in all moral matters, which are contingent matters of action. Hence there is only one virtue, prudence, for directing moral actions.[8] But the object of the appetitive power is a desirable good, which differs in kind according to the diverse relationship it has to reason as directing it.

Reply to 2: This formality is one in genus on account of the unity of the agent, but it is diverse in species because of the various relations of the receiving matter to the agent, as we have just explained above.

Reply to 3: Moral actions are not specified by the ultimate end, but by proximate ends which, though infinite in number, nevertheless are not infinite in kind.

---

[6] This argument may be considered appropriate as resting on a fictive example.

[7] Cf. Aristotle, *Nicomachean Ethics* I, 13 (1102b 13; b 26). The appetites, both the will and sense appetite, not being rational essentially, that is, not being knowing powers, nevertheless are rational by participation inasmuch as they are subject to direction by reason.

[8] Prudence is one virtue when considered as individual or personal prudence. But political prudence, as distinguished from individual prudence, is divided into various kinds. Cf. II-II, question 48.

Second Article

ARE MORAL VIRTUES ABOUT OPERATIONS DISTINCT FROM MORAL VIRTUES ABOUT PASSIONS?

It seems that moral virtues are not distinguished into those about operations and those about passions.[9]

1. Moral virtue is "an operative habit by which we tend to do what is best in matters of pleasure or sorrow."[10] But pleasure and sorrow are passions, as we have said.[11] Therefore a virtue which concerns the passions is also a virtue which concerns operations, since it is an operative habit.

2. The passions are principles of exterior operations. If, therefore, certain virtues rectify the passions, they must, as a consequence, also rectify the operations. Therefore the same moral virtues are about both passions and operations.

3. The sense appetite is moved well or badly toward every external operation. But the movements of sense appetite are passions. Therefore the same virtues which are about operations are also about passions.

On the contrary: The Philosopher maintains that justice is about operations, whereas temperance, fortitude, and mildness are about the passions.[12]

Response: Operation and passion can be related to virtue in two ways. First, by way of effect, and in this way every moral virtue has some good operations which it produces, as well as some accompanying delight or sorrow, which are passions, as we have said.[13]

Second, operation can be viewed in relation to moral virtue as the matter about which virtue is concerned, and from this point of view moral virtues which are about operations are different from those about passions. The reason for this is that the good or evil of certain operations is in terms of the operations themselves, no matter how man feels in regard to them, inasmuch as the good and evil in these operations depends on their being commensurate with something else. In such operations, there must be some virtue which directs the operations in themselves; for example, in buying and selling, and other actions of the kind

---

[9] The term "operations" signifies exterior actions by which one person is engaged with another, for example, the actions of buying and selling or the payment of a debt. The question, then, is whether the moral virtues concerned with such actions are of a different sort from those virtues which bring about order in the movement of passions themselves, which are interior to man.

[10] Aristotle, *Nicomachean Ethics* II, 3 (1104b 27).

[11] Question 31, article 1; question 35, article 1.

[12] Cf. *Nicomachean Ethics* II, 7 (1107a 33); IV, 5 (1125b 26); V, 1 (1129a 3).

[13] Question 49, article 4, reply to 1.

which involve a consideration of what is owed or not owed to another. This is the reason justice and its various kinds are strictly about operations, as their proper matter. In some operations, however, the good or evil is based only on a commensuration with the agent, and hence good and evil in such actions depend on whether man is affected well or badly toward them. For this reason, in these operations virtue must be principally about interior affections, which are called passions of the soul; such is evidently the case with the virtues of temperance, fortitude, and others like them.

It may happen, however, in operations which are directed to someone else, that the good of virtue is neglected because of some inordinate passion. In such instances, justice is forfeited insofar as the due measure of the external action is forfeited; moreover, some other virtue is lost insofar as the due measure of the interior passions is lost. For example, when one man strikes another out of anger, justice is lost by the unwarranted blow, and mildness is lost because of the immoderate anger. The situation is the same in regard to other virtues.

The foregoing remarks are sufficient for replying to the arguments given at the beginning. The first argument treats operation as it is an effect of virtue; the other two of operation and passion as concurring in the same effect. In some cases, however, virtue is principally about the operation while in others it is about passions, for the reason given in the body of this article.

Third Article

IS THERE ONLY ONE MORAL VIRTUE ABOUT OPERATIONS? [14]

It seems that there is only one moral virtue about operations.

1. The rightness of all external operations seems to pertain to justice. But justice is one virtue. Therefore there is only one virtue about operations.

2. Those operations which are ordered to the good of one and those which are ordered to the good of many seem to differ most of all. But such a difference does not diversify moral virtues, for the Philosopher says that legal justice, which orders human actions to the common good does not differ, except according to reason, from virtue which orders man's action to the good of only one.[15] Therefore diversity of operations does not cause a diversity of moral virtues.

3. If there are different moral virtues about different operations, then it would follow that in conformity with the diversity of operations there

---

[14] This is a question about justice, as to whether it is one virtue in all respects, or different in its kinds.

[15] Cf. *Nicomachean Ethics* V, 1 (1130a 12).

would have to be diversity of moral virtues. But this is clearly false, for it is the function of justice to establish a rightness in the various kinds of transactions between men, and also in distributions [of honor or money] among men [in political society].[16] There are not, therefore, different virtues about different operations.

On the contrary: Religion is a virtue different from piety, yet both are about operations.

Response: All the moral virtues which are about operations agree in the general notion of justice, which concerns what is due to another, but they are distinguished according to their different special notions. The reason for this is that in external operations the order of reason is governed, as we have said,[17] not according to how man feels in regard to them, but on the fittingness of the thing itself; and from such fittingness we derive the notion of something due, from which the notion of justice is established, for it seems to pertain to justice that one render what is due to another. Consequently, all such virtues about operations realize in some way the notion of justice.

What is due, however, is not of the same kind in all these virtues. For something is due to an equal in one way, to a superior in another way, and to an inferior in still another; and what is due differs also as it arises from a contract, a promise, or from some benefit that has been received. And corresponding to these different kinds of what is due, there are different virtues. For example, religion is the virtue by which we render what is due to God; piety, that by which we render what is owed to our parents or to our country;[18] gratitude, that by which we render what is due our benefactors, and so on.

Reply to 1: Properly speaking, justice is one special virtue which has regard to the whole notion of what is due, for which there can be an equivalent return. Nevertheless, the word "justice" can be extended to any rendering of what is due, and in this sense it is not one special virtue.[19]

Reply to 2: The justice which intends the common good is a different virtue from the justice which is ordered to the private good of an individual; accordingly, a common right is distinguished from a private right, and Cicero acknowledges piety[20] as a special virtue which orders man to the good of his country.[21] However, the justice directing man to the

---

[16] Cf. Aristotle, *op. cit.*, V, 2 (1130b 30).   [17] In the preceding article.

[18] "Piety" refers first to filial piety; second to what we now call "patriotism." In modern times, we have tended to restrict "piety" to devoutness or dutifulness in regard to religious observance.

[19] That is, taking into account the various degrees of rendering what is due to another, in a proportional way as well as by strict equality, justice is a common virtue realized variously, as indicated in the second part of the body of the article.

[20] In the sense of patriotism.   [21] *On Rhetorical Discovery*, II.

common good is a general virtue because of its act of command, since it orders all acts of virtue to its own end, the common good. And the virtues, insofar as they are commanded by such justice, also receive the name of justice. Accordingly, virtue and legal justice differ only by a distinction of reason, just as a virtue operating of itself and a virtue operating at the command of another virtue differ only by a distinction of reason.[22]

Reply to 3: The same notion of what is due is found in all operations relating to particular justice. Hence there is the same virtue of justice, especially with regard to transactions between men; it may be, however, that distributive justice is specifically different from commutative justice, but we shall consider this matter later.[23]

Fourth Article

ARE THERE DIFFERENT MORAL VIRTUES ABOUT DIFFERENT PASSIONS?

It seems that there are not different moral virtues about different passions.

1. There is one habit about things that admit of the same principle and end, as is evident especially in the sciences. But there is one principle of all passions, namely, love; and all passions terminate in the same end, either joy or sorrow, as we have said.[24] Therefore there is only one moral virtue for all the passions.

2. If there were different moral virtues for the different passions, there would be as many moral virtues as passions. But this is clearly false, since one and the same virtue is about opposite passions; for example, fortitude about fear and daring, temperance about pleasure and sorrow. Therefore there do not have to be different moral virtues for different passions.

3. Love, desire, and joy are specifically different passions, as we have pointed out.[25] But one virtue concerns all these passions, namely, tem-

---

[22] A fuller discussion of this point is given in II-II, question 58, article 6. This discussion can be summarized as follows: If legal justice is understood as ordered properly and per se to the common good, then it is a specific virtue, distinct from all other virtues. Since any virtue, however, can also be ordered to the common good in some way, any virtue can be regarded as a form of legal justice, and it is in this sense that legal justice is said to be the same as all virtue, though still distinguished by reason from any specific virtue.

[23] II-II, question 61, article 1. In this article, St. Thomas definitely states that commutative justice, justice between two equals in regard to private transactions, and distributive justice, the dispensing of honors and rewards rendered according to proportion, are specifically different kinds of particular justice.

[24] Question 35, articles 1 and 2.   [25] Question 23, article 4.

perance. Therefore there are not different moral virtues about different passions.

On the contrary: Fortitude is concerned with fear and daring, temperance with concupiscible desire, gentleness with anger, as the Philosopher points out.[26]

Response: It cannot be maintained that there is only one moral virtue dealing with all the passions. For the passions pertain to different powers, some to the irascible and others to the concupiscible, as we have said.[27]

On the other hand, it does not follow that every sort of diversity among the passions is sufficient to diversify moral virtues. For in the first place, some passions are in contrary opposition, such as joy and sorrow, fear and daring, and the like. And the virtue having to do with passions thus opposed must be one and the same virtue. The reason for this is that moral virtue consists in a kind of mean, and in contrary passions this mean stands in the same ratio to both, just as in physical things the mean between contraries is the same, for example, between white and black.

Secondly, different passions oppose reason in the same manner, either by impelling toward what is contrary to reason, or by withdrawing from what is in accord with reason. Consequently, the different passions of the concupiscible appetite do not relate to different moral virtues,[28] for their movements follow one another according to a certain order inasmuch as they are directed to the same thing, namely, to attaining a good or avoiding an evil; thus, from love we proceed to desire, and from desire we arrive at joy. The same holds for the opposite passions: from hatred follows avoidance or loathing, which in turn leads to sorrow. The irascible passions, however, do not all have one ordering, but are directed to different things. Boldness and fear, for instance, are related to some great danger; hope and desperation to some difficult good; and anger is directed to overcoming something adverse which has caused injury. Consequently different virtues govern these various passions; for example, temperance in regard to the concupiscible passions, fortitude in regard to fear and boldness, magnanimity in regard to hope and desperation, and gentleness in regard to anger.

Reply to 1: All the passions admit of one common principle and end, but not one proper principle or end. This is not enough for the unity of moral virtue.

---

[26] *Nicomachean Ethics* III, 5 (1115a 6); 10 (1117b 25); IV, 5 (1125b 26).

[27] Question 23, article 1.

[28] That is, temperance is the one principal virtue regarding the movement of the concupiscible appetite even though we can further distinguish different virtues under temperance, for example, chastity, sobriety, and so on. But even in ordinary speech we talk of being temperate in regard to food, drink, or sex.

Reply to 2: Just as in physical things, the same principle causes movement from one extreme and movement toward the other, and as in the rational order contraries have one common notion, so too in regard to contrary passions there is one moral virtue, which is like a nature in harmony with reason.

Reply to 3: These three passions are directed to the same object according to a certain order, as we have said,[29] and hence they pertain to the same moral virtue.

Fifth Article

ARE MORAL VIRTUES DISTINGUISHED ACCORDING TO THE DIVERSE OBJECTS OF THE PASSIONS?

It seems that the moral virtues are not distinguished according to the objects of the passions.

1. Just as there are objects of the passions so there are objects of operations. But moral virtues about operations are not distinguished according to the objects of those operations, for buying and selling, whether it be of a house or a horse, concerns the same virtue of justice. Therefore neither are moral virtues about passions diversified by the objects of those passions.

2. The passions are acts or movements of the sense appetite. But a greater diversity is needed for diversity of habits than for diversity of acts. Hence, if diverse objects do not differentiate a passion in species, they will not differentiate a moral virtue in species. Thus there will be one moral virtue dealing with all pleasurable objects, and the same holds for the other passions.

3. More and less do not change a species.[30] But various objects of pleasure differ only by way of more or less. Therefore all pleasurable objects are related to one kind of virtue and, for the same reason, all fearful objects relate to one kind, and so of the others. Therefore moral virtue is not distinguished according to the objects of the passions.

4. Just as virtue tends to produce good, so it tends to obstruct evil. But there are different virtues with respect to the goods desirable to the sense appetite; for example, temperance deals with delight in pleasures of touch, well-bred insolence[31] with recreative pleasure. Therefore there should also be different virtues about fears of evil.

---

[29] In the body of this article.

[30] For example, what is more white or less white is still white; what is more sweet or less sweet is still sweet. There is no change of kind or species.

[31] *Eutrapelia* in the original, a Greek word signifying a special quality of wit in conversation and amusing pastimes. Cf. Aristotle, *Nicomachean Ethics* IV, 8 (especially 1128a 9 *et seq.*).

On the contrary: Chastity is about sexual pleasures, abstinence about delight in food, and well-bred insolence about recreative pleasure.

Response: The perfection of a virtue depends upon reason while the perfection of a passion depends on the sense appetite itself. Hence virtues must be differentiated according to their ordering to reason, whereas passions are differentiated according to their relation to appetite. Therefore the objects of the passions, as related in different ways to sense appetite, cause passions that are different in kind, but as related to reason they cause virtues different in kind. Now the movement of reason is not the same as that of sense appetite. Accordingly, a difference of objects causing a diversity among passions need not cause a diversity among virtues, as when one virtue is about several passions, as we have seen;[82] furthermore, a difference of objects causing a diversity among virtues need not cause a diversity among passions, since different virtues may be related to one passion, for example, pleasure.

Now because diverse passions belonging to diverse powers always pertain to different virtues, as we have said,[33] hence a diversity of objects, which corresponds to a diversity of powers, always diversifies the kinds of virtues; for example, the difference between something good simply and something good but difficult to attain. Moreover, since reason directs the lower powers of man in a certain order, extending even to external things, hence a single object of the passions—as apprehended by sense or imagination or even reason, and again, depending on whether it pertains to the soul, the body, or external things—is diversely related to reason, and consequently is of such a nature as to diversify virtues. Consequently, man's good, which is the object of love, desire, and pleasure, can be taken as referred either to a bodily sense or to some interior apprehension of the soul, and this same good may be ordered to the good of man himself, whether of body or soul, or ordered to the good of man in his relationship with others. Every such diversity, because of a different ordering to reason, differentiates virtue.

Accordingly, if we take a good and it be something discerned by the sense of touch, and pertinent to maintaining human life either in the individual or in the species (for example, the pleasures of food or sex), it will concern the virtue of temperance. On the other hand, pleasures belonging to other senses, not being so intense, do not present any difficulty to reason; consequently, there is no virtue corresponding to them, for virtue, like art, deals with what is difficult.[34]

But a good apprehended by an interior power, not by an external sense, and pertinent to man in himself, like money or honor—money by its nature being usable for the good of the body whereas honor depends

---

[82] In the preceding article.   [83] *Ibid.*
[34] Cf. Aristotle, *Nicomachean Ethics* II, 3 (1105a 9).

upon the apprehension of the mind—such a good can be considered either simply, in which case it concerns the concupiscible appetite, or as being difficult to attain, in which case it concerns the irascible appetite. This distinction, however, is not relevant to pleasurable objects of touch, for a good of this kind is of a low type and belongs to man as he is assimilated to irrational animals. Accordingly, in regard to money as a good, taken simply, and as the object of desire or pleasure, or of love, the virtue is liberality.[35] But if this same good is taken as difficult to attain, and thus the object of hope, the virtue is magnificence.[36] With regard to the good we call honor, if it is taken simply, as the object of love, we have the virtue called *philotimia*,[37] that is, a love of honor. But if we take this same good as difficult to attain and as the object of hope, the virtue is magnanimity. Hence liberality and love of honor are seen to be in the concupiscible part of man, magnificence and magnanimity in the irascible part.

The good of man in his relationship with others does not seem to be something arduous, but is understood as taken simply, as the object of the concupiscible passions. This good can be the pleasure had in disposing oneself toward another in serious matters, that is, in actions directed by reason to their appropriate end, or in diversions, that is, in actions directed to pleasure only, which are not related in the same way to reason as the first type is. Now a man disposes himself toward another in serious matters in two ways. First, by being agreeable, through becoming speech and action, and this refers to a virtue which Aristotle calls friendliness,[38] which may be rendered as affability. In a second way, by being frank in speech and action, and this refers to another virtue, which Aristotle calls truthfulness.[39] For frankness is closer to reason than pleasure, and closer to what is serious than to what is playful. Therefore there is another virtue having to do with diversions which Aristotle calls well-bred insolence.[40]

It is therefore evident that according to Aristotle there are ten moral virtues connected with the passions: fortitude, temperance, liberality, magnificence, magnanimity, love of honor, gentleness, friendliness, truthfulness, and well-bred insolence. They are all distinguished according to

---

[35] A certain freedom in regard to the desire for money that prevents a person from being mean or covetous.

[36] This term signifies the quality of dealing in a high-minded manner with regard to money matters; a greatness of soul in obtaining and using of money. One who donates a large amount of money for a worthy cause is "magnificent," or makes a "magnificent" contribution; hence, great generosity for a worthwhile purpose.

[37] This Greek word, taken from Aristotle in his *Nicomachean Ethics* (II, 7 1107b 32), refers to a right love of honor, as distinct from vanity, as one extreme, and self-abasement as the other extreme.

[38] *Nicomachean Ethics* II, 7 (1108a 28).   [39] *Ibid.*, (1108a 20).

[40] *Ibid.*, (1108a 24). See note 31 above.

their different matter or passions or objects, and if we add justice, which deals with external operations, there will be eleven in all.

Reply to 1: All objects of the same kind of operation have the same relation to reason, but not all objects of the same kind of passion do, for operations do not offer resistance to reason as the passions do.[41]

Reply to 2: The grounds for diversifying the passions and the virtues is not the same, as we have explained.[42]

Reply to 3: The more and the less do not cause a change in species except by reason of a different relationship to reason.

Reply to 4: Good is a more powerful mover than evil, for evil does not cause action except in virtue of the good, as Dionysius says.[43] Hence an evil does not cause a difficulty for reason, which requires virtue, unless the evil be predominant, and there seems to be one such evil with regard to each kind of passion. Accordingly, for every form of anger, there is the one virtue of gentleness, and likewise for all forms of rashness there is the one virtue of fortitude. What is good, on the other hand, offers difficulty, which requires the aid of virtue, even though it is not a predominant good in a given kind of passion. Hence there are different moral virtues with regard to the concupiscible emotions, as we have said.[44]

---

[41] That is, the passions at times go against the direction of reason, but they can also follow the direction of reason. There is a kind of contrariety between the movement of passion and reason that is lacking between external operations and reason.

[42] In the body of this article. [43] *On the Divine Names* IV, 31.

[44] In the body of this article.

The Cardinal Virtues

(In Five Articles)

SHOULD THE MORAL VIRTUES BE CALLED CARDINAL OR PRINCIPAL VIRTUES? [1]

It seems that moral virtues should not be called cardinal or principal virtues.

1. "Things which are opposed to one another within the same genus are simultaneous in nature," [2] and thus one does not rank before another. But all virtues, as dividing the genus of virtue, are opposed to one another. Therefore none of the moral virtues should be called principal virtues.

2. The end is superior to the things which are for the sake of the end. But the theological virtues are about the end whereas the moral virtues are about what is for the sake of the end. Therefore the theological virtues rather than the moral should be called cardinal or principal virtues.

3. What is essentially so ranks before what is so by participation. But intellectual virtues pertain to what is rational essentially whereas moral virtues pertain to reason by participation, as we have said. [3] Therefore the intellectual virtues rather than the moral are the principal virtues.

On the contrary: In explaining the words *Blessed are the poor in spirit* (*Luke 6:20*), Ambrose says: "We know that there are four cardinal virtues: temperance, justice, prudence, and fortitude." [4] Now these are moral virtues. Therefore the moral virtues are cardinal virtues.

Response: When we speak about virtue unqualifiedly, we are understood to be speaking about human virtue. Now human virtue, as we have

---

[1] The word "cardinal" derives from the Latin *cardinalis*, which first means "pertaining to a door-hinge," i.e., something pivotal, and then was extended to mean "that on which something depends." Accordingly, the question is whether there are some principal virtues on which all other virtues depend primarily. Cf. St. Thomas in his opusculum, *On the Virtues in Common*, article 12, reply to 24.

[2] Aristotle, *Categories*, 13 (14b 33).

[3] Question 46, article 6, reply to 2; question 58, article 3; question 59, article 4, second argument.

[4] *Commentary on Luke* V, verse 6:20.

said,[5] is virtue as it corresponds to the perfect notion of virtue, which requires rectitude of appetite, for such virtue not only confers the faculty of doing well but also causes the performing of a good action. But virtue which does not require rectitude of the appetite corresponds to virtue in an imperfect sense because it confers only the faculty of doing well but does not cause the performing of a good action.[6] Now clearly what is perfect ranks before what is imperfect, and hence those virtues which involve rectitude of appetite are called principal virtues. Such virtues are the moral virtues and, of the intellectual virtues, prudence alone, for in a certain respect it is also a moral virtue as regards its matter, as we have said.[7] Hence some of the moral virtues are appropriately said to be principal or cardinal virtues.

Reply to 1: When a univocal genus is divided into its species, then the dividing parts are related equally to the notion of the genus even though in the real order one species is more principal and more perfect than the others, as man is in relation to other animals. But when the division is of something analogously named, which is said of many things according as they are prior and posterior, then there is nothing to prevent one being more principal than another even according to the common notion, as *being* applies to substance more principally than to accident. Such is the division of virtue into its various kinds, since the good of reason is not found in the same way in all virtues.

Reply to 2: The theological virtues are above man, as we have said.[8] Hence they are not properly called human virtues, but "superhuman" or divine virtues.[9]

Reply to 3: The intellectual virtues, except for prudence, though more principal than the moral virtues in regard to their subject,[10] do not rank before them as virtues, for virtue as such refers to the good, which is the object of appetite.[11]

---

[5] Question 56, article 3.

[6] Such virtue is intellectual virtue, dealing with knowledge; and precisely because it does not require right appetite, it does not realize fully the nature of virtue.

[7] Question 57, article 4; question 58, article 3, reply to 1.

[8] Question 58, article 3, reply to 3.

[9] Although the theological virtues are higher virtues, they are not acquired by man of himself (on this point, see question 62, article 1). Among the virtues that can be acquired by man, the cardinal virtues are therefore the principal virtues with respect to leading the good moral life.

[10] That is, the subject in which they exist, the intellect.

[11] Thus the intellectual virtues are higher than the moral virtues in the sense that the intellectual power is higher than the appetitive powers. On the other hand, the moral virtues are virtues unqualifiedly, since it belongs to the nature of virtue to refer to the good rather than to the true. Furthermore, as this article makes clear, moral virtue causes the performing of a good work whereas intellectual virtue only makes a power act well without necessarily being put to good use. For example, a brilliant scientist could use his knowledge to destroy life wantonly.

Second Article

ARE THERE FOUR CARDINAL VIRTUES?

It seems that there are not four cardinal virtues.

1. Prudence is directive with respect to the other moral virtues, as was said above.[12] But that which directs others is first in rank. Therefore only prudence is a principal virtue.

2. The principal virtues are in some way moral. But we are ordered to moral action by practical reason and right appetite.[13] Therefore there are only two cardinal virtues [i.e., one for practical reason and one for appetite].

3. Even among other virtues,[14] one ranks higher than another. But in order that a virtue be called principal, it is not necessary that it be principal in relation to all others, but only in regard to some. Therefore it seems that there are many more principal virtues [than four].

On the contrary: Gregory says: "The whole structure of good works is founded on four virtues." [15]

Response: Things can be numbered either according to their formal principles or according to their subjects; taken in either way, we find that there are four cardinal virtues.

Now the formal principle of virtue which we are speaking of here is the good determined by reason. This can be considered in two ways: first, as realized in the very act of reasoning, and thus we will have one principal virtue which is called *prudence;* and second, according as the ordering of reason is put into something else, either into operations, and then we have *justice,* or into the passions, and then there must be two virtues. For the need of the ordering of reason in the passions is seen when we consider the ways in which they may oppose reason, which is twofold. First, by the passions inciting to something contrary to reason, and then the passions need restraining, and *temperance* is denominated from this. Second, by the passions withdrawing us from what reason dictates—for example, the fear of dangers or of hardships—and then man has to be strengthened in regard to what reason requires, so that he will not turn back, and *fortitude* is denominated from this.

We find again the same number of virtues if we consider the subjects of virtue. For there are four subjects of the virtue of which we are speaking now: the power which is rational essentially,[16] which *prudence* perfects; that which is rational by participation, and is divisible into the will, the subject of *justice;* the concupiscible appetite, the subject of *temperance;* and the irascible appetite, the subject of *fortitude.*

[12] Question 58, article 4.   [13] Cf. Aristotle, *Nicomachean Ethics* VI, 2 (1139a 24).
[14] I.e., other than the virtues usually listed as cardinal.   [15] *Moral.* II, 49.
[16] I.e., practical reason.

Reply to 1: Absolutely speaking, prudence is more principal than all other virtues, but each of the other virtues is principal in its own genus.

Reply to 2: What is rational by participation is divisible into three, as explained in this article.

Reply to 3: All the other virtues, among which one is more principal than another, are reduced to the four mentioned above, both with respect to their subjects and to their formal aspects.

Third Article

SHOULD ANY OTHER VIRTUES BE CALLED PRINCIPAL RATHER THAN THESE?

It seems that other virtues should be called principal rather than the ones we have indicated.

1. Whatever is maximum in any genus seems to be more principal. But "magnanimity has great influence on all the virtues." [17] Therefore magnanimity more than any other should be called a principal virtue.

2. The virtue which strengthens the others would seem most of all to be a principal virtue. But humility is such a virtue, for Gregory says that "he who collects other virtues without humility is like one who carries straw against the wind." [18] Therefore humility seems above all to be a principal virtue.

3. What is most perfect seems to be most principal. But this refers to patience, for "Patience has its perfect work" (*James 1:4*). Therefore patience should be put down as a principal virtue.

On the contrary: Cicero reduces all other virtues to the four cardinal virtues.[19]

Response: As we have said,[20] the four virtues that are considered cardinal are taken from the four formal principles of virtue, as we are now speaking of virtue.[21] These principles are found primarily in certain acts and passions. Thus the good which is realized in the act of reasoning is found principally in reason's command, not in its deliberation or its judgment, as we have said.[22] Further, the good of reason which is put into our operations as something right and due according to reason appears principally in exchanges and distributions in respect to another on a basis of equality. The good of restraining the passions is found principally in those passions which are most difficult to restrain, namely, the pleasures connected with touch. The good of persisting firmly in the

---

[17] Aristotle, *Nicomachean Ethics* IV, 3 (1123b 30).   [18] *In Evang.* I, sermon 7.
[19] Cf. *Rhetoric* II, 53.   [20] Article 2.
[21] The phrase "as we now speak of virtue" emphasizes that we are now treating human virtue, consisting in the good of reason, as distinct from supernatural virtue bestowed through grace.
[22] Question 57, article 6.

good of reason against the impulse of passion is found especially in dangers which may involve death, which are most difficult to withstand.

Hence these four virtues can be considered in two ways. First, in regard to their common formal notions. In this way, they are called principal, as being common, to all the virtues, so that, for instance, any virtue which causes good in reason's consideration is called prudence; any virtue which realizes the good of what is right and due in operations is called justice; any virtue which curbs and restrains the passions is called temperance; and any virtue which strengthens the soul against any passion whatsoever is called fortitude. This is the way many holy doctors as well as philosophers speak of these virtues, and in this way all the other virtues are contained under them. Hence the arguments stated at the beginning of this article are invalid.

In a second way, however, these virtues can be taken according as each is denominated from what is primary in its respective matter, and thus they are specific virtues, divided off from other virtues. Nevertheless they are still referred to as principal in comparison with other virtues because of the primacy of their matter. Thus prudence is the virtue which commands, justice the virtue which deals with due actions between equals, temperance the virtue which curbs desires for the pleasures of touch, and fortitude the virtue which strengthens one in the face of danger of death. And thus again the initial arguments do not hold, for the other virtues may be principal in some other way, but these virtues are called principal by reason of their matter, as we have explained.

Fourth Article

DO THE FOUR CARDINAL VIRTUES DIFFER FROM EACH OTHER?

It seems that the four cardinal virtues are not different virtues, and are not distinct from each other.

1. "There is no real prudence which is not just, temperate, and brave; nor perfect temperance which is not brave, just, and prudent; nor complete fortitude which is not prudent, temperate, and just; nor true justice which is not prudent, brave, and temperate." [23] Now this would not be the case if these four virtues were distinct from each other, for different species of the same genus are not denominated from each other. Therefore these virtues are not distinct from each other.

2. Things are distinct from each other when what belongs to one is not attributed to another. But that which belongs to temperance is attributed to fortitude, for Ambrose says, "Rightly do we speak of fortitude when a man conquers himself and is not softened or bent by allure-

---

[23] Gregory, *Moral.* XXII, 1.

ment." [24] He says also of temperance that "it preserves the manner or order in everything we decide to do or say." [25] Therefore it seems that these virtues are not distinct from each other.

3. The Philosopher says that the following are required for virtue: "First, a man should have knowledge; secondly, he must choose the acts, and choose them for this end; and thirdly, he must act in a firm and steadfast manner." [26] But the first of these conditions seems to belong to prudence, which is right reasoning about what is to be done; the second, namely, choice, to temperance so that with his passions restrained a man acts not from passion but from choice; the third, that a man should act for a due end implies a certain rectitude, which seems to belong to justice; and the last, firmness and steadfastness, which belong to fortitude. Therefore each of these virtues is general in respect to all virtues. Hence they are not distinguished from each other.

On the contrary: Augustine says that "virtue is fourfold in meaning, corresponding to a certain diverse state of the affection of love itself," [27] and he connects this with the above mentioned virtues. Therefore these virtues are distinct from each other.

Response: As we have said, [28] these four virtues are understood in different ways by various authors. Some take them as signifying certain general conditions of the human soul to be found in all the virtues. Thus prudence is simply a rectitude of discretion in any action or matter whatsoever; justice a rectitude of soul whereby man does what he should in any matter; temperance a disposition of soul which imposes a measure on any passions or operations so that they do not go beyond certain limits; fortitude a disposition of soul by which one is steadfast in regard to what is according to reason, against any incitement from the passions or hardships involved in action.

Now distinguishing these four virtues in this way fails to convey that justice, temperance, and fortitude are diverse virtuous habits. For every moral virtue, by the fact that it is a *habit,* has a certain firmness such that it is not moved by something contrary to it, which is said to belong to fortitude. From the fact that it is a *virtue,* it is ordered to the good, which implies the notion of what is right and due, and this is said to belong to justice. By the fact that it is a *moral* virtue, participating in reason, it observes the order of reason in all matters and does not exceed its limits, which is said to belong to temperance. Only having discretion, which is attributed to prudence, seems to be distinguished from the other three inasmuch as this belongs to reason essentially whereas the other three virtues imply a certain participation in reason by way of some kind of application of reason to passions or operations. According to this explanation, then, prudence indeed would be a virtue distinct from the

---

[24] *De Off. Ministr.* I, 36.   [25] *Op. cit.* I, 24.   [26] *Nicomachean Ethics* II, 4 (1105a 31).
[27] *The Morals of the Catholic Church,* 15.   [28] Article 3.

other three, but these latter would not differ from each other, for clearly one and the same virtue is a habit, a virtue, and moral.

Others, however, and more correctly, take these four virtues as they are related to specific matters, each of them to its own matter in which that general condition is principally exemplified, from which the name of the virtue is taken, as we have said.[29] And in this way it is clear that these virtues are different habits, differentiated by the diversity of their objects.

Reply to 1: Gregory is speaking of these four virtues taken in the first way given above.[30] Or it can be said that these four virtues are denominated from each other by a kind of overflowing of one to the other. For what is proper to prudence overflows into the other virtues insofar as they are directed by prudence. And each of the others overflows into the rest by reason of the fact that one who is capable of what is more difficult is also capable of what is less difficult. Hence whoever can restrain his desires for the pleasures of touch so that they do not exceed the proper limits, which is very hard to do, for this very reason is more able to moderate his daring in the face of dangers which may involve death, so as not to go too far, which is far easier, and in this respect bravery is said to be temperate. Temperance is likewise said to be brave by an overflowing of fortitude into temperance inasmuch as he whose soul is strengthened by fortitude against perils of death, which is very hard, is more able to stand firm against the incitement of pleasures.[31] Cicero therefore says, "it would not be consistent for a man unbroken by fear to be overcome by lust or that he should be conquered by lust when he has shown himself to be unconquered by toil." [32]

Reply to 2: The reply to the second argument is evident from the foregoing. For temperance holds to the mean in all things and fortitude keeps the soul unyielding with regard to the allurement of pleasure, either insofar as these virtues connote certain general conditions of virtue or in the way that they overflow into each other, as we have explained.

Reply to 3: The four general conditions of virtue which the Philosopher lays down are not peculiar to the virtues we are discussing. But these conditions can be appropriated to those virtues in the manner in which we have indicated.[33]

---

[29] *Ibid.*   [30] According to the first way considered in the body of this article.

[31] This reply brings out how intimately the different virtues are connected with each other, and how a thoroughly good person is good in all respects. This passage also indicates how the virtues mutually affect and strengthen each other. St. Thomas discusses this point more at length in question 65, especially article 1.

[32] *De Offic.,* 20.   [33] In the body of this article.

Fifth Article

ARE THE CARDINAL VIRTUES APPROPRIATELY DIVIDED INTO POLITICAL, PURIFYING, PERFECT, AND EXEMPLAR VIRTUES? [34]

It seems that these four virtues are not fittingly divided into exemplar, perfect, purifying, and political virtues.

1. Macrobius says, "the exemplar virtues are those which exist in the divine mind itself." [35] But the Philosopher says that "it is ridiculous to attribute justice, fortitude, temperance, and prudence to God." [36] Therefore these virtues cannot be exemplar virtues.

2. Perfect virtues of the soul are said to be those which are without passions. For Macrobius says that "in the purified soul, it does not belong to temperance to restrain worldly desires but to be wholly oblivious of them; and it belongs to fortitude to be unacquainted with passions, not to overcome them." [37] Now it was said above that these virtues cannot exist without the passions.[38] Therefore there cannot be such perfect virtues in the soul.

3. Macrobius says that the purifying virtues are those of a person "who by a flight from human affairs attaches himself to divine things alone." [39] But this seems wrong to do, for Cicero says, "I think that it is not only unpraiseworthy but wrong for men to say that they despise what most men admire, that is, office and power." [40] Therefore there are not any purifying virtues.

4. Macrobius says that the political virtues are "those by which good men work for the commonweal and safeguard the city." [41] But only legal justice is ordered to the common good, as the Philosopher says.[42] Therefore other virtues should not be called political.

On the contrary: Macrobius says, "Plotinus, along with Plato, the foremost among the teachers of philosophy, says: 'There are four kinds of virtue. First are those called political, second the purifying, third the perfect, fourth the exemplar virtues.' " [43]

Response: As Augustine says, "the soul must follow something so that

---

[34] The Latin for "purifying" virtues is *purgatorias*, literally, "purging" or "cleansing" virtues. The Latin for "perfect" virtues is *purgati animi*, literally, virtues of "a soul now purged or cleansed." The explanation in the body of the article justifies the English translation made of these terms.

[35] *In Somn. Scipion.* I, 8. The work referred to here is *The Dream of Scipion* by Cicero; Macrobius wrote a commentary on this work. He was a neo-Platonic writer who lived at about the beginning of the fifth century, and was well known in the Middle Ages for this commentary on Cicero's *The Dream of Scipion.*

[36] *Nicomachean Ethics* X, 8 (1178b 10).   [37] *In Somn. Scipion.* I, 8.

[38] Question 59, article 5.   [39] *In Somn. Scipion.* I, 8.   [40] *De Off.* I, 21.

[41] *In Somn. Scipion.* I, 8.   [42] *Nicomachean Ethics* V, 1 (1129b 15).

[43] *In Somn. Scipion.* I, 8.

virtue can be born in it; and this something is God, and if we follow Him we shall live a moral life." [44] Hence the exemplar of human virtue must pre-exist in God, just as the exemplars of all things pre-exist in Him. In this way, therefore, virtue can be considered as existing in its highest exemplification in God, and in this fashion we speak of *exemplar* virtues. Thus the divine mind in God can be called prudence, while temperance is the turning of the divine attention to Himself, just as in us temperance is that which conforms the concupiscible appetite to reason. The fortitude of God is His immutability, while God's justice is the observance of the eternal law in His works, as Plotinus has said. [45]

Now because man is a political animal by nature, virtues of this type, inasmuch as they exist in man according to the condition of his nature, are called *political* virtues, since man comports himself rightly in human affairs by these virtues. It is in this manner that we have been speaking about virtues up to this point. [46]

But because it belongs to man to strive as much as possible to attain what is divine, as even the Philosopher says, [47] and Scripture commends to us in many places—for example, "Be ye perfect as your heavenly Father is perfect" (*Matthew 5:48*)—hence we must have some virtues midway between the political virtues, which are human, and the exemplar virtues, which are divine. These intermediate virtues are distinguished by a difference of movement and term. Some are virtues of those who are on the way and tending toward a likeness of what is divine, and these are called *purifying virtues.* Thus prudence, by contemplating divine things, counts all worldly things as nothing and directs all thought of the soul only to what is divine; temperance puts aside the customary needs of the body so far as nature permits; fortitude prevents the soul from being afraid of withdrawing from bodily needs and rising to heavenly things; and justice brings the whole soul's accord to such a way of life.

In addition, there are the virtues of those already attaining a divine likeness, which are called *perfect* virtues. Thus prudence now sees only divine things, temperance knows no earthly desires, fortitude is oblivious to the passions, and justice is united with the divine mind in an everlasting bond, by imitating it. These are the virtues we attribute to the blessed or to those who are most perfect in this life.

Reply to 1: The Philosopher is speaking of these virtues as concerned with human affairs; and thus, justice deals with buying and selling,

---

[44] *The Morals of the Catholic Church* I, 6.   [45] Cf. Macrobius, *In Somn. Scipion.* I, 8.

[46] That is, St. Thomas has been treating virtue in its most evident and familiar sense, which is human virtue as divided primarily into the four cardinal virtues. He now proceeds to extend the meaning of virtue to qualities perfecting man in a way that is beyond his human nature. In the following question, he will then consider the theological virtues, which are infused by grace.

[47] *Nicomachean Ethics* X, 7 (1177b 26).

fortitude with fears, and temperance with desires; for in this sense it would be ridiculous to attribute such virtues to God.

Reply to 2: Human virtues are about the passions, which is to say they are virtues of men passing their life in this world. But the virtues of those who have attained beatitude or full happiness are without passions. Hence Plotinus says that "political virtues mollify the passions," i.e., they bring them to a mean; "the second kind," namely, the purifying virtues, "remove the passions; the third kind," which perfect the soul, "know nothing of the passions; while in regard to the fourth kind," namely, the exemplar virtues, "it is abominable to mention the passions." [48] It may also be said that Plotinus is speaking here of the passions as they signify certain disordered movements.

Reply to 3: To neglect human affairs when they require attending to is wrong; otherwise it is virtuous. Hence Cicero says, a little before the quoted passage, "Perhaps one should make some allowance for lack of interest in the affairs of state in those who because of outstanding talent have devoted themselves to learning, as well as in those who have withdrawn from public life because of failing health or for some even weightier motive, when such men would yield to others the administration of power and authority." [49] This agrees with what Augustine says: "The love of truth needs a sacred leisure; the force of love demands just deeds. If no one places a burden upon us, then we are free to know and contemplate truth; but if such a burden is put upon us, we must accept it because of the demands of charity." [50]

Reply to 4: Legal justice alone directly relates to the common good, but by commanding it draws all the other virtues to the common good, as the Philosopher says.[51] For we must take into account that it belongs to the political virtues, as we are speaking of them here, not only to function well in regard to the community, but also in regard to the parts of the community, namely, the home or an individual person.

---

[48] Cf. Macrobius, *In Somn. Scipion.* I, 8.   [49] *De Off.* I, 21.
[50] *The City of God* XIX, 19.   [51] *Nicomachean Ethics* V, 1 (1129b 31).

The Theological Virtues

(In Four Articles)

First Article

ARE THERE THEOLOGICAL VIRTUES?

It seems that there are not any theological virtues.

1. "Virtue is the disposition of the perfect for the best, and by perfect I mean what is disposed according to its nature." [1] But that which is divine is above the nature of man. Therefore the theological virtues are not virtues belonging to man.

2. Theological virtues are in a way divine virtues. But divine virtues are exemplars, as we have said,[2] which indeed are not in us but in God. Therefore the theological virtues are not virtues of man.

3. The theological virtues are said to be those by which we are ordered to God, Who is the first principle and ultimate end of everything. But man is ordered to the first principle and ultimate end by the very nature of his reason and will. There is no need, therefore, for any habits of theological virtue to order his reason and will to God.

On the contrary: The precepts of law deal with acts of virtue. But there are precepts of the divine law[3] concerning acts of faith, hope, and charity, for "you that fear the Lord, believe Him," and again, "hope in Him," and again, "love Him" (*Ecclesiasticus 2:8, et seq.*). Therefore faith, hope, and charity are virtues ordering us to God, and hence are theological virtues.

Response: Man is perfected by virtue for those acts which lead to happiness, as we have said.[4] Now man's beatitude or happiness is of two kinds, as we have also said.[5] One kind is proportioned to human nature, which man can arrive at by the principles of his nature. The other kind is a happiness surpassing man's nature, which man can arrive at only by the power of God, by a certain participation in divinity, and so it is

---

[1] Aristotle, *Physics* VII, 3 (246a 13).   [2] Question 61, article 5.

[3] Divine law is distinct from human law and eternal law. Divine law enables man to share more perfectly in eternal law, the governing of the whole universe by divine reason. Divine law is given by revelation and is distinguished into the Old Law, that of the Old Testament, and the New Law, that of the New Testament. Cf. question 91, especially articles 1-5.

[4] Question 5, article 7.   [5] Question 5, article 5.

written that by Christ we are made "partakers of the divine nature" (*II Peter 1:4*). Now because happiness of this kind is beyond the capacity of human nature, man's natural principles, by which he proceeds to act well in proportion to his capacity, are not sufficient for ordering man to this happiness. Hence certain additional principles must be given by God to man by which he can thus be ordered to supernatural happiness, just as by natural principles he is ordered to a connatural end, though not without divine help. These additional principles are called theological virtues: first, because they have God as their object, inasmuch as by them we are rightly ordered to God; secondly, because they are infused in us by God alone; and finally, because these virtues are made known to us only by divine revelation in Sacred Scripture.

Reply to 1: A nature can be attributed to a thing in two ways. First, essentially, and thus these theological virtues exceed human nature. Second, participatively, for example, as ignited wood participates in the nature of fire, and thus, after a fashion, man partakes of the divine nature, as we have explained.[6] And so these virtues belong to man as he is made a participant of a nature.

Reply to 2: These virtues are called divine, not as though by them God is virtuous, but rather because by them God makes us virtuous and directs us to Him. Hence these virtues are not exemplars, but exemplifications.

Reply to 3: Reason and will are naturally ordered to God inasmuch as He is the principle and end of nature, though in proportion to nature. But reason and will by their nature are not sufficiently ordered to God as He is the object of supernatural happiness.

Second Article

SHOULD THE THEOLOGICAL VIRTUES BE DISTINGUISHED FROM THE INTELLECTUAL AND THE MORAL VIRTUES?

It seems that the theological virtues should not be distinguished from the intellectual and the moral virtues.

1. If the theological virtues are in the human soul, they must perfect either the intellectual or the appetitive part of the soul. But virtues which perfect the intellectual part are called the intellectual virtues, while those which perfect the appetitive part are called moral virtues. Therefore the theological virtues should not be distinguished from the moral and intellectual virtues.

2. Those virtues are called theological which order us to God. But there is an intellectual virtue which orders us to God, wisdom, which is about divine things inasmuch as it considers the highest cause. There-

---

[6] In the body of this article.

fore theological virtues should not be distinguished from intellectual virtues.

3. Augustine makes clear how there is an *order of love* in the four cardinal virtues.[7] But love is charity, which is acknowledged to be a theological virtue. Therefore the moral virtues should not be distinguished from the theological virtues.

On the contrary: What is above the nature of man should be distinguished from what is according to the nature of man. But the theological virtues are above the nature of man, whereas the intellectual and moral virtues belong to the nature of man, as we have explained.[8] Therefore the theological virtues should be distinguished from them.

Response: As we have said,[9] habits are specifically distinguished by a formal difference of objects. Now the object of the theological virtues is God Himself, Who is the ultimate end of things as exceeding the knowledge of our reason. But the object of the intellectual and moral virtues is something which can be grasped by human reason. Hence the theological virtues are specifically distinguished from the moral and intellectual virtues.

Reply to 1: The intellectual and moral virtues perfect the human intellect and appetite in proportion to human nature, but the theological virtues do so supernaturally.

Reply to 2: The wisdom which the Philosopher lists as an intellectual virtue considers divine things insofar as they can be investigated by human reason.[10] But a theological virtue treats them as they surpass human reason.

Reply to 3: Although charity is love, not all love is charity. When it is said, therefore, that all virtue is the order of love, this can be understood either of love generally or of the love of charity. If taken as love generally, then any virtue is said to be an ordering of love inasmuch as ordered affection is required for any cardinal virtue, and the root and principle of affection is love, as we have said.[11] But when taken as the love of charity, we are not then given to understand by this that any other virtue essentially is charity, but that all other virtues in some way depend on charity, as we shall explain later.[12]

---

[7] *The Morals of the Catholic Church* I, 13.   [8] Question 58, article 3.

[9] Question 54, article 2, reply to 1.   [10] Cf. *Nicomachean Ethics* VI, 3 (1139b 17).

[11] Question 27, article 4; question 28, article 6, reply to 2; question 41, article 2, reply to 1.

[12] Question 65, articles 2 and 4; II-II, question 23, article 7.

Third Article

ARE FAITH, HOPE AND CHARITY APPROPRIATELY PROPOSED
AS THEOLOGICAL VIRTUES?

It seems that faith, hope, and charity are not appropriately proposed
as the three theological virtues.

1. Theological virtues are related to divine happiness as natural inclination is to connatural end. But among the virtues ordered to the connatural end, only one virtue is natural,[13] the understanding of principles. Therefore there needs to be only one theological virtue.

2. The theological virtues are more perfect than the intellectual and
moral virtues. Faith, however, is not represented as an intellectual virtue,
but is something less than a virtue, since it is imperfect knowledge. Likewise, hope is not represented as a moral virtue, but is something less than
a virtue, since it is a passion. Therefore with much less reason should
they be listed as theological virtues.

3. The theological virtues order man's soul to God. But man's soul
cannot be ordered to God except through the intellectual part, in which
the intellect and will are. Therefore there can only be two theological
virtues: one which perfects the intellect and the other which perfects the
will.

On the contrary: The Apostle says, "Now there remain these three,
faith, hope, and charity" (*I Corinthians 13:13*).

Response: As we have said,[14] the theological virtues order man to
supernatural happiness in the same way as man is ordered to an end connatural to him by a natural inclination. This latter ordering occurs in
respect to two things. First, in respect to reason or intellect, inasmuch
as the intellect comprehends the first universal principles known to us
by the natural light of the intellect, from which our reasoning proceeds
in both speculative and practical matters. Second, through the rectitude
of the will which naturally tends to the good known by reason.

But these two ways are not sufficient for the order of supernatural
happiness, according to Scripture: "Eye has not seen nor ear heard, nor
has it entered into the heart of man, what things God has prepared for
those who love him" (*I Corinthians 2:9*). Hence it was necessary with
respect to both intellect and will that something be added supernaturally
to direct man to a supernatural end. First, with respect to the intellect,

---

[13] "Natural" here can be taken as opposed to supernatural, but in another sense,
"natural" is applied to the virtue of understanding principles. This virtue is then
set off from the virtues of science and wisdom in that man "naturally" has this virtue
with little or no discourse, whereas science and wisdom require a reasoning process. Cf.
question 57, article 2.

[14] Article 1.

certain supernatural principles held by means of divine light were added to man, and these are the things to be believed, with which faith is concerned. Second, the will is directed to this end both with respect to the movement of intention, which looks to that end as something possible to attain, which pertains to hope; and also with respect to a certain spiritual union, through which the will is transformed in a certain way into that end, which is effected by charity. For the appetite of a thing is naturally moved and tends to an end connatural to it, and this movement comes from a certain conformity of the thing with its end.

Reply to 1: The intellect requires intelligible species,[15] by means of which it understands, and hence there must be a natural habit in addition to the power. But the very nature of the will suffices for its natural ordering to the end, whether with respect to intending the end or being conformed to the end. But in relation to those things above its nature, the will's natural power is insufficient in regard to either of these. Hence there must be a supernatural habit added to the power in regard to both of these.[16]

Reply to 2: Faith and hope do imply a certain imperfection, for faith is about things which are not seen and hope is about things which are not yet had. Consequently, to have faith and hope about things which are subject to human power falls short of the nature of virtue. But to have faith and hope about things which are beyond the power of human nature surpasses all virtue proportionate to man, according to Scripture: "The foolishness of God is stronger than men" (*I Corinthians 1:25*).

Reply to 3: Two things belong to the appetite: movement toward the end and conformity with the end through love. Therefore it is necessary to have two theological virtues in the human appetite, hope and charity.

Fourth Article

IS FAITH PRIOR TO HOPE AND HOPE TO CHARITY?

It seems that there is not an order among theological virtues such that faith is prior to hope and hope is prior to charity.

1. The root is prior to what comes from the root. But charity is the root of all the virtues, for all "is rooted and founded in charity" (*Ephesians 3:17*). Therefore charity is prior to the other virtues.

2. Augustine says, "No one can love that which he does not believe exists. If, however, he believes and loves by doing good deeds, he will

---

[15] I.e., forms by means of which we know intellectually the objects we sense.

[16] That is, hope with respect to attaining the end and charity with respect to being conformed to the end.

show that he also hopes." [17] Therefore it seems that faith precedes charity and charity hope.

3. Love is the principle of all affection, as we have said.[18] But hope signifies a kind of affection, for it is a passion, as we have pointed out.[19] Therefore charity, which is love, is prior to hope.

On the contrary: The Apostle enumerates the virtues in this order: "Now there remain faith, hope, and charity" (*I Corinthians 13:13*).

Response: There are two kinds of order, one of generation and the other of perfection. In the order of generation, where matter is prior to form and the imperfect to the perfect, in one and the same subject, faith precedes hope, and hope charity, in regard to their acts (for the habits of each are infused simultaneously). For we cannot tend to something by appetitive movement, whether by hope or love, unless it is apprehended by sense or intellect. Now the intellect apprehends by faith what we hope for and love. Hence in the order of generation, faith must precede hope and charity. In like manner, from the fact that a man loves something, he apprehends it as a good for him. Now by the fact that a man hopes to be able to obtain something good from someone, he regards the one in whom he has hope as a certain good of his own. Hence by hoping in someone, a man proceeds to love him. In this way, in the order of generation and with respect to the acts of the virtues, hope precedes charity.

But in the order of perfection, charity precedes faith and hope in that both faith and hope are formed by charity and so acquire the perfection of virtue. Charity is thus the mother and root of all virtues insofar as it is the form of all virtues, as we shall explain later.[20]

Reply to 1: The response is clear from what has been said.

Reply to 2: Augustine is speaking of the hope by which someone hopes through merits already had that he will achieve happiness, and this belongs to a hope formed by charity and following upon it. But one can have hope before having charity, not from merits already possessed, but from merits he hopes to have.

Reply to 3: As we have said earlier when treating of the passions,[21] hope refers to two things. The first is its principal object, the good hoped for. With respect to this, love always precedes hope, for a good is never hoped for unless it is desired and loved. Secondly, hope also refers to the person from whom one hopes to be able to obtain a good. And in respect to this, hope precedes love at first, although afterward hope is increased by love. For when a man reflects on the fact that he can obtain something good through someone, he begins to love him, and by reason of loving him he hopes all the more in him.

---

[17] *On Christian Doctrine* I, 37.   [18] Article 2, reply to 3.   [19] Question 23, article 4.
[20] II-II, question 23, articles 7 and 8.   [21] Question 40, article 7.

The Cause of Virtue

(In Four Articles)

DOES VIRTUE EXIST IN US BY NATURE?

It seems that virtue is in us by nature.

1. Damascene says, "The virtues are natural and exist equally in all." [1] And Anthony says, in a sermon to monks, "If the will goes against nature, there is perversity; if nature is followed, there is virtue." [2] Finally, a gloss on *Matthew 4:23* ("Jesus went about," etc.) says, "He taught them natural virtues, namely, chastity, justice, and humility, which man has naturally."

2. The good of virtue is to be in conformity with reason, as we have said.[3] But that which is according to reason is natural to man, since reason is man's nature. Therefore virtue is in man by nature.

3. Something is said to be natural to us which is in us from birth. But virtues are in some persons from birth, for it is said in Scripture: "From my infancy mercy grew up with me, and it came out with me from my mother's womb" (*Job 31:18*). Therefore virtue is in man by nature.

On the contrary: Whatever is in man by nature is common to all men and is not destroyed by sin, for natural good remains even in demons, as Dionysius says.[4] But virtue is not in all men, and is expelled by sin. Therefore virtue is not in man by nature.

Response: With regard to corporeal forms, some have said that they come wholly from within, as with those who hold the position that there are latent forms.[5] Others, however, held that they came wholly from without, as with those who maintain that corporeal forms come from some separated cause.[6] Still others held that they came partly from within inasmuch as they exist potentially in matter, and partly from without insofar as they are brought into act by some agent.[7]

So also with regard to the sciences and the virtues, some held that they

---

[1] *On the Orthodox Faith* III, 14.   [2] Cf. St. Athanasius, *Vita S. Antonii.*
[3] Question 55, article 4, reply to 2.   [4] *On the Divine Names* IV, 23.
[5] The early Greek philosopher Anaxagoras may be one source referred to; cf. I, question 45, article 8. Cf. also Aristotle, *Physics* I, 4 (187a 29).
[6] Cf. I, question 45, article 8.   [7] Cf. *ibid.*

came wholly from within,[8] such that all virtues and sciences pre-exist naturally in the soul, but the impediments blocking the development of science and virtue, which accrue to the soul because of the burden of the body, are removed by study and practice, just as iron is brightened by filing. This was the opinion of the Platonists.[9] Others, however, said that they came wholly from without, i.e., from the influence of the agent intellect, as Avicenna held.[10] Still others said that the sciences and the virtues, with respect to our aptitude for having them, are in us by nature, but not in their perfect state, as the Philosopher says,[11] and this view is closer to the truth.

In order to explain this, we must observe that something is said to be natural to man in two ways: first, from his specific nature; second, from his individual nature. Now because anything has its species from the form and is individuated by the matter, and since the form of man is his rational soul and the matter is his body, then whatever belongs to man by reason of his rational soul is natural to him in respect to his species while that which is natural to him by reason of the determinate temperament of his body is natural to him in respect to his individual nature. For whatever is natural to man on the part of the body in accord with his species, is referred in a certain way to the soul insofar as such a body is proportioned to such a soul.

Now in each of these ways virtue is natural to man in an incipient state. Virtue is natural to man in respect to his specific nature insofar as certain naturally[12] known principles in regard to both thought and action are in man's reason naturally, which are like the seeds of intellectual and moral virtues, and insofar as there is in the will a certain natural appetite for good in conformity with reason. Virtue is natural to man also by reason of his individual nature insofar as by certain bodily dispositions some are disposed either better or worse to certain virtues. This is because the acts of some sense powers are acts of certain parts of the body, the condition of which helps or hinders such powers in their functioning and, as a consequence, the rational powers, which these

---

[8] Cf. I, question 84, article 3, obj. 3. [9] Cf. Plato, *Meno.*

[10] *On the Soul* V, 5. Avicenna (980-1037) was an Arabian commentator on Aristotle. He maintained that the agent intellect is substantially separate from the soul. For a criticism of this view of the agent intellect and how St. Thomas treated the agent intellect, cf. I, question 79, article 4.

[11] *Nicomachean Ethics* II, 1 (1103a 25): "Not by nature nor contrary to nature do the virtues come to be in us; rather, we are adapted by nature to receive them and are perfected by habit."

[12] I.e., known with little or no discourse. Such common principles—for example, the principle of noncontradiction in the speculative order, or the principle to seek the good and avoid the evil in the practical order—are known immediately, as it were, from an instance or two. Hence such principles are regarded as "naturally' present to the human mind.

sense powers serve. And corresponding to this way, man has a natural aptitude for science, another for fortitude, and another for temperance. In such manner, both intellectual and moral virtues, according to a certain incipient aptitude, are in us by nature, but not in their perfection. The reason for this is that nature is determined to one way of acting, and the fulfillment of these virtues is not brought about by one mode of acting, but by various modes, corresponding to the different matters with which the virtues are concerned and according to the varying circumstances.

It is therefore evident that the virtues are in us by nature in an incipient state and by way of aptitude, but not in a perfect state—except the theological virtues, which are wholly from without.

The replies to the initial arguments are clear from what we have said. For the first two positions argue that the virtues are in us by nature in the manner of seeds, inasmuch as we are rational. The third position argues that because of the natural disposition the body has from birth, one person has an aptitude for mercy, another for living temperately, and another for some other virtue.

Second Article

IS ANY VIRTUE CAUSED IN US BY OUR ACTIONS BEING HABITUATED?

It seems that virtues are not caused in us by our actions being habituated.

1. A gloss of Augustine on *Romans 14:23* ("All that is not of faith is sin") says: "The entire life of an unbeliever is a sin, and nothing is good without the supreme good. Where knowledge of truth is lacking, virtue is false even in the best behavior." [13] Now faith cannot be acquired by works but is caused in us by God, according to Scripture: "By grace you are saved through faith" (*Ephesians 2:8*). Therefore no virtue can be acquired in us by our actions being habituated.

2. Since sin is contrary to virtue, it is not compatible with virtue. But man cannot avoid sin except by the grace of God, for "I knew that I could not otherwise be continent, except God gave it" (*Wisdom 8:21*). Therefore virtues cannot be caused in us by our actions being habituated, but only by the gift of God.

3. Acts which are without virtue lack the perfection of virtue. But an effect cannot be more perfect than its cause. Therefore a virtue cannot be caused by acts preceding the virtue.

On the contrary: Dionysius says that good is more powerful than evil.[14]

---

[13] *Gloss ordin.* (VI, 30B).   [14] *On the Divine Names* IV, 20.

But habits of vice are caused by evil acts. Therefore much more can habits of virtue be caused by good acts.

Response: We have already spoken in a general way about the generation of habits from acts.[15] Now with respect to virtue in particular, we must consider that, as we have said,[16] human virtue perfects man in regard to the good. But since the notion of good consists in *mode, species, and order,* as Augustine says,[17] or in *number, weight, and measure,* as Scripture says,[18] the good of man must be considered in relation to some rule. This rule is twofold, as we have said:[19] human reason and divine law.[20] And because divine law is the superior rule, hence it covers more things, so that whatever is ruled by human reason is ruled also by divine law, but not conversely.[21]

Accordingly, human virtue, as ordered to the good which is measured by the rule of human reason, can be caused by human acts insofar as acts of such virtue proceed from reason, under whose power and rule such good is established. However, the virtue ordering man to a good as measured by divine law, and not by human reason, cannot be caused by human acts whose principle is reason, but only by divine operation in us. Hence, defining virtue of this kind, Augustine put the following phrase in the definition of virtue, "which God works in us without us." [22]

Reply to 1: This argument holds in regard to the virtue ordering man to a good as measured by divine law.

Reply to 2: Divinely infused virtue, especially when considered in its perfection, is not compatible with mortal sin. But virtue humanly acquired is compatible with a sinful act, even a mortal one, because the use of a habit in us is subject to our will, as we have said,[23] and the habit of an acquired virtue is not destroyed by one sinful act, since it is not an act, but a habit, that is directly contrary to a habit. Consequently, although without grace man cannot avoid mortal sin, so as never to sin mortally, yet he is not hindered from acquiring a habit of virtue whereby he can abstain from evil deeds for the most part, and especially from those which are very much opposed to reason. There are also some mortal sins which man in no way can avoid without grace, namely, those directly opposed to the theological virtues, which are gifts of grace in us. How this happens, however, will be explained later.[24]

Reply to 3: As we have said,[25] the seeds or principles of acquired virtues

---

[15] Question 51, articles 2 and 3.   [16] Question 55, articles 3 and 4.
[17] *On the Nature of the Good,* III.   [18] *Wisdom 11:21.*
[19] Question 19, articles 3 and 4.
[20] On the meaning of divine law, see note 3 of question 62.
[21] I.e., some things ruled by divine law exceed the grasp of reason.
[22] *Commentary on Psalms;* Psalms 118, sermon 26. *On Free Will* II, 19.
[23] Question 49, article 3.   [24] Question 109, article 4.
[25] Article 1; question 51, article 1.

pre-exist in us by nature. These principles are superior to the virtues acquired through them, just as the understanding of speculative principles
is superior to the knowledge of conclusions acquired through them, and
the natural rectitude of reason is superior to the rectitude of appetite
which arises from the appetite's participation in reason, which rectitude
belongs to moral virtue. Therefore human acts, insofar as they proceed
from higher principles, can cause acquired human virtues.

Third Article

ARE ANY MORAL VIRTUES INFUSED IN US?

It seems that apart from the theological virtues no other virtues are
infused in us by God.[26]

1. Whatever can be done by secondary causes is not done immediately
by God except perhaps sometimes miraculously because, as Dionysius
says, "it is the law of God to bring about the end through what is a
means to it." [27] But the intellectual and moral virtues can be caused in
us by our own acts, as has been said.[28] Therefore it is not fitting for them
to be caused in us by being infused.

2. There is much less of what is superfluous in the works of God than
in the works of nature. But the theological virtues are sufficient for ordering us to the supernatural good. Therefore no other supernatural virtues
need to be caused in us by God.

3. Nature does not use two things to accomplish what can be done by
one, and much less does God. But God has sown the seeds of virtue in
our soul, as a gloss says.[29] Therefore God does not need to cause other
virtues in us by infusion.

On the contrary: "She [i.e., Wisdom] teaches temperance and prudence
and justice and fortitude" (*Wisdom 8:7*).

Response: Effects must be proportionate to their causes and principles.
Now all virtues, intellectual and moral, which are acquired by our actions, proceed from certain natural principles which pre-exist in us, as
we have said.[30] In place of these natural principles, God has bestowed
on us theological virtues whereby we are ordered to a supernatural end,
as we have also said.[31] Hence it was necessary that other habits, corresponding proportionally to the theological virtues, be caused in us by
God which are related to the theological virtues as the moral and intellectual virtues are to the natural principles of virtues.

Reply to 1: Some moral and intellectual virtues can indeed be caused

[26] It is already clear from question 62 that the theological virtues of faith, hope, and
charity are infused by God. The question now is whether any other virtues we possess
are infused by God.
[27] *De Cael. Hier.,* IV, 3.   [28] Article 2.   [29] On *Hebrews 1:6.*
[30] Article 1; question 51, article 1.   [31] Question 62, article 1.

in us by our actions, but they are not proportioned to the theological virtues. Hence we need other virtues that are proportioned to them, caused immediately by God.

Reply to 2: The theological virtues order us sufficiently to a supernatural end in an incipient way, that is, to God Himself. Other infused virtues, however, are needed to perfect the soul with respect to other things, but in relation to God.

Reply to 3: The power of the principles naturally in us does not extend beyond the capacity of nature. Consequently, in relation to a supernatural end, man needs to be perfected by other principles in addition to these.

Fourth Article

IS THE VIRTUE WE ACQUIRE FROM HABITUAL ACTS THE
SAME IN KIND AS INFUSED VIRTUES?

It seems that infused virtues are not different in kind from the acquired virtues.

1. From what has been said before,[32] it seems that infused and acquired virtues do not differ except according to an ordering to an ultimate end. But habits and human acts are specified by a proximate end, not by the ultimate end. Therefore the infused moral or intellectual virtues do not differ in kind from the acquired virtues.

2. Habits are known through their acts. But the act of infused and acquired temperance is the same, that is, to moderate desires for the pleasure of touch.[33] Therefore they do not differ in kind.

3. Acquired and infused virtue differ as that which is done immediately by God and that which is done by a creature. But man whom God formed and whom nature generates is the same in kind, and the eye which God gave to the man born blind and one produced by the power of nature is the same in kind. Therefore it seems that acquired and infused virtue are the same in kind.

On the contrary: If the difference stated in a definition is changed, the species is changed. But we find expressed in the definition of infused virtue the words "which God works in us without us," as we have indicated.[34] Therefore acquired virtue, to which these words do not apply, is not the same in kind as infused virtue.

Response: Habits are distinguished in species in two ways. First, according to the special and formal ordering of their objects, as we have

---

[32] Article 3.
[33] Moderation of the pleasure of touch is given as the principal, though not the exclusive, concern of temperance.
[34] Article 2; question 55, article 4.

pointed out.[35] Now the object of any virtue is the good considered in the matter proper to that virtue; for example, the object of temperance is the pleasurable good relevant to desires of touch.[36] The formal ordering of this object comes from reason, which determines the mean in such desires, while the material object comes from the desires. Now it is clear that the mean which is imposed on such desires in conformity with the rule of human reason is different from that determined according to divine rule. In the eating of food, for instance, the mean established by human reason is that food should not harm the health of the body nor hinder the activity of thinking, whereas according to the rule of divine law man should "chastise his body and bring it into subjection" (*I Corinthians 9:27*), by abstaining from food, drink, and the like. Hence it is plain that infused and acquired virtue differ in kind, and for the same reason the other virtues do also.

The second way in which habits differ specifically is in regard to what they are ordered to, for the health of a man and of a horse is not of the same species, because of the different natures to which the health of each is ordered. In a similar way, the Philosopher says that the virtues of citizens differ according as they are well ordered to different forms of government.[37] And in this way also the infused moral virtues, by which men are ordered well as "citizens with the saints and members of God's household" (*Ephesians 2:19*) differ in kind from the acquired virtue by which men are ordered well in regard to human affairs.

Reply to 1: Infused and acquired virtue differ not only in their ordering to the ultimate end but also in regard to their ordering to their objects, as we have said.[38]

Reply to 2: Acquired and infused temperance moderate desires for the pleasure of touch in a different way, as we have said.[39] Hence they do not have the same act.

Reply to 3: God made the eye of the man born blind from birth for the same activity as the eye formed by nature, and hence it was of the same kind. And the reasoning would be the same if God willed miraculously to cause in man the virtues which are acquired by acts. But this is not the point at issue in the matter we are discussing, as we have explained.[40]

---

[35] Question 54, article 2; question 56, article 2; question 60, article 1.
[36] See note 33 above.   [37] Cf. *Politics* III, 2 (1276b 31).   [38] In the body of this article.
[39] *Ibid.*   [40] *Ibid.*

The Mean of Virtue

(In Four Articles)

DO THE MORAL VIRTUES OBSERVE A MEAN? [1]

It seems that the moral virtues do not observe a mean.

1. The notion of a mean is opposed to that of an extreme.[2] But it belongs to the nature of virtue to be an extreme, for "virtue is the maximum of a power." [3] Therefore moral virtue does not observe a mean.

2. Whatever is a maximum is not a mean. But some moral virtues tend to the maximum; for example, magnanimity is concerned about the greatest honors, and magnificence about great expenditures.[4] Therefore not every moral virtue observes a mean.

3. If it were of the nature of moral virtue to observe the mean, then it would have to follow that moral virtue could not be perfected, but rather destroyed, by tending to an extreme. Now some moral virtues are perfected by tending to an extreme; for example, virginity abstains from all sexual pleasure and thus observes an extreme and is the most perfect form of chastity; similarly, to give all one has to the poor is the most perfect form of mercy or liberality. Therefore it is not of the nature of moral virtue to be in the mean.

---

[1] The order of procedure might be noted. Question 55 treated the essence of virtue. Question 56 examined the subject of virtue, where it was noted that since a power of the soul is the proper and immediate subject of virtue, virtue is found principally in the human will, or in a power moved by the will, the intellect, or the irascible and concupiscible powers which can have a conformity to reason. Questions 57-62 therefore consider the different kinds of virtue: moral, intellectual, and theological. Question 63 then investigates the cause of virtue, as we have just seen. Now in question 64 we begin examining certain properties characteristic of virtue, of which the first is that virtue is realized in a certain mean between extremes.

[2] The word for "extreme" in Latin is *ultimum.* The word "extreme," rather than the English word "ultimate" conveys better the force of the argument being advanced here. We shall see, in the reply to this argument, that the argument being given here plays upon the ambiguity of what is an "extreme" or what is "ultimate" in the moral order.

[3] Aristotle, *On the Heavens* I, 11 (281a 11).

[4] Cf. Aristotle, *Nicomachean Ethics* IV, 2 (1122a 18); 3 (1123a 34).

On the contrary: The Philosopher says that "moral virtue is the habit of choosing the mean." [5]

Response: As we have said,[6] virtue of its very nature directs man to good. Now moral virtue is properly a perfection of the appetitive part of the soul in regard to some determinate matter, and the measure and rule of the movement of appetite with respect to appetible objects is reason itself. But the goodness of what is measured and ruled consists in its conformity to its rule, just as the good of works of art is in following the rule of art. Consequently, in matters of this kind, evil results from a thing's not being in accord with its rule or measure, which can happen either by exceeding the measure or by falling short of it, as is clearly apparent in all things which are ruled and measured. Hence it is evident that the goodness of moral virtue consists in conformity to the rule of reason. Now it is clear that the mean between an excess and a defect is an equality or conformity. Hence it is manifest that moral virtue observes a mean.

Reply to 1: Moral virtue derives its goodness from the rule of reason whereas its matter is the passions or the operations. Accordingly, if moral virtue is compared to reason, then with regard to what it has from reason it is considered as one extreme, a conformity, while the excess and defect are considered as the other extreme, a deformity. But if moral virtue is considered in regard to its matter, then it is considered as a mean insofar as it restores the passions to the rule of reason.[7] Hence the Philosopher says that "in respect to its substance, virtue is a mean," inasmuch as the rule of virtue is maintained in the proper matter, but "with regard to what is best and right, it is an extreme," namely, as to its conformity with reason.[8]

Reply to 2: The mean and extremes in actions and passions depend on the differing circumstances. Consequently, there is nothing to prevent something from being extreme in a virtue as to one circumstance and yet a mean in respect to other circumstances, by being conformed to reason.

---

[5] *Op. cit.,* II, 6 (1106b 36).   [6] Question 55, article 3.

[7] The foregoing distinction is important by way of removing a common misapprehension of moral virtue as a mean. Such a mean is not reducible to mediocrity nor to an average achievement. The moral mean refers to the *right* ordering of the passions and operations by conforming to the direction of reason, thus avoiding the excess or defect. Attaining such a mean in the movement of appetite is a perfection *morally,* and this perfection comes from order being introduced into the movement of the appetite itself by reason. Hence moral virtue is also an *extreme* in the sense that it is the best morally; at the same time, what is best morally is the *mean* between excessive or defective movement of appetite. Aristotle himself is very clear on this point; cf. *Nicomachean Ethics* II, 6 (110-6b 36-1107a 8). Despite Aristotle's careful and explicit explanation, some persist in thinking that Aristotle's notion of virtue as a mean amounts to making virtue "average" or "ordinary" in regard to achieving moral excellence. Such a view is exactly contrary to Aristotle's position.

[8] *Nicomachean Ethics* II, 6 (1107a 7). See preceding note.

Such is the case with magnificence and magnanimity. If we consider the absolute quantity of the object to which the magnanimous or magnificent[9] person tends, we would call it extreme and a maximum. But if we consider the quantity in relation to other circumstances, it then has the aspect of a mean, because these virtues tend to that maximum according to the direction of reason, that is, by taking into account such circumstances as *where* it is right [to give large sums of money], *when* it is right, and *why* it is right. There would be excess if one tended to this maximum when it is not right, or where it is not right, to do so, or when the end in view is not right; and there would be something defective if one did not tend to this maximum where it was right to do so and when it was right. And this agrees with what the Philosopher says: "the magnanimous person is at an extreme in respect to greatness of his actions, but at a mean in regard to the rightness of them." [10]

Reply to 3: The same reasoning holds with respect to virginity and poverty as for magnanimity. For virginity abstains from all sexual pleasures and poverty from all wealth for a right end according as one ought, that is, according to the commandment of God and for the sake of eternal life. But if these things be done not according as they should be— from some illicit superstition, for example, or vainglory—they will be an excess. And if they are not done when they should be or as they should be, then they become a vice by defect, as happens in breaking the vows of virginity or poverty.

Second Article

IS THE MEAN OF MORAL VIRTUE A REAL MEAN OR A MEAN OF REASON? [11]

It seems that the mean of moral virtue is not a mean of reason but a real mean.

1. The goodness of moral virtue consists in its being in the mean. But the good is in things themselves.[12] Therefore the mean of moral virtue is a real mean.

2. Reasoning is a power of apprehending. But moral virtue does not observe a mean in regard to apprehensions, but a mean in regard to operations and passions. Therefore the mean of moral virtue is not a mean of reason but a real mean.

---

[9] On this use of the word "magnificent," see note 36 in question 60, article 5.

[10] *Nicomachean Ethics* IV, 3 (1123b 13).

[11] A real mean is one that is established on the part of things or objects, as an arithmetic mean. A mean of reason is one established in conformity to man's reason as directing his appetite. The latter type is a proportional mean; the former is one of strict equality.

[12] Cf. Aristotle, *Metaphysics* VI, 4 (1027b 26).

3. The mean taken according to an arithmetic or geometric proportion is a real mean. But such is the mean of justice.[13] Therefore the mean of moral virtue is not a mean of reason, but a real mean.

On the contrary: The Philosopher says that "moral virtue consists in a mean relative to us, determined by reason." [14]

Response: The mean of reason can be understood in two ways. First, as the mean exists in the very act of reason, as the act itself of reason is made to observe a mean. When the mean is so understood, then since moral virtue perfects not the act of reason, but the act of an appetitive power, the mean of moral virtue is not the mean of reason. Second, the mean of reason can be understood as that which reason appoints in some matter, and in this sense every mean of moral virtue is a mean of reason; for, as we have pointed out,[15] moral virtue is said to observe a mean by conforming with right reason.

It may sometimes happen, however, that the mean of reason is also a real mean, and then the mean of moral virtue must be a real mean, as it is in the case of justice. But sometimes the mean of reason is not a real mean, but is taken in relation to ourselves, and this is the sort of mean found in all other moral virtues. The reason for the foregoing difference is that justice is about operations dealing with external things wherein what is right has to be established simply and unqualifiedly, as we have said.[16] Consequently, the mean of reason in justice is the same as the real mean inasmuch as justice renders to each one what is due, neither more nor less. The other moral virtues, however, are about interior passions wherein what is right cannot be determined in the same way, because men differ in regard to their passions. Accordingly, rectitude of reason must be established in the passions with due regard to ourselves, for we are affected in proportion to our passions.

The foregoing remarks will suffice for replying to the initial arguments. The first two arguments are based on the mean of reason as it is found in the very act of reason; the third on the mean as it is found in justice.

Third Article

DO THE INTELLECTUAL VIRTUES OBSERVE A MEAN?

It seems that the intellectual virtues do not observe a mean.

1. The moral virtues observe a mean insofar as they conform to the rule of reason. But the intellectual virtues are in reason itself, and so they do not appear to have a superior rule. Therefore the intellectual virtues do not observe a mean.

2. The mean of moral virtue is determined by intellectual virtue, for

---

[13] Cf. Aristotle, *Nicomachean Ethics* V, 4 (1132a 2); 3 (1131b 13); II, 6 (1106b 28).
[14] *Op. cit.,* II, 6 (1106b 36).   [15] In the preceding article.   [16] Question 60, article 2.

"virtue consists in a mean determined by reason as a man of practical wisdom would determine it." [17] Accordingly, if intellectual virtue were also to consist in a mean, it would be necessary to determine a mean for it by some other virtue, and thus there would be an endless series of the virtues.

3. The mean is properly between contraries, as the Philosopher makes evident.[18] But there does not seem to be any contrariety in the intellect, for even contraries themselves, as they are in the mind, are not in opposition, but are understood at the same time, as white and black, healthy and sick. Therefore there is no mean in the intellectual virtues.

On the contrary: "Art is an intellectual virtue," [19] and yet "there is a mean in art." [20] Therefore intellectual virtue observes a mean.

Response: The goodness of something consists in its being in a mean in conformity with a rule or measure in respect to which there may be excess or defect, as we have noted.[21] Now intellectual virtue, like moral virtue, is ordered to a good, as we have said.[22] Hence, the good of intellectual virtue is subject to a mean insofar as it is subject to a measure. Now the good to which intellectual virtue is ordered is the true: in the case of speculative virtue, what is true absolutely;[23] in the case of practical virtue, what is true in conformity with right appetite.

The truth of our intellect, if we consider it absolutely, is measured by the thing, for things are the measure of our intellect.[24] For by the fact that a thing is so or not, there is truth in what we think and say. In this way, then, the good of speculative intellectual virtue observes a certain mean, through conformity with things themselves, according as the intellect expresses that what is, is, and what is not, is not; for this is what truth is. There is excess when there is a false affirmation, as in saying that something is when it is not. There is defect when there is a false negation, as in saying something is not when it is.

The truth of practical intellectual virtue, when compared to things, has the aspect of being measured, and thus in both speculative and practical intellectual virtues, the mean consists in conformity with things. But if we consider this truth in relation to appetite, it has the character of a rule and a measure. Hence, rectitude of reason is the mean of moral virtue and also the mean of prudence, but in respect to prudence this mean stands as ruling and measuring, while moral virtue is measured and ruled by the mean.[25] Likewise, the excess and defect are taken differently in each case.

---

[17] Aristotle, *Nicomachean Ethics* II, 6 (1106b 36).   [18] Cf. *Metaphysics* X, 7 (1057a 30).
[19] Aristotle, *Nicomachean Ethics* VI, 3 (1139b 16).   [20] *Op. cit.,* II, 6 (1106b 13).
[21] Article 1.   [22] Question 56, article 3.
[23] Cf. Aristotle, *Nicomachean Ethics* VI, 2 (1139a 29).
[24] Cf. Aristotle, *Metaphysics* X, 1 (1053a 33).
[25] In prudence, right reason as establishing the mean is the measure of the move-

Reply to 1: Intellectual virtue also has its own measure, as we have said,[26] and its mean consists in conforming to this measure.

Reply to 2: There is no need to have an endless succession of virtues, for the measure and rule of intellectual virtue is not some other kind of virtue, but is things themselves.

Reply to 3: Contrary things do not have contrariety in the mind, for one contrary is the reason for knowing the other.[27] However, there is in the intellect contrariety of affirmation and negation, which are contraries.[28] For although *to be* and *not to be* are not opposed as contraries, but as contradictories, as long as we consider what they signify in reality —for the one is *being* and the other wholly *non-being*—yet if they are referred to the act of the mind, each posits something. Hence *to be* and *not to be* are contradictories. But the opinion by which we think a good is good is contrary to the opinion by which we think a good is not good, and it is between contraries of this kind that intellectual virtue is a mean.[29]

Fourth Article

DO THE THEOLOGICAL VIRTUES OBSERVE A MEAN?

It seems that a theological virtue observes a mean.

1. The good of the other virtues consists in a mean. But a theological virtue surpasses the other virtues in goodness. Therefore much more does a theological virtue observe a mean.

2. The mean of moral virtue depends on the appetite being ruled by reason while the mean of intellectual virtue depends on our intellect being measured by reality. But a theological virtue perfects both the intellect and appetite, as we have said.[30] Therefore a theological virtue also observes a mean.

3. Hope, a theological virtue, is the mean between despair and presumption; similarly, faith holds a middle position between contrary heresies.[31] Thus, our belief that there is one person and two natures in

---

ment of appetite; the mean in moral virtue, accordingly, is to be measured by this right reason. Because prudence is an intellectual virtue, right reason is directive in relation to appetite; because moral virtue is in the appetite, it is directed by right reason.

[26] In the body of this article.

[27] For example, healthy and sick are contraries, but to understand what it is to be sick one must know what it is to be healthy.

[28] Cf. Aristotle, *On Interpretation*, 14 (23a 27).

[29] Aristotle discusses at length (*op. cit.*, 14, 23a 40—24b 9) how the opinion "everything good is good" is contrary to the opinion "nothing good is good," whereas the contradictory of the first opinion is "not everything good is good."

[30] Question 62, article 3.   [31] Cf. Boethius, *De Duabus Naturis*, VII.

Christ is a mean between the heresy of Nestorius, who held that there were two persons and two natures, and the heresy of Eutyches, who said that there was one person and one nature. Therefore a theological virtue observes a mean.

On the contrary: Whenever a virtue consists in a mean, one can sin by excess as well as by defect. But it is not possible to sin by excess with respect to God, the object of theological virtue, for "Blessing the Lord, exalt him as much as you can; for he is above all praise" (*Ecclesiasticus 43:33*). Therefore a theological virtue does not observe a mean.

Response: As we have said,[32] the mean of virtue is based on conformity with its rule or measure inasmuch as one may go beyond or fall short of it. Now a twofold measure of theological virtue can be noted. One is taken from the very nature of the virtue, and in this way the measure and rule of theological virtue is God Himself. Thus, our faith is regulated by divine truth, charity by divine goodness, and hope by the immensity of His divine omnipotence and loving kindness. Now this is a measure exceeding all human capability, and so we can never love God as much as He should be loved, nor believe or hope in Him as much as we should. Hence, with much less reason can there be any excess in these matters. Accordingly, the good of such virtue does not consist in a mean; rather, the more one approaches the extreme of it the better one becomes.

The other rule or measure of theological virtue is on our part. For although we are not moved toward God as much as we should be, nevertheless we should approach Him by believing and hoping in Him, and loving Him, in the measure of our condition. Hence in an accidental way and on our part, a mean and extremes can be found in theological virtue.

Reply to 1: The good of intellectual and moral virtue consists in a mean in conformity with a rule or measure which can be exceeded, whereas in theological virtue, properly speaking, this cannot happen, as we have explained.[33]

Reply to 2: The moral and intellectual virtues perfect our intellect and appetite in relation to a created measure and rule while the theological virtues do so in relation to an uncreated measure and rule. Hence the comparison is not the same.

Reply to 3: Hope is a mean between presumption and despair when considered in relation to us. Thus a man is said to be presumptuous insofar as he hopes for a good from God beyond his condition, or he is said to despair because he does not hope for what he could according to his condition. But there cannot be too much hope in relation to God,

---

[32] Article 1.   [33] In the body of this article.

whose goodness is unlimited. Likewise, faith is a mean between contrary heresies, not with respect to God as its object, in whom we cannot believe too much, but insofar as a human opinion is a mean between contrary opinions, as we have said.[34]

---

[34] Article 3.

The Connection of the Virtues

(In Five Articles)

ARE THE MORAL VIRTUES CONNECTED WITH EACH OTHER?

It seems that the moral virtues are not necessarily connected.

1. The moral virtues are sometimes caused by exercising the acts.[1] But a man can thus do the acts of one virtue without doing the acts of another. Therefore it is possible to have one moral virtue without another.

2. Magnificence and magnanimity are moral virtues. But one can have other moral virtues without having magnificence and magnanimity. For the Philosopher says, "a poor man cannot be magnificent," [2] although he can have some other virtues; and "he who is worthy of little things and thinks himself worthy of little things is temperate, but not magnanimous." [3] Therefore the moral virtues are not connected.

3. Moral virtues perfect the appetitive part of the soul as intellectual virtues perfect the intellectual part. But the intellectual virtues are not connected, for a man can have one science without having another. Therefore the moral virtues are also not connected.

4. If the moral virtues were connected with each other, this would happen only by their being joined together in prudence. But this is not enough to connect the moral virtues, for a man can be prudent about what to do in regard to one virtue without being prudent about what is to be done with respect to another virtue. Similarly, one can have the art of making some things without having the art of making other things. Now prudence is right reasoning about what is to be done. Therefore the moral virtues are not necessarily connected with each other.

On the contrary: Ambrose says, "The virtues are connected and joined together in such a way that he who has one seems to have many." [4] Augustine likewise says that "the virtues in the human soul in no way are separated from each other." [5] And Gregory says that "one virtue without the others is either nothing at all or is quite imperfect." [6] Finally, Cicero

---

[1] Cf. Aristotle, *Nicomachean Ethics* II, 1 (1103a 31).   [2] *Op. cit.*, IV, 2 (1122b 26).
[3] *Op. cit.*, IV, 3 (1123b 5).   [4] *Commentary on Luke* 6:20.   [5] *The Trinity* VI, 4.
[6] *Moral.*, XXII, 1.

says, "If you admit to not having one particular virtue, you will necessarily not have any at all." [7]

Response: We can consider moral virtue in either a perfect or an imperfect state. A moral virtue in an imperfect state (for example, temperance or fortitude) is simply the inclination we have for that good work, whether the inclination arises in us by nature or from custom. Taken this way, the moral virtues are not connected, for we observe that some persons, by reason of natural temperament or of being accustomed to do so, are prompt in acts of generosity but not so prompt regarding acts of chastity.

But moral virtue in its perfect state is a habit inclining one to do a good act well, and taken in this way, we must say that the moral virtues are connected, as nearly everyone agrees. Two reasons are given for this position, corresponding to the different ways in which the cardinal virtues are distinguished. For, as we pointed out,[8] some distinguish them according to certain general characteristics of virtues; for example, discretion pertains to prudence, rectitude to justice, moderation to temperance, firmness to fortitude, in any matter in which these are considered to be. So considered, the reason for the connection of the virtues is apparent, for firmness is not commended as virtuous if it is without moderation or rectitude or discretion, and so with the others. Gregory also assigns this as the reason for their connection: "The virtues, if they are not connected, cannot be perfect" as virtues, "for there is no true prudence without justice, temperance, and fortitude." [9] Augustine also gives the same reason.[10]

Others, however, distinguish these virtues according to their matter, and in this way Aristotle assigns the reason for their connection,[11] for, as we have said,[12] there can be no moral virtue without prudence since it belongs to moral virtue, as an elective habit, to make a right choice. Now right choice requires not only an inclination to an appropriate end, which arises directly from the habit of moral virtue, but also the correct choice of means to the end, which is made by prudence, which deliberates, judges, and commands in regard to the means. Likewise, one cannot have prudence without having the moral virtues since prudence is right reasoning about what is to be done, whose starting point is the end of action, to which we are rightly disposed by the moral virtues. Hence, just as we cannot have a speculative science without understanding its principles so we cannot have prudence unless we have the moral virtues. From all this, it clearly follows that the moral virtues are connected.

Reply to 1: Certain moral virtues perfect man according to his common

---

[7] *Tusculan Disputations* II, 14.   [8] Question 61, articles 3 and 4.   [9] *Moral.,* XXII, 1.
[10] Cf. *The Trinity* VI, 4.   [11] Cf. *Nicomachean Ethics* VI, 13 (1144b 36).
[12] Question 58, article 4.

state of life, that is, with respect to what needs to be done in any kind of human life. To that end, man has to exercise acts at the same time in the matters of all moral virtues. And if he does well in so acting in all these matters, he will acquire the habits of all moral virtues. Now if he exercises himself well in regard to one matter, but not another—well with respect to matters of anger but not with respect to those of concupiscence —he will indeed acquire a habit of restraining his anger, but this habit will not achieve the state of a virtue because of the absence of prudence, which is vitiated in matters of concupiscence. In a similar way, natural inclinations fail to achieve the complete state of virtue if prudence is absent.

But there are some virtues which perfect man with respect to an eminent state, such as magnificence and magnanimity. And because activity about matters related to such virtues does not happen to everyone generally, a man can have other moral virtues without having the habits of these virtues actually, if we are speaking about the acquired virtues.[13] Nevertheless, once one has acquired the other virtues, he is proximately in potency to having these virtues. Thus, when a man becomes adept in practicing liberality in moderate gifts and spending, if he comes into a large sum of money he would acquire the habit of magnificence with little practice, just as a geometer with little study acquires scientific knowledge of a conclusion which he had never previously given thought to. Indeed, we are said to *have* a thing when we can *readily* have it, according to what the Philosopher says: "That which is barely lacking, seems not to be lacking at all." [14]

Reply to 2: The foregoing is sufficient for this reply.

Reply to 3: The intellectual virtues deal with different subject matters that are not ordered to each other, as is evident in the different sciences and arts. Accordingly, we do not find in them the connection there is in the moral virtues, which deal with passions and operations, and are clearly related to each other. For all the passions proceed from certain primary ones, love and hate, and terminate in certain other ones, joy and sorrow. Similarly, all operations, which are the matter of moral virtue, are related to each other and also to the passions. And so it is that the whole matter of moral virtue falls under the direction of prudence.

All intelligible objects, however, are related to first principles. In this respect, then, all the intellectual virtues depend upon the understanding of principles, as prudence does upon the moral virtues, as we have said.[15] But the universal principles, with which the virtue of understanding is concerned, do not depend upon conclusions, with which the other intellectual virtues are concerned, whereas the moral virtues do depend on

---

[13] As distinguished from the infused virtues. See the following two articles.
[14] *Physics* II, 5 (197a 29).   [15] In the body of this article.

prudence inasmuch as the appetite in a way moves reason, and reason appetite, as we have explained.[16]

Reply to 4: The things which the moral virtues incline to are related to prudence as principles whereas the products of art are not related to art as principles, but as matter. Now it is clear that although reason can be right in regard to one part of the matter and not in another, nevertheless it can in no way be called right reason if it is deficient with respect to any principle whatever. For example, if one is in error about the principle *Every [quantitative] whole is greater than its part,* he could not attain the science of geometry, because in subsequent matters he would have to deviate from the truth.

Furthermore, things which are *done* are related to each other, whereas things which are *made* are not, as we have explained.[17] Consequently, a lack of prudence in regard to one part of what is to be done would lead to a lack of prudence in regard to other things to be done. This situation does not occur with respect to things which are to be made.

Second Article

CAN THE MORAL VIRTUES EXIST WITHOUT CHARITY?

It seems that the moral virtues can exist without charity.

1. "Every virtue except charity can be common to good and bad persons."[18] But "charity can exist only in the good," as is stated in the same passage. Therefore the other virtues can be had without charity.

2. Moral virtues can be acquired by human acts.[19] But charity can be had only by being infused, according to Scripture: "The charity of God is poured forth in our hearts by the Holy Spirit Who has been given to us" (*Romans 5:5*). Therefore the other virtues can be had without charity.

3. The moral virtues are connected with each other insofar as they depend on prudence. But charity does not depend on prudence; rather, it surpasses prudence, according to Scripture: "Christ's charity, which surpasses knowledge" (*Ephesians 3:19*). Therefore the moral virtues are not connected with charity, but can exist without charity.

On the contrary: "He who does not love abides in death" (*I John 3:14*). But the spiritual life is perfected by the virtues, for "it is by the virtues that we live rightly."[20] Therefore the virtues cannot exist without the love of charity.

---

[16] Question 9, article 1; question 58, article 5, reply to 1.

[17] Reply to 3, first paragraph, where passions and operations, which are what is meant by things *done,* are shown to have an ordering among themselves. Things which are *made* refer to products of art. St. Thomas merely points out here as something evident that products of the different arts are not related to each other.

[18] Prosper of Aquitaine, *Sent.* VII.

[19] Cf. Aristotle, *Nicomachean Ethics* II, 1 (1103a 31).

[20] Augustine, *On Free Will* II, 19.

Response: As we have said,[21] the moral virtues, inasmuch as they are productive of good works ordered to an end which does not surpass the natural capacity of man, can be acquired by human actions. And acquired in this way they can be without charity, as has happened with many pagans. But insofar as they are productive of good works in relation to a supernatural last end, and thus truly and perfectly attain the nature of virtue, they cannot be acquired by human acts but are infused by God. Moral virtues of this kind cannot exist without charity. For, as we have already said,[22] the other moral virtues cannot exist without prudence nor prudence without the moral virtues inasmuch as the moral virtues make man well disposed to certain ends, from which the reasoning of prudence proceeds. Now for the right reasoning of prudence it is much more necessary that man be well disposed to the ultimate end, which is the result of charity, than that he be well disposed to other ends, which is the result of moral virtue, just as sound reasoning in speculative matters requires most of all the first indemonstrable principle, namely, that *contradictory statements cannot at the same time be true.* Hence it becomes evident that infused prudence cannot exist without charity; nor, consequently, the other moral virtues, for they cannot exist without prudence.

Accordingly, it is clear from what has been said that only the infused virtues are perfect virtues and are to be called virtues unqualifiedly, for they order man to his ultimate end absolutely. The other virtues, the acquired ones, are virtues in a restricted sense, and not unqualifiedly, for they order man well regarding the ultimate end in some particular kind of action, but not in regard to the ultimate end absolutely. Hence on the passage in Scripture, "all that is not from faith is sin" (*Romans 14:23*), a gloss of Augustine reads: "Where knowledge of truth is lacking, virtue is false even in those with the best behavior." [23]

Reply to 1: The virtues, in the passage quoted, correspond to imperfect virtue. Besides, if moral virtue be understood in its perfect state, "it makes the one who possesses it good," [24] and consequently cannot be found in evil persons.

Reply to 2: The argument is based upon the acquired moral virtues.

Reply to 3: Although charity surpasses science and prudence, nevertheless prudence depends upon charity, as we have explained,[25] and consequently, all the infused moral virtues also depend on charity.

---

[21] Question 63, article 2.   [22] Article 1; question 58, articles 4 and 5.
[23] *Gloss ordin.* (VI, 30 B). Cf. also Prosper of Aquitaine, *Sent.* CVI.
[24] Cf. question 55, article 3, *On the contrary.*   [25] In the body of this article.

Third Article

CAN CHARITY EXIST WITHOUT THE MORAL VIRTUES?

It seems possible to have charity without the moral virtues.

1. When one thing is sufficient for something, it is unreasonable to adopt many. But charity alone is sufficient for the fulfillment of all the works of virtue, as is clear from Scripture: "Charity is patient, is kind," etc. (*I Corinthians 13:4*). Therefore it seems that when one has charity, other virtues are superfluous.

2. One who has the habit of charity readily does the works of virtue, and the works of virtue themselves are pleasing to him. Hence, "a sign of having a habit is the pleasure with which the work is done." [26] But many who have charity, being without mortal sin, still have difficulty in doing the works of virtue, nor are the works pleasing of themselves but only as they are referred to charity. Therefore many have charity without having other virtues.

3. Charity is found in all the saints. Yet there are some saints who lack certain virtues, for Bede says that the saints are more humbled with respect to the virtues they do not have than they are exalted with respect to the virtues they have.[27] Therefore it is not necessary that one who has charity have all the moral virtues.

On the contrary: The whole Law is fulfilled by charity, for "He who loves his neighbor has fulfilled the Law" (*Romans 13:8*). But it is not possible to fulfill the whole Law without having all the moral virtues, for law gives rules about all acts of virtue.[28] Therefore one who has charity has all the moral virtues. Augustine also says in a letter that charity includes all the cardinal virtues.[29]

Response: All the moral virtues are infused together with charity. The reason for this is that God does not act less perfectly in works of grace than in works of nature. Thus, we observe in the works of nature that a thing does not have a principle for certain works without also having whatever is necessary for carrying them out; for example, animals have certain organs enabling them to do the works which their souls[30] empower them to do. Now it is clear that charity, inasmuch as it directs man to his ultimate end, is the principle of all the good works that are referable to his ultimate end. Hence it is necessary that along with charity there be infused at the same time all the moral virtues by which man can perform each kind of good work.

Thus it is clear that the infused moral virtues are connected not only

---

[26] Aristotle, *Nicomachean Ethics* II, 3 (1104b 3).   [27] *In Luc.* V, 17:10.
[28] Cf. Aristotle, *Nicomachean Ethics* V, 1 (1129b 23).   [29] *Epist.* CLXVII.
[30] Taken in the common sense of principles of life, and specifically of animal life.

because of prudence, but because of charity as well; and it is also evident that he who loses charity through mortal sin loses all the infused moral virtues.

Reply to 1: In order that an act of a lower power be perfect, there must not only be perfection in the higher power but also in the lower, for if the principal agent were rightly disposed, perfect action would not follow if the instrument were not also well disposed. Hence, for man to act well in regard to what is for the sake of an end, it is necessary not only that he have the virtue whereby he is well ordered to the end, but also the virtues whereby he is well ordered in regard to the means to the end, for the virtue concerning the end is the primary and moving principle in respect to those things that are for the sake of the end. Hence it is necessary to have the moral virtues along with charity.

Reply to 2: It sometimes happens that someone who has a habit finds difficulty in acting, and as a consequence does not experience delight and satisfaction in the act because of some extrinsic impediment. For example, a person with the habit of science may have difficulty in understanding because of being sleepy, or from some other weakness. Similarly, the habits of the infused moral virtues now and then have difficulty in operating because of certain opposing dispositions remaining from previous acts. Such difficulty does not occur in the acquired moral virtues because the exercise of the acts by which the virtues are acquired also removes opposing dispositions.[31]

Reply to 3: Some saints are said not to have certain virtues insofar as they have difficulty in performing acts of those virtues, for the reason we have given,[32] although they have the habits of all the virtues.

Fourth Article

CAN THERE BE FAITH AND HOPE WITHOUT CHARITY?

It seems that there can never be faith and hope without charity.

1. Since faith and hope are theological virtues, they seem to be more worthy than the moral virtues, even the infused moral virtues. But there cannot be infused moral virtues without charity, and hence neither can there be faith or hope without charity.

2. "No one believes unless he wills to do so." [33] But charity is in the will as its perfection, as we have said.[34] Therefore there cannot be faith without charity.

3. Augustine says that "there can be no hope without love." [35] But love

---

[31] For example, the acts leading to the acquiring of fortitude remove, in proportion as the virtue becomes established, acts of undue fear and cowardice.

[32] Reply to 2.   [33] Augustine, Tract XXVI; *super Joann.* 6:44.

[34] Question 62, article 3.   [35] *Enchiridion,* VIII.

is charity, for it is of such love that he speaks. Therefore there cannot be hope without charity.

On the contrary: A gloss on *Matthew 1:2* says that "faith generates hope, and hope charity." [36] But that which generates precedes that which is generated. Therefore there can be faith without hope, and hope without charity.

Response: Faith and hope, like the moral virtues, can be considered in two ways. First, in a beginning state; second, as perfect virtues. Now, since virtue is ordered to doing a good work, a virtue is said to be perfect by the fact that it is capable of producing a completely good work, which consists not only in doing what is good, but also in doing it well. Otherwise, if what is done is good, but not done well, it will not be completely good; hence neither will the habit, which is the principle of such a work, be characterized as perfect virtue. For instance, if someone does what is just, what he does is good, but it will not be a work of perfect virtue unless he does it well, i.e., by choosing rightly, which is accomplished through prudence; hence, justice without prudence cannot be a perfect virtue.

Accordingly, faith and hope can exist in some way without charity, but they are not characterized as perfect virtues without charity. For, since the work of faith is to believe in God, and to believe is to assent to something by one's own will, if one does not will as he ought, the work of faith will not be perfect. Now to will something as one ought results from charity, which perfects the will, for every right movement of the will proceeds from a right love, as Augustine says.[37] Hence there can indeed be faith without charity, but not as a perfect virtue, just as there can be temperance or fortitude without prudence. The same is to be said about hope. For the act of hope consists in looking forward to future happiness from God. This act is perfect if it is based on the merits one has, which cannot exist without charity. But if one expects future happiness from merits he does not yet have, but proposes to get in the future, the act will be imperfect, and this is possible without charity.

Consequently, there can be faith and hope without charity, but without charity they are not virtues properly speaking, for the nature of virtue requires that we not only do a good act, but do it well.[38]

Reply to 1: The moral virtues depend on prudence, but infused prudence cannot have the character of prudence without charity inasmuch as it will be lacking the due relation to the first principle, which is the ultimate end. But faith and hope, in their proper natures, do not depend on either prudence or charity.[39] Consequently, they can be without

[36] *Glossa interl., super Matt. 1:2.*   [37] *The City of God* XIV, 9.
[38] Cf. Aristotle, *Nicomachean Ethics* II, 6 (1106a 23).
[39] Hence charity is not the intrinsic or essential form of faith, but an external form; cf. II-II, question 4, article 3.

charity, although they are not virtues without charity, as we have explained.[40]

Reply to 2: The argument given is based upon faith as it is a perfect virtue.

Reply to 3: Augustine is there speaking about the hope by which one looks to future happiness because of merits he already has, which does not occur without charity.

Fifth Article

CAN THERE BE CHARITY WITHOUT FAITH AND HOPE?

It seems that there can be charity without faith and hope.

1. Charity is the love of God. But God can be loved in a natural way without presupposing faith or hope in future happiness. Therefore there can be charity without faith and hope.

2. Charity is the root of all the virtues, which are "rooted and founded in charity" (*Ephesians 3:17*). But a root is sometimes without branches. Therefore there can sometimes be charity without faith, hope, and the other virtues.

3. There was perfect charity in Christ, yet He did not have faith and hope, because He saw and enjoyed the divine essence, as we shall point out later.[41] Therefore there can be charity without faith and hope.

On the contrary: The Apostle says, "Without faith it is impossible to please God" (*Hebrews 11:6*), which especially belongs to charity, according to Scripture: "I love them that love me" (*Proverbs 8:17*). Further, hope leads to charity, as we have said.[42] Therefore we cannot have charity without faith and hope.

Response: Charity signifies not only love of God, but also a kind of friendship with Him, which adds besides love a returning of love for love along with a certain communing of one with another.[43] That this belongs to charity is evident from Scripture: "He who abides in love abides in God, and God in him" (*I John 4:16*), and "God is trustworthy, by him you have been called into fellowship with his Son" (*I Corinthians 1:9*). Now this fellowship of man with God, which consists in a kind of intimate living with Him, is begun here in our present life through grace and will be brought to completion in the future life by glory, each of which matters we hold by faith and hope. Consequently, just as one could not have friendship with another if he should disbelieve in, or have no hope of, the possibility of fellowship or intimate association with him,

---

[40] In the body of this article.   [41] III, question 7, articles 3 and 4.
[42] Question 62, article 4.
[43] Cf. Aristotle, *Nicomachean Ethics* VIII, 2 (1155b 28); 12 (1161b 11). Aristotle's doctrine of perfect friendship in Books VIII and IX is profitable to read by way of understanding the natural counterpart to charity.

so one cannot have friendship with God, which is charity, unless he have faith, by which he believes in such fellowship and intimate association of man with God, and the hope of possessing this fellowship. Thus in no way can there be charity without faith and hope.

Reply to 1: Charity is not any sort of love of God, but that love of God by which He is loved as the object of eternal happiness, to which we are directed by faith and hope.

Reply to 2: Charity is the root of faith and hope inasmuch as it gives them the perfection of virtue. But faith and hope, as such, are presupposed for charity, as we have explained.[44] And in this way, without them there cannot be charity.

Reply to 3: There was neither faith nor hope in Christ because of the imperfection there is in them. In place of faith Christ had clear vision, and in place of hope He had full comprehension; and so there was perfect charity in Christ.

---

[44] Question 62, article 4.

The Equality of the Virtues

(In Six Articles)

CAN ONE VIRTUE BE GREATER OR LESS THAN ANOTHER?

It seems that one virtue cannot be greater or less than another.

1. It is said in Scripture (*Apocalypse 21:16*) that the walls of the city of Jerusalem are equal. A gloss says that "walls" here signifies the virtues. Therefore all virtues are equal, and hence one virtue cannot be greater than another.

2. A thing whose nature consists in a maximum cannot be greater or less. But the nature of a virtue consists in a maximum, for virtue is the "limit of a power," [1] and Augustine says that "virtues are the greatest goods, which no one can use badly." [2] Therefore it seems that one virtue cannot be greater or less than another.

3. The greatness of an effect is measured by the power of the agent. But perfect virtues, which are infused, come from God, whose power is uniform and infinite. Therefore it seems that one virtue cannot be greater than another.

On the contrary: Wherever there can be an increase and great abundance, there can be inequality. But there is great abundance and increase in the virtues, for "Unless your justice exceeds that of the Scribes and Pharisees, you shall not enter the kingdom of heaven" (*Matthew 5:20*), and "In abundant justice there is the greatest strength" (*Proverbs 15:5*). Therefore it seems that one virtue can be greater or less than another.

Response: The question whether one virtue can be greater than another can be understood in two ways. In one way as applying to virtues of different species, and if it is so taken, clearly one virtue is greater than another, for a cause is always more powerful than its effect, and among effects, the closer an effect is to the cause the more powerful it is. Now it is evident from what has been said,[3] that the cause and root of human good is reason. Accordingly, prudence, which perfects reason, surpasses in goodness the other moral virtues which perfect the appetitive power, insofar as it participates in reason. And among the moral virtues, one is

---

[1] Aristotle, *On the Heavens* I, II (281a 11; a 18).   [2] *On Free Will* II, 18.

[3] Question 18, article 5; question 61, article 2.

better than another to the extent it approaches reason. Thus justice, which is in the will, ranks before the other moral virtues, and fortitude, which is in the irascible appetite, before temperance in the concupiscible appetite, which participates less in reason.[4]

The question can be understood in another way, as referring to virtues of the same species. And in this way, in conformity with what was said when treating the intensity of habits,[5] virtue may be said to be greater or less in two ways: in one way, of itself; in another way, on the part of the participating subject. Accordingly, if we consider a virtue as such, its being greater or less is based on the things to which it extends. For whoever has a certain virtue—temperance, for example—has it in respect to everything temperance extends to. But this is not the case with science and art, for not everyone who knows grammar knows everything pertaining to grammar. In this respect, the Stoics were right in saying that moral virtue cannot be more or less whereas science or art can,[6] because the kind of thing virtue is, is a maximum.

But if we consider virtue on the part of the subject participating in it, then it can be more or less, either at different times in the same person or in different persons. For, one man is better disposed than another to attain the mean of virtue which is in conformity with right reason, either because the habit is more developed in him, or because of a better natural disposition or a more discerning judgment of reason; or, finally, because of a greater gift of grace, which is given to each one "according to the measure of Christ's bestowal" (*Ephesians 4:7*). And in this regard the Stoics were mistaken, for they thought that no one should be called virtuous unless he were in the highest degree disposed to virtue. For, the nature of virtue does not require attaining the mean of right reason as though it were an indivisible point, as the Stoics thought; it is sufficient that the mean be approached.[7] Furthermore, this one and the same indivisible mark is reached more nearly and more readily by one person than by another, as is evident when archers aim at a given target.

Reply to 1: The equality spoken of is not one of absolute quantity, but must be understood as proportional, for all virtues grow proportionally in man, as we shall point out.[8]

Reply to 2: The maximum which pertains to virtue can have the aspect of more or less good in the ways we have explained, since the maximum is not something indivisible, as we have said.[9]

Reply to 3: God does not act according to necessity of nature, but according to the order of His wisdom by which He distributes a varying measure of virtue to men, as Scripture says: "But to each one of us grace was given according to the measure of Christ's bestowal" (*Ephesians 4:7*).

---

[4] Cf. Aristotle, *Nicomachean Ethics* VII, 6 (1149b 1).   [5] Question 52, article 1.
[6] Cf. Simplicius, *In Categ.*, 8.   [7] Cf. Aristotle, *Nicomachean Ethics* II, 9 (1109b 18).
[8] In the following article.   [9] In the body of this article.

Second Article

ARE ALL THE VIRTUES IN ONE MAN EQUAL?

It seems that not all virtues in one and the same man are equally intense.

1. The Apostle says, "Each one has his own gift from God, one in this way, and another in that" (*I Corinthians 7:7*). But one gift would not be more proper than another to someone if God infused equally all the virtues in each man. Therefore it seems that the virtues are not all equal in one and the same man.

2. If all virtues were equally intense in one and the same man, it would follow that whoever surpassed someone in one virtue would surpass him in all other virtues. But this is plainly false, for different saints are especially praised for different virtues, as Abraham for faith (*Romans 4:1*), Moses for meekness (*Numbers 12:3*), and Job for patience (*Job 2:12*). Hence the Church in her liturgy says of each Confessor: "There was not found his like in keeping the law of the most High," [10] in that each one is outstanding for one virtue or another. Therefore the virtues are not all equal in one and the same person.

3. The more intense a habit is the more delightedly and readily one acts in conformity with it. But it is clear from experience that a man performs the act of one virtue with more delight and readiness than another. Therefore the virtues are not all equal in one and the same man.

On the contrary: Augustine says that "those who are equal in fortitude are equal in prudence and temperance," [11] and the same holds for the others. This would not be so unless all the virtues of a man were equal. Therefore all virtues are equal in a man.

Response: Whether virtues are greater or less can be considered in two ways, as we have said.[12] First, according to their specific kind, and in this way there is no doubt that one virtue is greater than another in a man, for example charity is greater than faith or hope. Second, according to the participation of the subject, insofar as a virtue increases or diminishes in the subject. In this respect, all the virtues of one man are equal proportionally inasmuch as they increase equally in a man; in this respect, they are like the fingers of a hand which are quantitatively unequal but equal proportionally in that they grow in proportion to one another.

Now the nature of this equality is to be explained in the same way as the connection of the virtues, for equality is a certain connection of the virtues as to quantity. Now we have said that a twofold connection of virtues can be assigned.[13] First, according to the view of those who un-

---

[10] Cf. the Epistle in the Mass *Statuit* in the Dominican Missal.   [11] *The Trinity* VI, 4.
[12] In the previous article.   [13] Question 65, article 1.

derstand the four cardinal virtues as four general conditions of virtue, any one of which is found simultaneously with the others in any matter.[14] And thus a virtue, whatever its matter, cannot be called equal unless it have all these conditions equally. Augustine gives the reason for this equality of virtues when he says, "If you say that these men are equal in fortitude but that one surpasses another in prudence, it follows that the fortitude of this one is less prudent. But then they are not equal in fortitude either, since the former's fortitude is more prudent. And you will find this to be the same with the other virtues if you run through them in the same way." [15]

The other kind of connection of the virtues is based on the view of those who understand these virtues to have their own determinate matter.[16] In this way, the reason for the connection of the moral virtues is prudence, and for the infused virtues charity, and not the inclination in the subject, as said above.[17] Thus the notion of the equality of virtues can be considered on the part of prudence, with regard to that which is formal in all the moral virtues.[18] Accordingly, in one and the same man, as long as his reasoning has the same degree of perfection, the mean will be proportionally determined according to right reason in each matter of virtue. But in regard to what is material in the moral virtues, namely, the inclination to the act of virtue, a man may be readier to do the act of one virtue than the act of another, either by nature, or from custom, or through a gift of grace.

Reply to 1: The words of the Apostle can be taken as referring to gifts of grace given gratuitously, which are not common to all nor all equal in one and the same man. Or his words can refer to the measure of sanctifying grace by which one person has all the virtues in greater abundance than another, because of his greater abundance of prudence, or also of charity in which all the infused virtues are connected.

Reply to 2: One saint is praised especially for one virtue, and another saint for another, because of his exceptional readiness to do the act of one virtue rather than that of another.

Reply to 3: The reply is clear from what has been said.

Third Article

DO THE MORAL VIRTUES SURPASS THE INTELLECTUAL VIRTUES?

It seems that the moral virtues surpass the intellectual virtues.

1. Whatever is more necessary and more permanent is better. But the

---

[14] Cf. question 61, article 4.   [15] *The Trinity* VI, 4.
[16] Cf. question 65, articles 1 and 2.   [17] *Ibid.*
[18] This refers to the ordering of reason which prudence realizes in the moral virtues, by which ordering of reason a moral virtue is changed in its formal condition however it is related to the matter, which is different for different virtues.

moral virtues are "more lasting than even the sciences," [19] which are intellectual virtues, and they are also more necessary for human life. Therefore moral virtues are preferable to intellectual virtues.

2. It belongs to the notion of virtue that it makes the one having it good. But a man is called good because of his moral virtues, not his intellectual virtues, with the exception perhaps of prudence. Therefore moral virtue is better than intellectual virtue.

3. The end is superior to what is for the sake of the end. But "moral virtue causes us to intend the right end, while prudence makes us choose the right means to the end." [20] Therefore moral virtue is superior to prudence, which is the intellectual virtue concerned with moral matters.

On the contrary: Moral virtue is in reason by participation whereas intellectual virtue is in reason essentially.[21] But what is rational essentially is superior to what is rational by participation. Therefore intellectual virtue is superior to moral virtue.

Response: Something can be called greater or less in two ways: absolutely, or in a certain respect. For nothing prevents something from being better absolutely, for example, "to know philosophy than to make money," but not better in a certain respect, i.e., "for one who lacks the necessities of life." [22] Now a thing is considered absolutely when it is considered according to its own specific nature. But a virtue is the kind of virtue it is because of its object, as we have said.[23] Hence, absolutely speaking, that virtue is superior which has a superior object. Now it is evident that the object of reason is superior to the object of appetite, for reason apprehends something universally whereas appetite tends to things themselves, whose being is restricted to the particular. Consequently, speaking absolutely, the intellectual virtues, which perfect reason, are superior to the moral virtues, which perfect the appetite.

But if we consider virtue in relation to its act, then moral virtue, which perfects the appetite, whose function is to move the other powers to act, as we have said,[24] is superior. And because virtue is so named from the fact that it is a principle of action, since it is the perfection of a power, it follows that the nature of virtue belongs more to the moral virtues than to intellectual virtues, although the intellectual virtues are, absolutely, superior.

Reply to 1: The moral virtues are more permanent than the intellectual virtues because they are exercised in matters pertaining to community life. But clearly the objects of science, which are necessary and stable, are more permanent than the objects of the moral virtues, which are certain individual things to be done. That the moral virtues are more

---

[19] Aristotle, *Nicomachean Ethics* I, 10 (1100b 14).
[20] Aristotle, *op. cit.,* VI, 12 (1144a 8).   [21] Cf. Aristotle, *op. cit.,* I, 13 (1103a 1).
[22] Cf. Aristotle, *Topics* III, 2 (118a 10).
[23] Question 54, article 2; question 60, article 1.   [24] Question 9, article 1.

necessary for human life shows that they are superior, not absolutely, but in a certain respect. The speculative intellectual virtues, on the other hand, from the fact that they are not ordered to something else, as what is useful is ordered to an end, are more excellent. And this is because with the intellectual virtues there is a sort of beginning in us of that happiness which consists in the knowledge of truth, as we have said.[25]

Reply to 2: The reason for saying that a man is good absolutely according to the moral, and not the intellectual, virtues is that the appetite moves the other powers to their acts, as we have said.[26] Hence this argument proves only that moral virtue is better in a certain respect.

Reply to 3: Prudence directs the moral virtues not only in choosing the means to an end, but also in prescribing the end.[27] Now the end of any moral virtue is to attain the mean in the proper matter, which mean prudence determines by right reasoning.[28]

Fourth Article

IS JUSTICE THE PRINCIPAL MORAL VIRTUE?

It seems that justice is not the principal moral virtue.

1. It is a greater act to give what is one's own than to return what is owned to another. The former act relates to liberality, the latter to justice. Therefore it seems that liberality is a greater virtue than justice.

2. The most eminent thing in any order seems to be that which is most perfect in that order. But "patience has its perfect work" (*James 1:4*). Therefore it seems that patience is greater than justice.

3. "Magnanimity brings about greatness in every virtue." [29] Therefore it enlarges even justice, and hence is greater than justice.

On the contrary: The Philosopher says that "justice is the greatest of virtues." [30]

Response: A virtue as to its species can be called greater or less either absolutely or in a certain respect. It is said to be greater, absolutely speaking, when a greater good of reason is reflected in it, as we have said,[31] and in this way justice surpasses all the moral virtues as being closer to

---

[25] Question 3, article 6.   [26] Question 56, article 3.

[27] Prudence does not prescribe the end of the moral virtues substantially and in general, for this is accomplished by what is called *synderesis,* the virtue by which we grasp the primary practical principles. (Cf. II-II, question 47, article 6 on how prudence presupposes the knowing of such principles.) Prudence directs the moral virtues in prescribing the end in regard to the manner of attaining the end and taking into account the particular circumstances by which the end is rightly achieved. For example, reason naturally dictates the end that one should live temperately, but it depends on prudence to find out how this is to be attained concretely in regard to the person concerned, the place, and the time.

[28] Cf. Aristotle, *Nicomachean Ethics* II, 6 (1107a 1); VI, 13 (1144b 21).

[29] Aristotle, *op. cit.,* IV, 3 (1123b 30).   [30] *Op. cit.,* V, 1 (1129b 27).   [31] Article 1.

reason. This is evident on the part of both the subject and the object. From the standpoint of the subject, because justice is in the will as its subject, and the will is the rational appetite, as we have shown.[32] In regard to its object or the matter, because justice is about the operations by which man establishes order not only in himself, but in relation to another. Hence "justice is the greatest of virtues." [33]

Among the other moral virtues, which deal with the passions, to the extent that in any one of them the movement of appetite, which is subjected to reason, concerns a more important thing, the more the good of reason is reflected in it. Now among the things pertaining to man the most important of all is life, on which all other things depend. Hence fortitude, which subjects the appetite's movement to reason in matters concerning life and death, ranks first among the moral virtues that are about the passions, although it is subordinate to justice. Hence the Philosopher says that "the highest virtues must be those which are most honored, for virtue is the power of doing good. For this reason, men honor most the just and the brave, for courage is useful in war and justice in both war and peace." [34] After fortitude comes temperance, which subjects the appetite to reason in matters directly affecting life, whether in the individual or the species, namely, in matters of food and sex. And so these three virtues, along with prudence, are called the principal virtues in worth as well.

A virtue is said to be greater in a certain respect in proportion as it supports or embellishes a principal virtue. Thus also, substance absolutely is deemed more worthy than accident, but in a certain respect a particular accident is more worthy than substance insofar as it perfects substance in some mode of accidental being.[35]

Reply to 1: An act of liberality must be founded on an act of justice, for "there would be no act of liberality if one did not give of what is his own." [36] Hence there could be no liberality without justice, which separates what is one's own from what is not, but there can be justice without liberality. Accordingly, justice absolutely is greater than liberality, as being more universal and the foundation of liberality, but liberality is greater in a certain respect, since it is a kind of embellishment of justice and a supplement to it.

Reply to 2: Patience is said "to have its perfect work" in tolerating evils, wherein it excludes not only unjust revenge (which is also excluded by justice), not only hatred (which is removed by charity), not only anger

---

[32] Question 8, article 1; question 26, article 1.

[33] Aristotle, *Nicomachean Ethics* V, 1 (1129b 27).   [34] *Rhetoric* I, 9 (1366b 3).

[35] Thus man, as a substance, is more worthy than any accident, absolutely speaking. But a quality, such as a moral virtue, is more worthy in that it makes man be as he should be.

[36] Aristotle, *Politics* II, 5 (1263b 13).

(which is tempered by gentleness), but it excludes also inordinate sadness, which is the root of all the foregoing. Hence patience is more perfect and greater because it destroys the root in such matter. But it is not more perfect absolutely than all the other virtues Thus fortitude not only bears up under trouble without being disturbed, which patience accomplishes, but also fights against it when this should be done. Hence, whoever is courageous is patient, but not conversely, for patience is just a part of fortitude.

Reply to 3: There cannot be magnanimity without the other virtues.[37] Hence it is compared to the other virtues like an embellishment of them. And thus in a certain respect it is greater than all the others, but not absolutely.

Fifth Article

IS WISDOM THE GREATEST OF THE INTELLECTUAL VIRTUES?

It seems that wisdom is not the greatest of the intellectual virtues.

1. The one who commands is greater than the one commanded. But prudence seems to command wisdom, for the political science which pertains to prudence,[38] "determines which sciences should be studied in states, and which kind each citizen should learn and to what extent." [39] Since wisdom is included among the sciences, it seems that prudence is greater than wisdom.

2. It is of the nature of virtue to direct man to happiness, for virtue is "the disposition of what is perfect to what is best." [40] But prudence is right reasoning in regard to what is to be done, through which man is brought to happiness, whereas wisdom does not deal with the human acts by which man attains happiness. Therefore prudence is a greater virtue than wisdom.

3. The more perfect the knowledge the greater it seems to be. But we can have a more perfect knowledge of human things, the subject of science, than we can of divine things, which wisdom treats, according to the distinction made by Augustine;[41] for divine things are incomprehensible: "Behold God is great, exceeding our knowledge" (*Job 36:26*). Therefore science is a greater virtue than wisdom.

4. The knowledge of principles is more eminent than the knowledge of conclusions.[42] But wisdom, along with the other sciences, reaches con-

---

[37] Cf. Aristotle, *Nicomachean Ethics* IV, 3 (1124a 2).
[38] Cf. Aristotle, *op. cit.*, VI, 8 (1141b 23).   [39] Aristotle, *op. cit.*, I, 2 (1094a 28).
[40] Aristotle, *Physics* VII, 3 (246a 13).   [41] Cf. *The Trinity* XII, 14.
[42] In the sense that principles are known immediately and are indemonstrable whereas knowledge of conclusions requires proof with ultimate dependence on self evident principles.

clusions from indemonstrable principles, attained by the virtue of understanding. Therefore understanding is a greater virtue than wisdom.

On the contrary: The Philosopher says that wisdom is the head, as it were, of the intellectual virtues.[43]

Response: As we have said,[44] we determine the greatness of a virtue, as to its kind, from its object. Now the object of wisdom is more eminent than the objects of all other intellectual virtues, for wisdom considers the highest cause, God.[45] And because we judge an effect in terms of its cause, and lower causes by higher causes, wisdom exercises judgment in regard to other intellectual virtues, directs them, and is architectonic, as it were, with respect to all of them.

Reply to 1: Since prudence is concerned with human affairs, and wisdom with the highest cause, it is impossible for prudence to be a greater virtue than wisdom, "unless man were the greatest thing in the world." [46] Hence we must say, as Aristotle also says in the same work,[47] that prudence does not command wisdom, but rather the reverse, for "the spiritual man judges all things, and he himself is judged by no man" (*I Corinthians 2:15*). For prudence is not adapted to the highest things which wisdom treats, but exercises direction over things ordered to wisdom, namely, how man should attain wisdom. In this way, then, prudence, that is, political prudence, ministers to wisdom, for it leads to wisdom, preparing the way for it, as an ambassador for a ruler.[48]

Reply to 2: Prudence deals with the means of arriving at happiness, but wisdom considers the very object of happiness, that which is highest in intelligibility. And if wisdom's consideration in regard to its object were perfect, there would be perfect happiness in the act of wisdom. But in this life the act of wisdom is imperfect in regard to its principal object, which is God, and hence the act of wisdom is a sort of beginning or participation in future happiness, and so is closer to happiness than prudence.

Reply to 3: As the Philosopher says, "one kind of knowledge is preferred to another either by reason of its greater nobility or because of its greater certitude." [49] Accordingly, if the subjects[50] are equal in goodness and nobility, the virtue which is more certain in its knowledge will be the greater virtue. But the virtue which is less certain about higher and greater things is preferable to the virtue which is more certain about inferior things. Hence the Philosopher says that it is better to be able to know something about heavenly matters even though by unconvincing and

---

[43] Cf. *Nicomachean Ethics* VI, 7 (1141a 19).   [44] Article 3.
[45] Cf. Aristotle, *Metaphysics* I, 1 (981b 28); 2 (982b 9; 983a 7).
[46] Aristotle, *Nicomachean Ethics* VI, 7 (1141a 27).   [47] *Op. cit.,* VI, 13 (1145a 6).
[48] In the original: *sicut ostiarius ad regem.*   [49] Aristotle, *On the Soul* I, 1 (402a 2).
[50] In the sense of subject matters dealt with.

probable reasoning.[51] He also says that "it is more pleasurable to know a little about more noble things than to know much about inferior things." [52] Hence wisdom, to which the knowledge of God pertains, cannot be perfectly attained by man in such a way that it belongs to him, especially in his present state of life, for "God alone can have this privilege." [53] Nevertheless, that modicum of knowledge which we can have of God through wisdom is preferable to all other knowledge.

Reply to 4: The truth and knowledge of indemonstrable principles depends upon the notions of the terms. Thus, as soon as we know what a whole is and what a part is, we know that every [quantitative] whole is greater than its part. Now to grasp the notion of being and nonbeing, of whole and part, and the other things which follow upon being, from which indemonstrable principles are constituted as to terms, belongs to wisdom, for universal being is the proper effect of the supreme cause, namely, God. Consequently, wisdom not only uses the indemonstrable principles, with which the virtue of understanding is concerned, by drawing conclusions from them, as other sciences do, but it also judges them and defends them against those who would deny them. Hence it follows that wisdom is a greater virtue than understanding.

Sixth Article

IS CHARITY THE GREATEST OF THE THEOLOGICAL VIRTUES?

It seems that charity is not the greatest of the theological virtues.

1. Since faith is in the intellect while hope and charity are in the appetitive power, as we have said,[54] it seems that faith is compared to hope and charity as an intellectual virtue is to a moral virtue. But an intellectual virtue is greater than a moral virtue, as is evident from what has been said.[55] Therefore faith is greater than hope and charity.

2. Whatever is constituted by way of addition to something else seems to be greater than it. But hope apparently is such as to be an addition to charity, for hope presupposes love, as Augustine says,[56] and adds a certain movement of reaching out to what is loved. Therefore hope is greater than charity.

3. A cause is more powerful than its effect. But faith and hope are causes of charity, for a gloss on *Matthew 1:2* says that faith begets hope, and hope charity. Therefore faith and hope are greater than charity.

On the contrary: The Apostle says: "So there abide faith, hope, and charity, these three; but the greatest of these is charity" (*I Corinthians 13:13*).

---

[51] Cf. Aristotle, *On the Heavens* II, 12 (291b 27).
[52] *On the Parts of Animals* I, 5 (644b 31).
[53] A saying of Simonides, quoted by Aristotle in *Metaphysics* I, 2 (982b 30).
[54] Question 62, article 3.   [55] Article 3.   [56] *Enchiridion*, VIII.

Response: As we have said,[57] the greatness of a virtue as to its species is determined by its object. Now since the three theological virtues look to God as their proper object, one cannot be called greater than another by reason of a greater object, but only by reason of being closer to the object than another. And in this way charity is greater than the others. For the others in their very nature imply a certain distance from the object; thus, faith is about what is not seen and hope is about what is not possessed. But the love of charity is about what is already possessed, for what is loved is in a certain way in the one who loves, and also the one who loves is drawn by affection to a union with what is loved. Hence, "He who abides in love abides in God, and God in him" (*I John 4:16*).

Reply to 1: Faith and hope are not related to charity in the same way as prudence is to moral virtue, for two reasons. First, the theological virtues have as an object something beyond the human soul while prudence and the moral virtues are about things below man. Now to love things above man is more noble than to know them. For knowledge depends on the known being in the knower whereas love is brought about by the lover being drawn to what is loved. But what is above man is more worthy in itself than it is in man because a thing is in something else according to the mode of the thing in which it is. The reverse holds in regard to things below man. Second, prudence moderates the appetitive movements pertaining to the moral virtues whereas faith does not moderate the appetitive movement tending to God, which movement pertains to the theological virtues, but only makes the object known. And this appetitive movement toward its object surpasses human knowledge, since "the charity of Christ surpasses knowledge" (*Ephesians 3:19*).

Reply to 2: Hope presupposes a love of that which man hopes to attain, and such is concupiscible love whereby the one who desires the good loves himself rather than something else. But charity implies the love of friendship, to which we are led by hope, as we have said.[58]

Reply to 3: A perfecting cause is more powerful than its effect, but not a disposing cause. Otherwise the heat of fire would be better than the soul, for which heat disposes matter, which is clearly false. It is in this way that faith begets hope, and hope charity, that is, as one is a disposition for another.

---

[57] Article 3. [58] Question 62, article 4. Cf. also note 43 of question 65.

The Duration of the Virtues after this Life[1]

(In Six Articles)

DO THE MORAL VIRTUES REMAIN AFTER THIS LIFE?

It seems that the moral virtues do not remain after this life.

1. In the future life of glory, men will be like angels, according to Scripture *(Matthew 22:30)*. But it is foolish to suppose that there are moral virtues in the angels, as Aristotle observes.[2] Therefore neither will there be moral virtues in men after this life.

2. The moral virtues perfect men in respect to the active life. But the active life does not continue after this life, for Gregory says, "The works of the active life pass away with the body." [3]

3. Temperance and fortitude, which are moral virtues, are in the irrational part of the soul.[4] But the irrational parts of the soul are corrupted when the body corrupts since they are acts of organs of the body. Therefore it seems that the moral virtues do not remain after this life.

On the contrary: "Justice is perpetual and immortal" *(Wisdom 1:15)*.

Response: As Augustine says, Cicero held that the four cardinal virtues would not exist after this life but that, as Augustine adds, in another life "men are made happy solely by the knowledge of that nature than which there is nothing better or more lovable, i.e., that nature which created all other natures." [5] Augustine subsequently concludes that the four virtues will remain in a future life, but in a different manner.

---

[1] Cf. note 1 on question 64. We are now finishing the consideration of certain properties which are characteristic of virtue. Question 64 treated the mean of virtue; question 65, the connection of the virtues; question 66, equality among the virtues; and, finally, in this question, the duration of the virtues.

[2] The reference cited is *Nicomachean Ethics* X, 8 (1178b 8): "We suppose the gods to be above all other beings blessed and happy; but what sort of activity should we assign them? Acts of justice? . . . Acts of a brave man? . . . Liberal acts? . . ."

[3] *Moral.,* VI, 37.

[4] Cf. Aristotle, *Nicomachean Ethics* III, 10 (1117b 23). The irrational part of the soul referred to here is the sense appetite which, though not in the rational part, is still subject to direction by the rational part.

[5] *The Trinity* XIV, 9.

In order to make this evident, we need to know that there is something formal and something material in these virtues. The material element in these virtues is the inclination of the appetitive part to the passions and operations according to a certain measure, and because this measure is determined by reason, the formal element in all these virtues is the ordering of reason.

Accordingly, we must point out that these moral virtues will not remain in the future life as far as their material element is concerned. For in the future life there will be no occasion for desire and pleasure in food and sex, nor any fear or boldness in the face of danger of death, nor any distributing or exchange of things needed for use in this life. But they will remain in a most perfect state in the blessed after this life as far as their formal element is concerned inasmuch as each one's reason will have utmost rectitude about things affecting him in that state, and his appetitive power will move wholly in conformity with the order of reason in matters pertaining to that state. Hence Augustine says that "there will be prudence without any danger of error, fortitude without the anxiety of sustaining evils, temperance without the opposition of desires, so that prudence will neither prefer nor make any good equal to God, fortitude will adhere to God with utmost firmness, and temperance will delight in God with no culpable defect." [6] With respect to justice, it is apparent what its act will be in that life, namely, *to be subject to God,* for even in this life subjection to a superior pertains to justice.

Reply to 1: The Philosopher is speaking there of the moral virtues in regard to what is material in them. He thus speaks of justice in terms of *exchanges and distributions,* of fortitude in terms of *terrors and dangers,* of temperance in terms of *disordered desires.*

Reply to 2: The same reply serves here, for those things which concern the active life belong to what is material in the virtues.

Reply to 3: There is a twofold state after this life: one before the resurrection, when the soul is separated from the body; the other after the resurrection, when the soul will again be united to the body. In the state of resurrection, the irrational powers will be in bodily organs as they are now, and hence it will be possible for fortitude to be in the irascible appetite and temperance in the concupiscible, inasmuch as each power will be perfectly disposed to follow reason. But in the state before the resurrection, the irrational parts will not actually be in the soul, but only radically[7] in its essence, as we have said.[8] Consequently, these virtues will not be actual except as to their root, that is, in reason and the will, in which they exist in a seminal form, as we have said.[9] Justice, however, being in the will, will remain actually. Accordingly, it is especially said of justice that it is perpetual and immortal, both by reason of its subject

---

[6] *Ibid.*   [7] In the etymological sense of *rootly.*   [8] I, question 77, article 8.   [9] *Ibid.*

in that the will is incorruptible, and also because its act will not change, as we said.[10]

Second Article

DO THE INTELLECTUAL VIRTUES REMAIN AFTER THIS LIFE?

It seems that the intellectual virtues do not remain after this life.

1. The Apostle says that "knowledge will be destroyed" (*I Corinthians 13:8*), the reason being that "we know in part" (*v.9*). But just as the knowledge of science is "in part," i.e., imperfect, so also is the knowledge acquired through other intellectual virtues, as long as this life goes on. Therefore all the intellectual virtues will cease after this life.

2. The Philosopher says that science, since it is a habit, is a quality difficult to displace, and is not easily lost except by some great change or disease.[11] But no bodily change is greater than that of death. Therefore science and the other intellectual virtues do not remain after this life.

3. The intellectual virtues perfect the intellect so that it does its proper act well. But there seems to be no act of the intellect after this life, for "the soul understands nothing without a phantasm." [12] But phantasms do not remain after this life since they exist only in bodily organs. Therefore the intellectual virtues do not remain after this life.

On the contrary: Knowledge of universal and necessary things is more steadfast than knowledge of the particular and the contingent. But knowledge of particular and contingent things remains in man after this life; for example, of what one has done or suffered, as Scripture says: "Son, remember that thou in thy lifetime hast received good things and Lazarus in like manner evil things" (*Luke 16:25*). Therefore much more does the knowledge of universal and necessary things remain, which pertains to science and other intellectual virtues.

Response: As we have said,[13] some held[14] that intelligible species[15] remain in the possible intellect only while the mind actually understands, nor is there any conserving of the species when actual consideration ceases except in the sense powers, i.e., the imagination and memory, which are acts of corporeal organs. Now such powers cease to exist when the body is corrupted, and so according to this view science in no way will remain once the body is corrupted, nor will any other intellectual virtue.

This opinion, however, is contrary to the view of Aristotle, who says that "the possible intellect is actualized by becoming each thing as it knows it, but even then it is in potentiality to considering it actually." [16]

---

[10] In the body of this article.   [11] *Categories* 8, (8b 31).
[12] Aristotle, *On the Soul* III, 7 (431a 16).   [13] I, question 79, article 6.
[14] Avicenna is the instance St. Thomas has in mind.   [15] I.e., concepts.
[16] *On the Soul* III, 4 (429b 6).

It is also contrary to reason, for intelligible species are received by the possible intellect in an immobile way, according to the mode of their recipient. Accordingly, the possible intellect is called "the locus of the species," [17] because it preserves the intelligible species.

But the phantasms, which in this life man must turn to in order to understand, by referring the intelligible species to them, as we have said,[18] are corrupted when the body is corrupted. Hence with respect to these phantasms, which are the material element, as it were, in the intellectual virtues, these virtues are destroyed when the body is corrupted, but in regard to the intelligible species, which are in the possible intellect, the intellectual virtues remain. Now the species are what is formal in the intellectual virtues. Hence the intellectual virtues remain after this life as regards what is formal in them, not what is material, as we said also about the moral virtues.[19]

Reply to 1: The words of the Apostle are to be understood as referring to what is material in science and to the manner of understanding, for the phantasms will not remain with the destruction of the body nor will science be exercised by referring to phantasms.

Reply to 2: Illness corrupts the habit of science as to what is material in science, i.e., the phantasms, but not with respect to the intelligible species, which are in the possible intellect.

Reply to 3: The separated soul after death has another way of knowing than by turning to phantasms, as we have said.[20] Accordingly, science remains, but it does not operate in the same way, as we have shown in regard to the moral virtues.[21]

Third Article

DOES FAITH REMAIN AFTER THIS LIFE?

It seems that faith remains after this life.

1. Faith is more noble than science. But science remains after this life, as we have said.[22] Therefore faith also remains.

2. "For other foundation no one can lay, but that which has been laid, which is Christ Jesus" (*I Corinthians 3:11*), that is, faith in Jesus Christ. But if the foundation is removed, the structure built upon it does not remain. Therefore, if faith did not remain after this life, no other virtue would remain.

3. The knowledge of faith and the knowledge that will be had in the state of glory[23] differ as imperfect and perfect. But imperfect knowledge can exist simultaneously with perfect knowledge. Thus, in the angel there

---

[17] *Ibid.,* (429a 27).   [18] I, question 84, article 7; question 85, articles 1 and 2.
[19] In the preceding article.   [20] I, question 89, article 1.   [21] In the preceding article.
[22] Article 2.   [23] The state of glory is the perfect enjoyment of God in heaven.

can be "evening" knowledge and "morning" knowledge,[24] and a man can have scientific knowledge of a conclusion through a demonstrative syllogism and at the same time have opinion about it through a dialectical syllogism. Therefore faith can likewise exist after this life along with the knowledge had in the state of glory.

On the contrary: The Apostle says that "while we are in the body we are exiled from the Lord—for we walk by faith and not by sight" (*II Corinthians 5:6, 7*). But those who are in the state of glory are not absent from the Lord but are present to Him. Therefore faith does not remain after this life in the state of glory.

Response: Opposition is the per se and proper cause of one thing being excluded from another inasmuch as every case of opposites involves opposition of affirmation and negation. Now in some things there is an opposition by way of contrary forms; for instance, white and black in colors. In other things, there is an opposition of perfect and imperfect. Hence in alterations, more and less are considered as contraries, as when something less hot becomes more hot.[25] And since perfect and imperfect are opposed, it is impossible that there be perfection and imperfection at the same time in respect to the same thing.

Now we must take note that sometimes imperfection pertains to a thing's very nature and belongs to its species; thus, the lack of reason belongs to the nature of the species horse or cow. And because a thing, while remaining one and the same, cannot go from one species to another, if such an imperfection be removed, the species of the thing is changed; thus, if it were to be rational, it would no longer be a cow or a horse. Sometimes, however, the imperfection does not belong to the nature of a species, but is accidental to the individual because of something else; thus, sometimes a man suffers a defect of reason inasmuch as his use of reason is impeded because of drowsiness or drunkenness, or something of the kind. Obviously, when this sort of imperfection is removed, the substance of the thing remains.

Now it is evident that imperfection of knowledge belongs to the nature of faith, for it is stated in the definition of faith that it "is the substance of things to be hoped for, the evidence of things that are not seen" (*Hebrews 11:1*). And Augustine says, "What is faith? To believe without seeing." [26] Now it belongs to imperfection of knowledge that it be inevident and without comprehension. Consequently, imperfection of knowledge belongs to the very nature of faith. Hence it is clear that faith, while remaining one and the same, cannot be perfect knowledge.

But we must also consider whether faith can exist simultaneously with

---

[24] The expressions "morning" and "evening" knowledge come from St. Augustine. The expressions are explained in the body of this article. Cf. also I, question 58, articles 6 and 7.

[25] Cf. Aristotle, *Physics* V, 2 (226b 2).   [26] Tract XL super *Joann.*, VIII, 32.

perfect knowledge, for there is nothing to prevent there being some imperfect knowledge along with perfect knowledge. Accordingly, we should note that knowledge can be imperfect in three ways: first, on the part of the knowable object; second, on the part of the means of knowing; third, on the part of the subject. A difference of perfect and imperfect knowledge on the part of the knowable object is found in the *morning* and *evening* knowledge of the angels. The *morning* knowledge is of things as they are in the Word while the *evening* knowledge is of things as they are in their own nature, which is imperfect compared to the first way of being. On the part of the means of knowing, the knowledge of a conclusion reached by demonstrative and by probable means differs as perfect and imperfect. The distinction of perfect and imperfect knowledge on the part of the subject applies to opinion, faith, and science. For it is essential to opinion that we assent to one of two opposite assertions with fear that the other may be true, and hence our adherence is not firm. The nature of scientific knowledge is such that there is firm adherence with an intellectual seeing, for its certitude results from an understanding of its principles. Now faith is in a middle position, for it surpasses opinion in that there is firm adherence, but it falls short of science in that there is not insight.

It is evident, then, that a thing cannot at the same time be perfect and imperfect in the same respect, but those things which differ as perfect and imperfect can be together in the same respect in some other thing. Accordingly, perfect knowledge on the part of the object is incompatible with imperfect knowledge about the same object. But the means of knowing can be the same and they can be in the same subject, for one man can have, at one and the same time, through one and the same means, perfect and imperfect knowledge about two things, one of which is perfect and the other imperfect, as knowledge of health and sickness, good and evil.[27] Similarly, knowledge which is perfect on the part of the means is incompatible with imperfect knowledge by one and the same means, but nothing prevents them being about the same object and in the same subject, for one man can know the same conclusion through a probable means and a demonstrative means. Likewise, knowledge which is perfect on the part of the subject is incompatible with imperfect knowledge in the same subject. Now faith of its very nature has an imperfection which is on the part of the subject in that the one who believes does not see what he believes, whereas eternal happiness of its very nature has a perfection which is on the part of the subject in that the blessed see that which makes them happy, as we have said.[28] Hence it

---

[27] Thus in the very knowing of what it is to be sick, one knows what it is to be healthy.

[28] Question 3, article 8.

is clearly impossible that there be faith and eternal happiness at one and the same time in the same subject.

Reply to 1: Faith is more noble than science on the part of the object, for its object is the primary truth. But science is more perfect as to its mode of knowing, which is not in opposition to the perfection of eternal happiness, namely, vision, as the way of knowing by faith is.

Reply to 2: Faith is a foundation inasmuch as it is knowledge. And hence when this knowledge is perfected, it will be more perfect as a foundation.

Reply to 3: The reply is evident from what has been said in this article.

Fourth Article

DOES HOPE REMAIN AFTER DEATH IN THE STATE OF GLORY?

It seems that hope remains after death in the state of glory.

1. Hope perfects the human appetite in a more noble way than the moral virtues do. But the moral virtues remain after this life, as is evident from Augustine.[29] Therefore much more does hope remain after this life.

2. Hope is opposed to fear. But fear remains after this life, and indeed in the blessed a filial fear remains forever while in the condemned the fear of punishment remains. Therefore hope, with equal reason, can remain after this life.

3. Hope is about a future good, just as desire is. But in the blessed there is the desire for a future good, both for the glorified state of the body, which the souls of the blessed desire, as Augustine says,[30] and also for the glorified condition of the soul, according to Scripture: "They that eat me, shall yet hunger: and they that drink me, shall yet thirst" (*Ecclesiasticus 24:29*), and also: "Into these things angels desire to look" (*I Peter 1:12*). Therefore it seems that hope can remain after this life in the blessed.

On the contrary: The Apostle says: "For how can a man hope for what he sees?" (*Romans 8:24*). But the blessed see what the object of hope is, namely, God. Therefore they no longer hope.

Response: As we have said,[31] whatever of its nature involves imperfection on the part of its subject cannot continue in the subject when the opposite perfection is realized. Thus it is clear that motion of its very nature implies imperfection of a subject, for motion is "the act of what is in potency inasmuch as it is in potency," [32] and hence when such potentiality is actualized, the motion ceases, for a thing does not continue to become white once it is made white. Now hope implies a certain

---

[29] Cf. *The Trinity* XIV, 9. [30] Cf. *De Genesi ad Litt.* XII, 35.
[31] In the preceding article. [32] Aristotle, *Physics* III, 1 (201a 10).

motion toward something not yet had, as is clear from what we said above about hope as an emotion.[33] Consequently, when we have what we have hoped for, namely, the enjoyment of God, hope will no longer be possible.[34]

Reply to 1: Hope is superior to the moral virtues as to its object, which is God. But the acts of the moral virtues are not opposed to the perfection of eternal happiness as the act of hope is,[35] unless perhaps by reason of their matter, but in this respect moral virtues do not remain. For moral virtue perfects the appetite not only in regard to what is not yet had, but also with respect to what is presently had.

Reply to 2: There are two kinds of fear, servile and filial, as we shall explain subsequently.[36] Servile fear is the fear of punishment, which we cannot have in the state of glory where no possibility of punishment remains. Filial fear, however, has two acts. One is the reverence for God, and in regard to this act, fear remains; the other is the fear of being separated from God, and with respect to this act, fear does not remain. For to be separated from God has the aspect of something evil, and there will be no evil there to fear, according to Scripture: "He shall enjoy abundance, without fear of evils" (*Proverbs 1:33*). Now fear is opposed to hope by an opposition of good and evil, as we have said,[37] and hence the fear which remains in the state of glory is not opposed to hope. But there can be more fear of punishment in the condemned than hope of glory in the blessed. For in the condemned there will be successive punishment, and in this way some notion of the future remains there, which is the object of fear, whereas the glory of the saints is without succession in that it is a certain participation in eternity, in which there is neither past nor future but only the present. And yet, in a proper sense, there is not fear in the condemned either. For as we have said,[38] fear is never without some hope of escape, which the condemned will in no way have. Accordingly, there will not be fear in them except in the general sense that any expectation of future evil is called fear.

Reply to 3: In respect to the glorified condition of the soul, there cannot be in the blessed any desire, according as desire looks to what is future, for the reason we have just given.[39] A hunger and a thirst, how-

---

[33] Question 40, articles 1 and 2.

[34] It follows from what has been said that hope, and faith also, would remain after this life for those in purgatory, whom St. Thomas is not considering in this article.

[35] That is, happiness not yet realized is accordingly not a perfection, and hope bears precisely on the desire for what is not yet had, and in this sense it is opposed to the perfection of happiness when realized.

[36] II-II, question 19, article 2.   [37] Question 23, article 2; question 40, article 1.

[38] Question 42, article 2.

[39] Reply to 2; specifically, the reason is that the state of glory is a participation in eternity in which there is properly no past nor future, but only the present; hence, there is no desire insofar as desire refers to what is future.

ever, are said to be in them through the removal of all aversion, and for the same reason desire is said to be in angels. With respect to the glorified state of the body, there can be desire for this in the souls of the saints, but not hope, properly speaking, neither hope as a theological virtue (whose object is God and not some created good), nor hope in its common meaning. For the object of hope is the arduous good, as we have said,[40] whereas a good whose unvarying cause we already possess does not present itself to us as something arduous. Thus, someone who has money is not properly said to hope for something which it is in his power to buy at once. Similarly, those who have that glorified condition of the soul are not properly said to hope for the glorified state of the body, but only to have desire for it.

Fifth Article

DOES ANYTHING OF FAITH OR HOPE REMAIN IN THE STATE OF GLORY?

It seems that something of faith or hope remains in the state of glory.

1. Whenever what is proper to a thing is removed, what is common remains, and thus "if rational is removed, living remains; and if living is removed, being remains."[41] But there is something faith has in common with eternal happiness, namely, knowledge, and also something which is proper to faith, obscurity, for faith is obscure knowledge. Therefore, with the obscurity of faith removed, the knowledge of faith still remains.

2. Faith is a certain spiritual light of the soul, for "the eyes of your mind enlightened . . . in the knowledge of God" (*Ephesians 1:17, 18*), but this light is imperfect in regard to the light of glory, of which it is said, "in Thy light, we shall see light" (*Psalms 35:10*). Now an imperfect light remains when a perfect light is added, for a candle is not extinguished when sunlight appears. Therefore it seems that the light of faith remains with the light of glory.

3. The substance of a habit is not removed when its matter is not present, for a man can retain the habit of liberality even with the loss of wealth, although he cannot act with liberality. Now the object of faith is the unseen first truth. Therefore, when this inevidence is removed by the first truth being seen, the habit of faith can still remain.

On the contrary: Faith is a simple habit. But what is simple is either wholly lost or it wholly remains. Since faith does not wholly remain, but

---

[40] Question 40, article 1.
[41] *De Causis* I. The *Liber de Causis,* at one time attributed to Aristotle, is largely an excerpt by an unknown author from the *Elementatio theologica* of Proclus (410-485). Proclus developed Neo-Platonism into its most complete form. St. Thomas, aware of the work's Neo-Platonic origin, wrote a commentary on it.

is removed, as we have said,[42] then it seems to follow that faith is wholly withdrawn.

Response: Some have said that hope is totally removed but that faith is withdrawn in part, namely, with respect to its obscurity, and remains in part, in regard to the substance of its knowledge.[43] If this is taken to mean that one and the same faith does not remain but that it remains generically, it is quite true, for faith belongs to the same genus as the Beatific Vision does, namely, knowledge. Hope, however, does not belong to the same genus as eternal happiness, for hope is compared to the fulfillment of happiness as motion to rest, as the term of motion.

But if this position means that the knowledge which belongs to faith remains precisely the same knowledge in heaven, this is absolutely impossible. For when the specific difference of a species is removed, the substance of the genus does not remain one and the same; for example, if the difference which constitutes the species white is removed, the substance of color does not remain one and the same such that one and the same color is sometimes white and sometimes black. For the genus is not related to the difference as matter to form so that the one and the same generic substance remains when the difference has been removed, as the substance of matter remains one and the same when the form is removed. This is because the genus and the difference are not parts of the species; if they were, they could not be predicated of the species. Now just as the species signifies the whole—the compound of matter and form in material things—so does the difference signify the whole, as also the genus; but the genus denominates the whole by signifying that which is material, the difference by signifying that which is formal, the species by signifying both. For example, in man sensitive nature is related as matter to intellectual nature; now, *animal* is said of that which has sensitive nature, and *rational* of that which has intellectual nature, but *man* of that which has both. And thus the same whole is signified by these three things, but not in the same way.

Hence it is evident that since the difference is a specific indication of the genus, if the difference is removed, the substance of the genus cannot remain the same; for the same animality does not remain if another kind of soul should constitute animal. Consequently, it is impossible that the knowledge which was previously obscure becomes clear vision. And so it is evident that nothing which is in faith remains numerically or specifically the same in heaven, but only generically.

Reply to 1: When *rational* is removed, *living* remains the same generically but not numerically, as we have just explained.

Reply to 2: The imperfection of candle light is not opposed to the

---

[42] Article 3.

[43] This position is attributed to William of Auxerre (d. 1231), in his *Summa Aurea* III, tr. 5, q. 5.

perfection of sunlight, since they do not refer to the same subject. But the imperfection of faith and the perfection of the state of glory are opposed to each other, for they do refer to the same subject. Accordingly, they cannot exist together simultaneously, as neither can light and darkness in the air.

Reply to 3: He who loses wealth does not lose the possibility of having wealth, and hence the habit of liberality appropriately remains. But in the state of glory not only is the object of faith, the inevident, actually removed, but also its possibility because of the unchanging character of eternal happiness. Accordingly, there is no point in such a habit remaining.

Sixth Article

DOES CHARITY REMAIN AFTER THIS LIFE IN THE STATE OF GLORY?

It seems that charity does not remain after this life in the state of glory.

1. The Apostle says, "when that which is perfect is come, that which is in part shall be done away," i.e., that which is imperfect (*I Corinthians 13:10*). But charity as we now have it is imperfect. Therefore it will be put aside when the perfection of the state of glory is achieved.

2. Habits and acts are distinguished according to their objects. But the object of love is the good as apprehended. Therefore, since the apprehension we have in this life is one thing, and the apprehension in the future life another, it seems that charity would not be the same in both.

3. Things which are one in nature can move by continuous increase from imperfection to perfection. But charity in this life can never reach perfection equal to that attained in heaven, however much it increases. Therefore it seems that the charity of this life does not remain in heaven.

On the contrary: The Apostle says: "Charity never fails" (*I Corinthians 13:8*).

Response: As we have said,[44] when the imperfection of a thing does not come from the nature of its species, nothing prevents one and the same thing advancing from imperfection to perfection, just as a man develops by growth, and whiteness by intensity. Now charity is love, which of its nature has no imperfection, for it may be for an object possessed or not, seen or not. Hence charity is not put aside by the perfection of the state of glory, but remains numerically the same.

Reply to 1: Imperfection is accidental to charity because imperfection does not belong to the nature of charity. Hence, the removal of its imperfection does not remove charity itself.

---

[44] Article 3.

Reply to 2: Charity does not have knowledge itself as its object, for if it did the charity of this life would not be the same as the charity of heaven; it has for its object the thing known, which remains the same, namely, God Himself.

Reply to 3: Charity in this life cannot by increasing become equal to the charity in heaven because of a difference on the part of the cause. For vision is a cause of love;[45] and the more perfectly God is known the more perfectly He is loved.

---

[45] Cf. Aristotle, *Nicomachean Ethics* IX, 5 (1167a 4).